CW00820271

Norfolk Record Society
Volume LXXXV for 2021

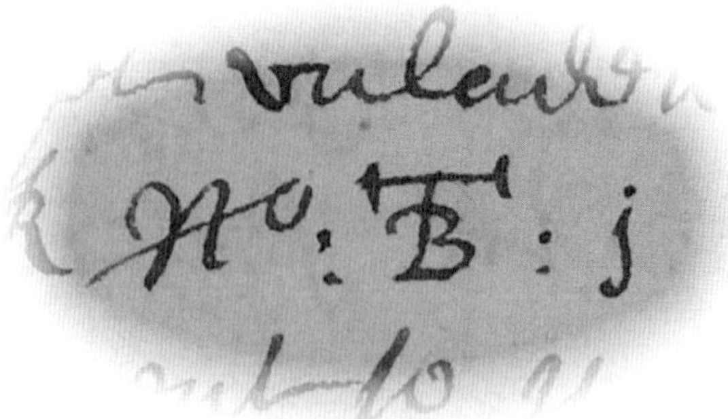

Thomas Baret

Rowland Cockey

Nathaniell Mathew

Merchant's marks, used for identifying parts of cargoes.
These are reproduced from letters on pp. 18, 33 and 165 of the letter-book.

The Letter-Book of Thomas Baret of Norwich

merchant and textile manufacturer, 1672–1677

Edited by Siobhan Talbott

General Editor
Jean Agnew

Norfolk Record Society
Volume LXXXV
2021

First published in 2021
by the Norfolk Record Society

ISBN 978-0-9957736-4-6

Typeset by Carnegie Book Production, Lancaster
Printed and bound by Short Run Press, Exeter

Contents

Illustrations

Preface and Acknowledgements

I first became aware of Thomas Baret's letter-book when visiting the Norfolk Record Office in 2012 for an entirely different project based at the University of Manchester. Since then, my interest in merchants' letters as a source for economic histories has only grown. Work on this volume has been intermittent over the subsequent years, taking place alongside lecturing at Keele University, an AHRC grant for another project, two periods of maternity leave, and with the text being finalised during the Covid-19 pandemic. I am very excited to see this volume come to fruition after spending nearly a decade with it. I would like to thank the Norfolk Record Society for their interest in this volume, their patience with multiple hiatuses and their encouragement as it neared completion. I would particularly like to thank Jean Agnew, the volume's general editor, who has been generous with her time and knowledge throughout this endeavour. Research seminar audiences at the University of Edinburgh and Keele University in October and November 2016 respectively offered valuable comments on this volume, for which I am very grateful. A return visit to the Norfolk Record Office in 2019, funded by Keele University, to finalise the transcription was made very enjoyable thanks to all of the staff at the archives. They could not have been more welcoming or helpful, and I must find an excuse to return. The NRO kindly re-photographed the pages of the letter-book used as illustrations on the cover and throughout this volume free of charge, and did so extremely efficiently, for which I am very grateful. As a historian of early-modern commerce but not by any means an expert in textiles, I would like to thank those scholars who offered their assistance as I strove to identify accurately the various commodities traded by Thomas Baret (despite his own inability to do so). Various pleas on Twitter led to interesting virtual conversations with a number of people far more expert in early-modern textiles than myself, and I thank them wholeheartedly for their generous assistance, in particular Lizzy Spencer, Sally Tuckett, Michael Pearce,

Gavin Robinson and Brodie Waddell. Finally, I would like to thank my family, who have put up with Baret for longer than originally anticipated. My husband Mark remains my most valued critic as well as my biggest champion, and our wonderful children, Alastair and Imogen, offered welcome (and sometimes unwelcome) respite from the headaches of seventeenth-century palaeography during the final stages of this project.

Siobhan Talbott

Introduction

I

Between the early sixteenth and early eighteenth centuries Norwich was England's largest provincial city, second only to London, with a population of c. 29,000 in 1700.[1] By 1728 Norwich had been eclipsed by Bristol, and by 1801 both Norwich and Bristol were being overtaken by the industrial towns of Manchester, Liverpool and Birmingham.[2] The rapidly changing ranking of Norwich – from second city in 1700 to 14th in 1851, 23rd in 1901 and 52nd in 1951 – has been described as 'the most dramatic change in terms of ranking that was experienced by any urban centre during this prolonged period of transformation'.[3] At the time of Norwich's ranking as the 'second city' in 1700, most of the other leading provincial cities were ports.[4] As an inland city, Norwich has left no commercial statistics (as inland trade was not subject to any fiscal or political control), and the official records of the Weavers' Company, the regulators of Norwich's staple industry, were destroyed in the eighteenth century when formal supervision of the industry ended.[5] In the absence of these records Penny Corfield has used the admissions to the freedom of Norwich between 1660–1749 to assess the size of its textile industry, and concluded that worsted weavers and those engaged in other stages of worsted production accounted for over 50% of all admissions by the early eighteenth century.[6]

---

1 P. Corfield, 'East Anglia', in P. Clark, ed., *Urban History of Britain II: 1540–1840* (Cambridge, 2000), p. 38; C. Daniell, *Atlas of Early Modern Britain, 1485–1715* (Oxford, 2014), pp. 101, 113.

2 P. Corfield, 'Norwich on the Cusp – from second city to regional capital', in C. Rawcliffe and R. Wilson, eds, *Norwich since 1550* (London, 2004), pp. 139–66.

3 Corfield, 'East Anglia', p. 41.

4 P. Corfield, 'A Provincial Capital in the late seventeenth century: the Case of Norwich' in P. Clark, ed., *The Early Modern Town* (New York 1976), p. 233.

5 Corfield, 'A Provincial Capital', pp. 233–4.

6 Corfield, 'A Provincial Capital', p. 243; U. Priestly, 'Marketing of Norwich Stuffs, c. 1660–1730', *Textile History* 22.2 (1991), p. 197.

Norwich's history of textile manufacturing dates back to the medieval period. Success in the industry was due in part to location – Norwich had access to the continent through the medieval ports of Yarmouth and King's Lynn, and linked important trade routes between London, Colchester, Ipswich and northeast England.[7] In the late sixteenth century, following an influx of Flemish and Dutch weavers, textile production shifted from traditional worsted stuffs to lighter, brighter 'New Draperies' influenced by Walloon tradition.[8] It has been said that Norwich 'found an ultimate escape route in the New Draperies': slumps in cloth exports in the 1550s and 1620s did not lead to a decline in the cloth industry in Norwich, largely because of the influence of foreign immigrants.[9] The Norwich textile industry continued to flourish throughout the seventeenth century, in contrast to other 'New Drapery' towns such as Colchester, whose bays industry was in decline by the late seventeenth century.[10] Following some peaks and troughs, from the 1660s domestic demand for Norwich's core manufactures of worsted, wool and linen peaked,[11] coinciding with Thomas Baret's foray into the textile trade.

Thomas Baret was born in 1636 into a family of minor Suffolk gentry who had settled in Norwich in the mid-sixteenth century. Both his grandfather Christopher (1562–1649) and his father Thomas (1597–1684) were mayors of Norwich, and both played a leading role in the events leading up to and following the Great Blow in April 1648.[12] His father was a mercer, and set up in trade with his son, our Thomas Baret, and a cousin; the former was described as a merchant when he became a freeman in 1661. When the letter-book begins in 1672, Thomas Baret was trading on his own account, and had also set up as a textile manufacturer exporting his own stuffs,

7 F. Williamson, *Social Relations and Urban Space: Norwich, 1600–1700* (Suffolk, 2014), p. 16.

8 Corfield, 'Norwich on the Cusp', pp. 139–68; J. Murray, 'The cultural impact of the Flemish Low Countries on sixteenth- and seventeenth-century England', *The American Historical Review*, 62.4 (1957), pp. 838–9; P. Clark and P. Slack, *English Towns in Transition, 1500–1700* (Oxford, 1976), p. 53; Priestly, 'Marketing of Norwich Stuffs', p. 194.

9 P. Slack, 'Great and good towns, 1540–1700', in Clark, *Urban History*, p. 355.

10 Corfield, 'A Provincial Capital', p. 244.

11 Williamson, *Social Relations and Urban Space*, p. 17; Clark and Slack, *English Towns*, p. 53.

12 On 24 April 1648, a day of rioting culminated in the explosion of 98 barrels of gunpowder in the county magazine, located in central Norwich, causing great damage and loss of life, *see* A. Hopper, J. Agnew and E. Alley, eds, *The Great Blow: Examinations and Informations relating to the Great Blow in Norwich, 1648* (Norfolk Record Society, lxxxii, 2018).

primarily trading with contacts in the Dutch Republic. Baret's business ventures were relatively short-lived: he ceased trading after 1677 in order to turn his attention to investment in land. Despite some disappointments, his tenacity and understanding of international trade, coupled with a well-timed lottery win in 1675, allowed him to purchase Heggatt Hall in that year, as well as further property in Horstead. His first wife, Hester Man, died in 1685, and he subsequently married Anne Yallop of Bowthorpe Hall, with whom he lived at Heggatt until his death in January 1711. Having no surviving children by either marriage, Baret named as his heir the husband of his niece Lydia Rayley, who was his cousin Thomas Baret of Ludham. When the latter predeceased him he made a complex will entailing his estates on their surviving and posthumous children, leading to protracted lawsuits.[13]

II

Norwich 'stuffs', the primary commodity featuring in Baret's letter-book, remain under-explored by historians. In 1985 Ursula Priestly remarked that there was no full-scale study devoted exclusively to Norwich textiles, and this remains the state of affairs thirty-five years on. There are, as pointed out by Priestly, good reasons for this – the lack of statistical records for the Norwich textile industry allows for no reliable assessment of output, growth, or the extent of the domestic or international export trade.[14] There are no known survivals of clothing made from Norwich stuffs, in part because it was relatively inexpensive and therefore not particularly valued, and because it was consumed primarily by the growing middle classes rather than the aristocracy. Compounding this, pattern books and samples of Norwich manufactures only survive from the 1760s, and there is no way of knowing with any certainty how far the stuffs produced and named in the eighteenth century can be equated with those of the previous century.[15]

We do know that the generic title of 'Norwich stuffs' included a range and variety of fabrics, with Thomas Fuller remarking that there were

13 Norfolk Record Office [hereafter NRO], NCC will register, Famm 353 (1710) (Thomas Baret), microfilm 95; P. Millican, *A History of Horstead and Stanninghall, Norfolk* (Norwich, 1937), pp. 97–8. *See Biographical notes*, p. 21.

14 U. Priestly, 'The Fabric of Stuffs: the Norwich textile industry, c. 1650–1750', *Textile History*, 16.2 (1985), p. 183.

15 Priestly, 'Marketing of Norwich Stuffs', pp. 195, 198; Priestly, 'The Fabric of Stuffs', p. 185.

'infinite varieties' of Norwich stuffs in his *History of the Worthies of England*, published posthumously in 1662.[16] Both Priestly and Corfield note the broad range of Norwich stuffs found in contemporary inventories of Norwich weavers, including: damasks, russells, satins, tamines, tammetts, cheyneys, paramides, callimancoes, crapes, camblets, druggets and faringdons.[17] Seventeenth-century Norwich stuffs were usually light and brightly coloured, made from long-staple wool that had been combed, spun, and dyed in the yarn.[18] As production of coarse worsteds expanded in Yorkshire, Norwich worsteds, following Walloon influence, became increasingly lighter, meaning that Yorkshire production complemented, rather than rivalled, production in Norwich.[19] 'Mixed' fabrics, made of worsted yarn integrated with fibres including linen, mohair or silk, became increasingly popular. The new fashion in Norwich of integrating silk with conventional worsted fabrics, reducing the use of more traditional secondary yarns like linen and mohair, further speaks to the influence of Walloon tradition – Flemish and Dutch weavers had been producing silk mixed fabrics since the sixteenth century.[20] From the 1670s, silk versions of a whole range of fabrics previously thought of as pure worsted were being produced, including 'silk sayes', 'silk druggets' and 'silk callimancoes', and by the 1690s Norwich was acknowledged as the leading manufacturing centre in Britain for silk-and-worsted stuffs.[21] Thomas Baret was part of this trend: in January 1674 he wrote to Rowland Cockey of a fabric 'strooke off with mixt wooll upon silke warpe', assuring Cockey that this would do 'mighty well' at market in Amsterdam [*p. 56*[22]]. Later that year Baret wrote to George Richards that his wares 'are fine wares closse strooke yett

16 T. Fuller, *The History of the Worthies of England*, volume II (London, 1662; 1840 edition), p. 488.

17 NRO, Case 33, Shelf e, Norwich Archdeaconry Inventories, Bundle iii, no. 200 (1674), Bundle iv, no. 69 (1692), cited in Corfield, 'A Provincial Capital', p. 247; Priestly, 'The Fabric of Stuffs', pp. 204–5.

18 The terms 'stuff' and 'cloth' did not become near synonyms until the nineteenth century. Cloth was heavier than stuff, which was made from finer, long-staple, worsted fibres; was combed instead of carded; and was often intermixed: Priestly, 'The Fabric of Stuffs', p. 193.

19 Corfield, 'A Provincial Capital', p. 247.

20 Priestly, 'Fabric of Stuffs', p. 186; Priestly, 'Marketing of Norwich Stuffs', p. 193; Corfield, 'A Provincial Capital', p. 247.

21 Priestly, 'Marketing of Norwich Stuffs', pp. 195–6.

22 Page numbers, *shown in italic*, refer to pages of the manuscript given in the transcripts, not of this publication. Page numbers of the manuscript can be found in the running header of the transcripts.

thinn & light beeinge half silke half worsted' [*p. 126*]. Although Walloon influence on the development of Norwich stuffs is widely accepted,[23] the extent of Huguenot influence, particularly following the Revocation of the Edict of Nantes in 1685, has been questioned. In the absence of any clear evidence for a substantial influx of Huguenots to Norwich after 1685, these developments in the textile trade have more convincingly been seen as a continuous process. Silk-worsted mixes, which have been assumed to be a product of Huguenot influence, were in fact well-established by the 1660s, and crapes and druggets, both of French origin, were already in production in Norwich in the 1670s.[24] Baret's trade in mixed silk stuffs and druggets in the 1670s supports this assessment [*e.g. pp. 56, 125–6, 165, 167, 238, 242*].

In addition to a lack of evidence for the specification of different types of stuffs, names were frequently updated or changed, particularly if a fabric performed badly when it was initially released to market and needed to be re-branded.[25] Indeed, Fuller asked his reader to 'expect not I should reckon up their several names, because daily increasing, and many of them are binominous, as which, when they began to tire in sale, are quickened with a new name'.[26] The proliferation of names in a period where records identifying these fabrics do not survive makes it very difficult to identify the characteristics of different fabrics.[27] This was also a problem for contemporaries. Baret did business in a broad range of textiles, including many of those identified by Priestly and Corfield [*see glossary*], but at times he professed himself unfamiliar with certain cloths or confused by terminology used. In March 1673 he wrote to William Fittz that his 'post[s]cript that Flemish linings are desired heere I can not answer you to because that at present I am a perfect stranger to those comodityes' [*p. 13*]. More than two years later Baret wrote to John Dey 'you are sorry that I send noe crowne rashes & truly I am sorry that I doe not know what you meane by them & therfore if you would have any you must send me a pattern of them or give me such description as I may understand for I am sure wee have noe such name for any comodity heere' [*p. 156*].

Baret traded primarily with associates in the Netherlands (some expatriate, some native), which raises important questions about the destinations of Norwich stuffs. It is commonly accepted that by the mid-seventeenth century

23 Corfield, 'Norwich on the Cusp', pp. 139–68.

24 Priestly, 'The Fabric of Stuffs', p. 187.

25 Priestly, 'Marketing of Norwich Stuffs', pp. 194–5; Priestly, 'The Fabric of Stuffs', pp. 184–5.

26 Fuller, *History of the Worthies of England*, II, p. 488.

27 Priestly, 'Marketing of Norwich Stuffs', pp. 194–5.

relatively little of Norwich's textile produce was being exported overseas, with the Norwich industry catering 'mainly for home demand', 'in marked contrast to both earlier and later times'.[28] In the early seventeenth century the expansion of the textile industry had been based on producing goods for foreign markets; by the 1730s increased domestic competition and decline in value of the home market meant that 'Norwich weavers turned their attention to overseas customers, so that by mid-century the export trade was dominant'.[29] By contrast, it is tentatively estimated that around three-quarters of Norwich's stuffs production between 1660 and 1731 was traded on the domestic market.[30] It has been said that 'the evidence for the importance of the home market in the late seventeenth century is incontrovertible',[31] and that 'there seems little reason to doubt that for much of the period under review home consumption continued to be by far the most important outlet for the city's textile production'.[32] It is suggested that 'evidence for an export trade in Norwich stuffs is either circumstantial or negative'.[33]

While the domestic market undoubtedly played a major role in Norwich's trade in stuffs in the seventeenth century, a lack of available data makes it difficult to assert with any certainty how much of Norwich's stuffs production remained on the domestic market, and the focus that has remained on Norwich's internal markets in the late seventeenth and early eighteenth centuries has not allowed for much discussion of the remaining quarter of produce said to have been sent to international markets. The patterns of trade highlighted by Baret's letter-book suggest that there is more to be said about the destinations of Norwich stuffs in this period. Crucially, Norwich's status as an inland port meant that any goods taken overseas needed first to travel to a port city. The 'obvious outlet' to continental markets was via Great Yarmouth and the Netherlands, though it is claimed that this was an under-used point of departure in the

28 J. Pound, *Tudor and Stuart Norwich* (Sussex, 1988), p. 64, Corfield, 'A Provincial Capital', p. 246.

29 Priestly, 'Marketing of Norwich Stuffs', p. 193.

30 Priestly, 'Marketing of Norwich Stuffs', p. 197; Priestly, 'The Fabric of Stuffs', p. 198. Both Priestly and Corfield suggest that, as this figure was estimated by the Weavers' Company at a time of dispute with alnage officials, and thus a time when it was in the interests of the industry to claim the maximum importance for export sales, the figure for domestic consumption was likely to have been higher. By contrast, the alnagers reported no exports of Norwich stuff, leaving the truth likely somewhere in between: *see* Corfield, 'A Provincial Capital', p. 246.

31 Corfield, 'A Provincial Capital', p. 246.

32 Priestly, 'The Fabric of Stuffs', p. 199.

33 Priestly, 'The Fabric of Stuffs', p. 198.

seventeenth century.[34] Thomas Baret evidently made use of the proximity of Great Yarmouth for his overseas business, in March 1673 writing to Nicholas Toll that 'per Mr Andress Vanderling the billander[35] from Yarmouth I have consigned to you a case of stuffs' [*pp. 17–18*]. There were additional, less obvious outlets to overseas markets. It has been suggested that the bulk of Norwich stuffs destined for the home market went to London for distribution,[36] but we have no way of knowing how much of this later went overseas – being classed as 'domestic' trade from Norwich but with an ultimate destination abroad. Even if we take the suggested 3:1 ratio as a fair indication of a split between domestic and foreign markets, it is highly likely that stuffs initially traded domestically were ultimately consumed overseas. Baret explicitly traded in this way, writing to Rowland Cockey in 1673 that 'I shall next weeke if not sooner send a pack to London to goe by way off Oostend & another to Yarmouth for the first oppertunity to send from thence' [*p. 31*]. Thus goods travelling from Norwich to Amsterdam went via London and Ostend as well as via Yarmouth, obscuring the start and end point of export, and disguising international as domestic trade. Such activity suggests that there may have been a greater proportion of Norwich's textile produce traded overseas than hitherto thought. Manuscripts such as Baret's letter-book are vital, particularly in the absence of statistical data, in allowing us to interrogate the fate of the portion of Norwich's seventeenth-century textile production that was traded overseas, though we will never be able to calculate accurately what proportion of stuffs went beyond domestic markets.

Acting as a manufacturer as well as a merchant, Baret's letter-book gives some insight into manufacturing practices in the Norwich textile industry in the seventeenth century. There is a lack of evidence for manufacturing costs, but the textile industry has been seen as the 'leading sector of the urban economy, productive of the greatest demand for labour in the city'.[37] Corfield suggests that the success of the Norwich industry and the absence of evidence for labour disputes over piecework rates indicates that labour costs were not prohibitively high.[38] Although Baret's letters reveal occasional concern over his workmen, these did not relate to pay. Instead, he expressed unease in the ability of his workmen to adapt to making goods for different markets [*p. 31*], and to problems caused by his attempts to manufacture

34 Priestly, 'The Fabric of Stuffs', p. 199.
35 A small double-masted European trading vessel, see *illustration* p. 44.
36 Priestly, 'The Fabric of Stuffs', p. 199.
37 Corfield, 'A Provincial Capital', p. 258.
38 Corfield, 'A Provincial Capital', p. 250.

a stuff 'soe difficult to make … that my workemen will leave rather than goe on' [*p. 77*]. In August 1674 Baret felt obliged to 'confess these No. 23 are not soe good as I would have had I putt new persons upon them whoe could not hitt right at first but you shall have better in future' [*p. 98*]. Manufacturing was not plain sailing for Baret, who also commented on his difficulties in procuring yarn, writing to Rowland Cockey in June 1674 that 'I can not gett yarne enough to supply my occasions that is of shuch collor as give you content' [*p. 77*], and in July that 'I find it difficult to geet good mixt wool yarnes to keepe those lombs that I have in worke' [*p. 85*]. Some stuffs were easier to make than others; he commented to Cockey that his 'No. 15 … is a very teedous comodity to make it swallows a vast deele of yarne & is 14 days to worke a piece' [*p. 85*]. It was common for manufacturers to undertake some of the procedures for finishing cloth, including yarn-processing, but less common for them to undertake more skilled techniques, like hot-pressing. Baret noted that he 'press[ed] none at all' [*p. 164*].

Norwich weavers were primarily craftsmen, overseeing all aspects of manufacturing and being present in their workshops,[39] whereas Baret was more heavily involved in marketing his produce than in the day-to-day process of manufacture. We can thus categorise him as one of the 'merchant-manufacturers' described by David Ormrod.[40] There are indications throughout Baret's letter-book that he prioritised his relationships with clients above overseeing his manufacturing operation. In November 1673 he wrote to Rowland Cockey that 'now I am come home I doe find that my workemen have made me since my departure about 40 pieces of No. 4 good wares & good sortment in collour which doe waite your advice for transportation' [*p. 45*]. Baret appears to have spent a great deal of his time dealing directly with consumers abroad and marketing his goods, consistently talking up the quality of the English manufacturing of his stuffs. In March 1673 Baret wrote to both Jacomo Lemo and Thomas Shephard, telling the former that 'the sorts I ordered to you are but a few of the many that I deale in to the Court of England as well as forraine parts', and the latter that 'if you incourage I will send you patterns of severall comodityes fitt to be worne by men by women by children for I deale in all sorts to the Court of England as well as to Amsterdam' [*pp. 16, 22*]. The following month Baret wrote to Cockey that 'the occasion of this is to send you some patterns

39 Priestly, 'The Fabric of Stuffs', p. 188.

40 D. Ormrod, *The Rise of Commercial Empires: England and the Netherlands in the Age of Mercantilism, 1650–1770* (Cambridge, 2003), pp. 138–9.

of such stuffs as are the mode with us especially the three patterns with orrange collour the patterne of chamolett I cutt of a piece I this day sent for London & I think is the best piece that ever you see of Norwich make'; he goes on to ask for specific orders from Cockey, and for any pattern that Cockey would like to send him to be made [*p. 23*]. This correspondence reveals cultural as well as economic exchange, as patterns for clothing, as well as the stuffs themselves, were shared among Baret's network. Baret had pride in the quality of his work – when he received a complaint from Rowland Cockey in June 1673 he responded that 'as to the old No. 15 bad collors pray retorne them by way of Yarmouth by first oppertunity for if I had them heere I question not but to make them saleable againe' [*p. 32*].

Many Norwich manufacturers had their own warehouses in the capital city,[41] and we know that Baret was one of them, as he instructed John Dey in September 1674 to draw money on 'John Burton at Mr Barets warehouse in Abb Church Lane in London' [*p. 117*]. We do not know how many looms Baret operated. It has been said that in 1661, having six looms was an 'unusually large number'.[42] We can glean from Baret's correspondence that he must have had at least four in 1674, at which point he had one loom making cloth No. 15 and one making No. 35, and he states that he 'sett others' (plural) to make No. 29 [*p. 91*]. Elsewhere Baret refers to 'all my loombs' [*p. 66, 74, 105*]. Although we don't know precisely how much Baret was worth, the amount of money mentioned at various points in his letter-book speaks to a wealthy individual; certainly by the time of his death he owned a substantial amount of land, purchased in part from proceeds from his textile business and in part from his lottery win in 1675 [*p. 247*].[43] For context, Ursula Priestly calculates that in 1661 a merchant awaiting payment of £174 for goods with a further £375 owed to him for debts was a successful merchant-manufacturer.[44] Throughout Baret's correspondence we see him dealing with large amounts of both goods and money. In December 1672 he shipped goods to Rowland Cockey worth over £106 [*p. 4*], three months later sending two more bundles of goods to Cockey amounting to £112 10s 6d and £120 5s respectively [*pp. 18, 19*]. Comparable figures feature throughout the letter-book, with an invoice sent to William Peacock in September 1675 amounting to over £98 and an invoice to Robert Pease in December of the same year totalling over £105 [*pp. 165, 197*]. Baret drew

41 Priestly, 'The Fabric of Stuffs', p. 199.

42 Priestly, 'The Fabric of Stuffs', p. 195.

43 Millican, *A History of Horstead and Stanninghall*, p. 98. Baret's will does not specify his worth: NRO, NCC will register, Famm 353 (1710) (Thomas Baret), MF 95.

44 Priestly, 'The Fabric of Stuffs', p. 195.

bills of exchange in large amounts, ordering John Langly to draw £200 upon Rowland Cockey in March 1673 [*p. 19*], and discussing a 'bill of exchange for £312 12s' in January 1674 [*p. 50*]. Most remarkably, in November 1674, Baret wrote to Cockey that 'by this accompt you have about £1,400 or £1,500 of myne in your hands … I have a verry considerable some of money to pay at Christmas neere £1,000 … therfore I depend upon you for £500 which pray remitt to me' [*p. 124*].

Baret's export trade was thus in stuffs, but he imported a range of commodities, as revealed particularly in the latter part of his letter-book. These included items linked to Baret's manufacturing operation: Baret accepted various qualities of madder, a natural red dye, ranging from crop madder (the best quality), through pipe madder, down to gameene madder (a low-grade quality of madder sold in powdered form).[45] Whalebone, used for stiffening stays and corsets, was imported, and Baret was aware of its most valuable form, writing to Thomas Shephard in September 1675 that 'the best may sell heere but cutt whalebone is looked upon as a cheate' [*p. 175*]. Baret imported a range of foodstuffs, including 'hambs of right Westphalia bacon about 12 or 13lb weight' [*p. 96*], beer, and various grades of sturgeon, both jowls (the head and shoulders, considered a delicacy in early-modern Britain) and rands (strips or slices of the meat of the fish) [*p. 100*]. Baret imported iron in various forms and from a variety of places, including Liège in Belgium, Stockholm in Sweden, and Bilbao in Spain. His imports also included copper, Flemish steel, brass pots, and latten (a mixed metal resembling brass). Tarras, a component for mortar and cement, commonly imported from Holland, was accepted by Baret, as were gravestones 'for tryall … the midling stones are the most vendible' [*p. 99*]; and at the other end of the scale, painted boxes, slat books, and Nuremburg 'toys' – small manufactured items for ornament or amusement – were imported. Shortly after purchasing the Heggatt estate, Baret requested 'clover grasseede … nonesuch seede & … saint foyne seede … to sow my grounds' [*p. 198*]. In a one-off letter to Captain John Clarke, Baret toyed with the possibility of branching out across the Atlantic Ocean and importing sugar from Barbados; a trade in which Baret noted that he was a 'stranger' [*p. 108*].

Despite his wealth, manufacturing outfit, and the range of commodities he traded in, Baret conceded in 1695 that he was 'not soe profitable … as I might have beene' [*p. 247*]. Timing was everything in business, and there are indications that he may simply have got his timing wrong, attempting

45 For more on grades of madder *see* R. Chenciner, *Madder Red: A history of luxury and trade* (Abingdon, 2000).

to operate during a recession in the industry between 1674 and 1676. Following this dip, the 1680s saw a 'prolonged boom',[46] but by this time Baret had ceased his trading and manufacturing operation. This is perhaps why he lamented to Sir Josiah Child, merchant and economist, in 1695 that he wished he had continued in trade: in his first letter to Child, he stated that 'I was not wholly negligent but as you truly observe had not land beene soe cheape I might have traded still & I really owne I wish I had continued it still' [*p. 247*]. Instead, though, Baret chose to invest his wealth in land. The final section of the letter-book comprises three letters from Baret to Child, written between April and December 1695. These are of a different tone to the rest of the volume, and written about twenty years after Baret ceased participation in Norwich's textile trade. Following his acquisition of Child's *A New Discourse of Trade* (1693), Baret felt compelled to write to Child to note the areas in which he disagreed, with a focus on land, rents, agriculture and coinage, indicating the shift in his interests. It is notable that Baret read and commented on Child's work on land, rather than his writings on trade, making no mention of Child's *Brief Observations concerning Trade and Interest of Money* (1668), nor his *An essay on wool and woollen manufacture* (1681), indicating that by the mid-1690s Baret had left his interlude in the textile trade behind.

III

As well as offering insights into the Norwich textile trade and the manufacturing of stuffs, the period when Baret operated adds an additional layer of interest to this manuscript. The seventeenth century was riven by conflict, and the numerous wars of the era have contributed to the century being termed one of 'general crisis' by a number of scholars.[47] Several scholars, including myself, have sought to analyse the impact of war on commercial exchanges.[48] Baret's letter-book spans a period encompassing the Third Anglo-Dutch War (1672–4) and the connected Franco-Dutch War (1672–8),

46 Corfield, 'A Provincial Capital', p. 251.

47 Notably E. Hobsbawm, 'The Crisis of the Seventeenth Century', *Past and Present*, 6 (1954), pp. 44–65; H. Trevor-Roper, 'The General Crisis of the Seventeeth Century', *Past and Present*, 16 (1959), pp. 31–64; G. Parker and L. Smith, eds, *The General Crisis of the Seventeeth Century* (London: Routledge, 1978).

48 S. Talbott, *Conflict, Commerce and Franco-Scottish Relations, 1560–1713* (London, 2014); P. Croft, 'Trading with the Enemy, 1585–1604', *Historical Journal*, 32.2 (1989), pp. 281–302; J. Levy and K. Barbieri, 'Trading with the enemy during wartime', *Security Studies*, 13.3 (2004).

making it an excellent resource for assessing the impact of these conflicts on the Anglo-Dutch textile trade.

The causes and nature of the Anglo-Dutch Wars have been fiercely debated in recent historiography.[49] While the three seventeenth-century conflicts (1652–4, 1665–7, 1672–4) continue to be broadly understood as commercial conflicts between two maritime powers seeking to control Europe's trade, shipping and wealth, there has been a recent shift away from considering the wars as solely economic, as the influence of other factors, including political pressure exerted by London's mercantile community, has been recognised.[50] It was during the third war, now interpreted as a planned war of political aggression against the backdrop of the larger Franco-Dutch conflict,[51] that Baret was operating as an international textile merchant.[52]

Whatever the cause of the conflicts, in practical terms there remains an assumption that they had a detrimental impact on commerce between England and the Dutch Republic.[53] There are several letters in Baret's letter-book that illuminate the concerns of merchants regarding the impact of the Third Anglo-Dutch War on business. In February 1673 Baret wrote to Rowland Cockey that despite Cockey's 'apprehentions of safety in Amsterdam … its my owne thoughts & all my friends that there can be noe long safety in that place unless the discource of peace' [*p. 8*]. Two months later Baret again wrote to Cockey declaring himself to be 'now againe full of feares conserning you for methinks the peace looke farther

49 Gijs Rommelse has provided succinct summaries of historiographical developments: G. Rommelse, *The Second Anglo-Dutch War* (Hilversum, 2006), pp. 11–12; G. Rommelse, 'The role of mercantilism in Anglo-Dutch political relations, 1650–74', *Economic History Review*, 63.3 (2010), pp. 591–5.

50 Rommelse, *The Second Anglo-Dutch War*, p. 12. *See also* G. Rommelse, 'Mountains of iron and gold: mercantilist ideology in Anglo-Dutch relations (1650–1674)' in D. Onnekirk and G. Rommelse, eds, *Ideology and Foreign Policy in Early Modern Europe (1650–1750)* (Farnham, 2011), p. 266; P. Seaward, 'The House of Commons Committee of Trade and the Origins of the Second Anglo-Dutch War, 1664', *The Historical Journal*, 30.2 (1987), pp. 437–52.

51 J. Jones, *The Anglo-Dutch Wars of the Seventeenth Century* (Essex, 1996), p. 13; S. Groenveld, 'The seventeenth-century Anglo-Dutch wars: economic or political issues?', *Low Countries: A yearbook*, 4 (1995–6), p. 174; G. Rommelse and R. Downing, 'Anglo-Dutch Mercantile Rivalry, 1585–1688', in M. Isenmann, ed., *Merkantilismus, Wiederaufnahme einer Debatte* (Stuttgart, 2014), p. 170.

52 S. Talbott, '"What cannot be helped must be indured": Coping with Obstacles to Business during the Anglo-Dutch Wars, 1652–1674', *Enterprise & Society*, 22 (forthcoming 2021).

53 J. Israel, *Dutch Primary in World Trade, 1585–1740* (Oxford 1989), pp. 293–4.

off us then we desire it should' [*p. 27*]. In June, he added that 'as to trade I see you have but little nor are you like to have much this beeing the time of action, I must confess I am some what unwilling to adventure any more goods as yet' [*p. 31*]. Baret's manufacturing was also impacted: 'you say that my goods are not soe good as formerley which shall be amended, the truth is the cessation of my Holland trade hath caused me to employ those workemen in English comodityes which I use to employ in Hollands comodityes' [*p. 31*]. In April Baret included a note to Cockey that he did 'not vallue the making of 20 pieces in hopes of peace', suggesting that he altered his manufacturing activities as a result of this climate [*p. 23*]. A month before peace was declared Baret lamented that his looms were 'almost at a stand' [*p. 50*], and by June 1674, despite peace between England and the Dutch, he struggled to acquire materials: 'I can not gett yarne enough … yet I use the utmost of my industry … I am dishertned in it' [*p. 77*]. These entries suggest both that Baret's own trade and manufacturing endeavours were impacted by the Third Anglo-Dutch War, and that the consequences of this warfare were felt along a whole spectrum of commercial activity – manufacturing and consumption as well as the physical act of exchange. This impact was felt beyond the lifespan of the conflict, as shown by Baret's final comment here regarding his difficulties in acquiring raw materials despite the coming of peace.

It is essential, however, to note that the repercussions of any 'crisis' of this period were not universally felt. Though it has been suggested that the impact of the Anglo-Dutch Wars on trading activity was necessarily negative,[54] Baret's letter-book shows how, when, where and with whom merchants were able to do business despite the conflict.[55] When rumours of peace reached Baret just halfway through the third war, he was proactive in altering his trading methods in anticipation of a change in context, entailing a halt to his wartime business. Baret explained that 'the present discourse of peace or rather a treaty dus incourage me to request you to send away noe more goods' [*p. 20*]. It was hoped throughout Baret's network that 'the good newse of a peace betwixt England & Holland … will revive trade' [*p. 59*]. By January 1674 Baret had started planning for business post-war: 'I am now in greate hopes wee shall have a peace & therfore if there be any comodityes fitt for my sale heere which would rise if a peace dus come … I would take the opportunity to draw before the exchange dus rise' [*p. 57*]. Baret's forward-planning involved capitalising on favourable rates available

54 Jones, *The Anglo-Dutch Wars*, pp. 130, 221.

55 Talbott, 'Coping with Obstacles to Business'.

during the conflict that would disappear with peace – crucially suggesting that the impact of warfare was not necessarily negative.

Despite the uncertainty caused by the war, business continued within Baret's network but was adjusted as necessary. Baret continued to encourage business with Rowland Cockey but requested 'you would not adventure above £2: or £300 vallue in one bottum unless you see safety in the conveyance & good convoy & then send as you thinke convenient' [*p. 8*]. Baret continued to use diversification as good business practice after the end of the war, instructing William Peacock in October 1676 that iron sent 'by way of Rotterdam' should 'for security … come in two severall vessells' [*p. 227*]. While Baret lamented that trade would 'be carried on with the hazard of but a small stock its truth the charges wilbe greate', he also noted that this might be 'helped by a raise of price which I suppose you may effect because few if any as the constitution of affairs now are will adventur to send any of these goods over' [*p. 12*]. By being proactive, exploiting fluctuations in supply and demand, and managing risk, participating in commerce during wartime could be a worthwhile endeavour. Importantly, we must move away from twentieth-century notions of warfare – as Peter Wilson has emphasised, in the early-modern period war was not 'total'; it did not 'entail the complete mobilisation of a belligerent's society and economy'.[56] Early-modern nations did not seek to cripple established international trade links; national economies were interdependent and whatever was occurring politically, nations needed economic relationships to survive.[57] The actions of individuals like Thomas Baret were never more significant than in periods that were ostensibly hostile to commerce, with patterns of trade being directed not solely by international political dynamics, but being largely dictated by the social contexts within which merchant networks operated.[58]

Indeed, throughout his letter-book Baret appears to have been angered and inconvenienced far more by the actions of his business associates than by problems caused by warfare. If information was not clear or forthcoming, it was difficult for Baret to calculate accounts or to do business efficiently. Baret regularly rebuked his contacts either for neglecting to send information, or for sending information that was difficult to understand. John Fittz was asked to send clearer accounts – Baret asked that 'as soone as convenently you can give me my accompt of sales & accompt currant

56 P. Wilson, 'Was the Thirty Years' War a "Total War"?', in E. Charters, E. Rosenhaft and H. Smith, eds, *Civilians and War in Europe, 1618–1815* (Liverpool: Liverpool University Press, 2012), p. 35.

57 Talbott, *Conflict and Commerce*, p. 2.

58 Talbott, *Conflict and Commerce*, p. 6.

that soe I may by it understand what I have in hand & charge my bookes accordingly' [*p. 141*]. Rowland Cockey was admonished numerous times for failing to send updated accounts, causing Baret to ask him in 1673 to 'send me one every six months for for want of it I doe not understand my selfe in the mannagement of my affaires' [*p. 46*]. Nonetheless, twelve months later Baret had still 'for many months beene desiringe an accompt from you after two yeares standinge' [*p. 123*]. In June 1675 Baret threatened to withhold commissions until the accounts were received, writing to Cockey that 'I have bound up my selfe by a resolution soe I will hould it not to send one piece more to you till I have my accompt stated & therfore heere they shall lay till I doe understand what you will doe which pray informe me quickly' [*p. 154*]. Eventually this led to the demise of Baret's trading relationship with Cockey, because 'if you doe not understand upon what accompt wee trade its best to leave off now whilst the accompt is small' [*pp. 168–9*]. Baret's relationship with Rowland Cockey was one of his primary grievances during this period. Tensions first came to light in November 1672, when Baret insisted that his money be 'remitted per exchange which please to doe per first conveniency for really I am in want' [*p. 3*]. By August 1675, following numerous pleas for Cockey to send updated accounts, Baret lamented that Cockey 'neglect it which is not the part of friend nor can it be called civill dealinge … it doth not turne to your reputation to have an accompt of towards five yeares now dependinge' [*p. 158*]. By October, Baret was lamenting to other associates – in this case William Peacock – that 'as to Rowland Cockey I wish he did deale otherwaise with his friends than he doth for at the last the discredit will light upon himselfe altho at present the loss light upon others I am sure' [*p. 178*].

In some cases, differences in convention between practices at home and practices abroad caused problems – in August 1675 Baret wrote to Nathaniell Mathew that 'at the present not fully understandinge your invoyce … I have tryed it all wayes that I can invent but can not give my selfe satisfaction about it & therfore by next pray cleare it to me' [*p. 161*]. Baret frequently asked for exchange rates, asking John Dey in January 1675 to 'pray informe of the corse of your exchange that is at what exchange when its mony for mony from England … how much one groat is off vallue in starlinge money' [*p. 135*]. On one occasion Baret admitted to Nathaniell Mathew that 'I doe not soe well understand the coarce of your exchange as I doe some others & therfore pray instruct me what coarce of exchange is even money with starlinge & how much every penny is in the rice or fall of the exchange' [*p. 162*]. When this information was not forthcoming Baret was not shy about revealing his displeasure, reprimanding William Peacock for sending a letter 'which had noe price current in it' [*p. 233*]. There was also a language barrier to contend with: Baret wrote to Thomas Shephard that the 'worthy person whome you have recommended Mr Jacomo Lemo whoe beeing a Dutch man may possibly be as farr from understanding my language as I should his' [*p. 21*]. Baret's unfamiliarity with the Dutch language perhaps explains why so many of his correspondents were expatriates.

IV

While Baret frequently had cause to complain about the behaviour of his trading partners, the restrictions posed by institutional bureaucracy were also a source of considerable frustration, and it would be remiss to conclude any discussion of the seventeenth-century trade in Norwich stuffs, or of Baret's business, without considering the role played by the Company of Merchant Adventurers. Founded in the fifteenth century, the Company of Merchant Adventurers of London (usually referred to as simply the Merchant Adventurers or, as by Baret, the Hamburg Company) were a trading company which had held a monopoly in the export of cloth from England since 1564. At the beginning of the seventeenth century, the Merchant Adventurers 'held unquestionable leadership in London's merchant community', monopolising the export market in semi-finished cloth.[59] During the seventeenth century, the company lost and then regained its privileges multiple times, notably in 1617, 1634 and 1662.[60] The Merchant Adventurers were one of a number of chartered companies operating in the period, with monopolies in various regions and in various commodities – other examples include the Levant Company, the Eastland Company and the Virginia Company. There were advantages to a system of chartered companies – competition was reduced, preventing the flooding of markets with goods and the lowering of prices, and it enabled the government to control trade to domestic advantage. Conversely, it hindered the expansion of trade and limited enterprise which tended to be encouraged by competition.[61] In the late seventeenth century, monopolistic trade declined. In the case of the Merchant Adventurers, this was in part because woollen production became increasingly diversified, and it became

59 R. Brenner, *Merchants and Revolution: Commercial Change, Political Conflict, and London's Overseas Traders, 1550–1653* (London, 2003), p. 3.

60 J. Cooper, 'Economic Regulation and the cloth industry in seventeenth-century England', *Transactions of the Royal Historical Society*, 20 (1970), p. 85; J. Bischoff, *A comprehensive history of the woollen and worsted manufactures* (London, 1968).

61 E. Lipson, *The History of the Woollen and Worsted Industries* (London, 1965), pp. 84–5.

harder to define the exact scope of permitted trade.[62] The position of the Merchant Adventurers weakened until, in 1689, a statute threw open the woollen trade, on what proved to be a permanent basis.[63] Following the dissolution of the Merchant Adventurers' monopoly, regulated trading in general was attacked by Parliament in the 1690s,[64] and by the end of the seventeenth century the Norwich textile industry had 'shed all internal restrictions'.[65] These events sparked an expansion in the international stuffs trade that came too late for Baret,[66] again suggesting that he may have got his timing wrong.

Baret's letters highlight the tensions between governmentally-controlled and non-governmentally controlled trade. Thomas Shephard operated in Hamburg as part of the Merchant Adventurers. In several letters, both to Shephard and about him, Baret complained about his exclusion from trade with Hamburg. In August 1673 Baret wrote to Shephard noting that 'if I were a member of the Hamborough Company you would afford me the utmost of your assistance … [but] amongst your selves you have made a resolution not to deale for any butt such as are of the Company' [*p. 42*]. While acknowledging that the charter of the Merchant Adventurers 'extends only to London', Baret protested that the 'City of Norwich hath always had Hamborough marchants … till within these last 40 years' [*p. 43*]. Baret echoed the fears of many of those opposed to trading monopolies in protesting that 'I doe thinke it some what hard in soe generous a Company as yours is to discourage the new inventions of our English manufactory' [*p. 34*].

Despite the Merchant Adventurers' monopoly, this was not a completely closed trade. In principle, admission to the Company was open on payment of an entry fee, which has been described as 'relatively nominal'.[67] Baret, however, despite eventually declaring himself 'very thankfull to your court for admitting the sale of my goods', decided that he was not willing to 'take up my freedome of the Company' [*p. 115*]. Baret objected to the oath of freedom, 'which dos particularly express Holland Zealand & the rest of the Low Contres with so large an obligation to the Company that I cannot take this oath & continue the trade which I now have in the Low Contry without breaking of it' [*p. 115*]. Baret was also reluctant to pay his entry fee, stating

62 Ormrod, *The Rise of Commercial Empires*, p. 126.
63 1 Wm & M. c. 32: Ormrod, *The Rise of Commercial Empires*, p. 126.
64 Ormrod, *The Rise of Commercial Empires*, p. 33.
65 Corfield, 'A Provincial Capital', p. 249.
66 Ormrod, *The Rise of Commercial Empires*, pp. 326–7.
67 J. Ball, *Merchants and Merchandise* (London, 1977), p. 34.

that 'to be out of money for a fredome before ever I can trye my experiment or be in a probable way to gett soe much by the trade seemeth a litle hard' [*p. 43*]. Baret ultimately declined to join the Company because he was not willing to compromise his existing trading activities, and he declared in August 1675 that 'my way of tradinge is not in company but either upon my particuler accompt or elce in commission' [*p. 163*], emphasising the importance to Baret of his personal connections in maintaining this overseas trade. Baret thus displays behaviour commonly attributed to those trading outside the monopolies of chartered companies, who have been referred to as 'interlopers'.[68] Baret assured Shephard that 'I have a minde to try to setle a trade in your parts & to doe it by our contrymens hands' [*p. 43*], indicating a desire to set up an independent trade in Hamburg, despite not being part of the Merchant Adventurers. It is telling that the institutional and bureaucratic barriers faced by Baret appear to have worried him more than any of the inconveniences caused by trading between two countries at war. Certainly they occupy far more space in his letter-book.

Excluded (at first by the monopoly and later by choice) from the Merchant Adventurers and operating during the Third Anglo-Dutch War, it was important that Baret traded within networks that he knew and trusted. In February 1673 Thomas Baret had ordered 'a totall withdrawinge my wholle conserns from Amsterdam', but on learning that Rowland Cockey – who at this stage was still (just) in Baret's good books – would 'still abide there & that there is some small trade to be driven there I will not totally desert you & that place but lett some small stock runn the fate of the place … I will keepe a small trade goeinge as long as you stay there' [*p. 11*]. In June Baret was adamant that he was 'unwilling to adventure any more goods as yet … the danger of the present warr dus make me at present unwilling', but asked nonetheless 'could your freinds give me any incouragement' [*pp. 31–2*]. Like many merchants, Baret made use of contacts both for practical assistance and to gauge the likelihood of future success.

V

The significance of Baret's letter-book is multi-layered. That no official data survives for Norwich relating either to the volume of stuffs production or the value of its domestic or overseas trade makes the evidence contained within this manuscript even more important, offering a way for historians

68 Lipson, *The History of the Woollen and Worsted Industries*, p. 85; Ormrod, *The Rise of Commercial Empires*, pp. 124–5.

to explore these issues. In this case, the methods by which Baret moved his manufactures overseas through a range of domestic ports suggests that the emphasis placed by scholars on the domestic market for textiles may need to be reconsidered. Baret's letters also illuminate activities in broader economic contexts, both in terms of operations during wars and in periods when the monopolists had the advantage. We can see that for Baret there were many obstacles that he had to face, and that most of his concerns stemmed from the actions of other individuals, rather than from the broader political context.

Despite the undoubted importance of this manuscript to our understanding of the Norwich stuffs trade and, more broadly, to our understanding of early-modern commercial practices, there are inevitably limitations to any single manuscript volume. Only Baret's side of the correspondence survives: we do not have replies to his letters, so do not always know whether Baret's business intentions were fulfilled (though some of this can be gleaned from the content of subsequent letters in the volume). Perhaps most pertinently, no manuscript pertaining so firmly to the activities of one individual can be taken as representative. The experiences Baret had were unique to his own life and work, though enough merchant out-letter-books and other correspondence survive for us to know that many aspects of Baret's activities, and his relationships with his business associates, are fairly typical of early-modern merchants.[69] Importantly, Baret's letter-book is an example of a type of source that is becoming more prevalent in studies of early-modern commerce and economies. Traditionally, economic histories have focused on quantitative issues such as calculating volumes of trade or quantifying economic growth: a macro-level approach relying on the use of customs records, port books and records of government legislation. More recently, some scholars have begun to prioritise micro-level methodologies, using merchants' letter-books, accounts and correspondence alongside more traditional sources of economic history.[70] By placing the actions of merchants, manufacturers and consumers – including individuals like Thomas Baret – at the heart of commercial histories, these studies have shed new light on historic commercial relationships.[71] Indeed, as

69 One example is the out-letter-book of John Clerk: S. Talbott, ed., 'The letter-book of John Clerk of Penicuik, 1644–1645', *Miscellany of the Scottish History Society*, XV (2014), pp. 1–54.

70 For a detailed discussion of these methodologies, *see* S. Talbott, 'Trade and Commerce', in J. Hogg, ed., *Using Primary Sources* (Liverpool University Press, 2016–).

71 Talbott, *Conflict and Commerce*; S. Haggerty, *'Merely for Money'?: Business Culture in the British Atlantic, 1750–1815* (Liverpool: Liverpool University Press, 2013); X. Lamikiz,

Stephanie Decker suggests, this sort of 'data collection (and analysis) stands up in comparison with what social scientists do', despite criticisms of the 'anecdotal' nature of qualitative historical research.[72] History benefits greatly from the perspective of the individuals who directly participated in it – and therefore heavily influenced it – and Baret's experiences as a textile merchant-manufacturer add a great deal to our understanding both of the Norwich stuffs trade and of early-modern commerce more broadly in the late seventeenth century.

Trade and Trust in the eighteenth-century Atlantic World: Spanish merchants and their overseas networks (Suffolk: Boydell & Brewer, 2010); H. de Bruyn Kops, *A Spirited Exchange: the wine and brandy trade between France and the Dutch Republic in its Atlantic framework, 1600–1650* (Leiden: Brill, 2007).

72 S. Decker, 'The silence of the archives: business history, post-colonialism and archival ethnography', *Management and Organisational History*, 8.2 (2013), p. 169.

Biographical notes

The Baret Family of Norwich[1]

Christopher Baret (1562–1649), of Norwich.
Second son of William Baret of Westhall, Suffolk, and his second wife Margaret Pettingale.

He was a grocer and lived in Suckling House which he purchased from his step-brother, Sir John Suckling. He became an alderman, mayor in 1634 and deputy mayor in 1648 in the aftermath of the Great Blow.[2]

He married (1588) Elizabeth (d. 1660), daughter of Allen Clarke of Hemmingstone, Lincs.

Their children included:

A William Baret (c. 1594–post 1661), comptroller of customs house in Great Yarmouth in 1633, whose grandson Thomas Baret (1665–1710), attorney at law of Ludham, Norfolk, married his cousin Lydia Rayley of Horstead (*see below*); their children inherited the Heggatt Hall estate.

B **Thomas Baret** (1597–1684), grocer, alderman, and mayor in 1650. Married (1625) Sarah (d. 1692), daughter of Francis Cocke of Norwich.

Their surviving children were:

1 Elizabeth Baret (baptized 1632), married William, son of John Rayley, merchant of Norwich.

Their children included Lydia Rayley (d. 1742), who married her cousin Thomas Baret of Ludham (*see above*).

1 Information from Millican, *A History of Horstead and Stanninghall*, pp. 104–9.

2 A. Hopper, J. Agnew and E. Alley, eds, *The Great Blow: Examinations and Informations relating to the Great Blow in Norwich, 1648* (Norfolk Record Society, lxxxii, 2018).

2 **THOMAS BARET** (1636–1711), textile manufacturer and merchant, author of the letter-book, purchased the Heggatt Hall estate in 1675, and was buried at Horstead on 21 January 1711.

He married (1) Hester, daughter of John Man or Mann of Norwich; she died in 1685 and their children died young; and (2) (1695) Anne, sister of Sir Robert Yallop of Bowthorpe Hall; she died in 1715.

Horstead Church, Norfolk. Drawing by John Sell Cotman, 1814
Norfolk Museums Collections

Editorial notes

The letter-book of Thomas Baret is a leather-bound volume comprising 245 pages of copies of out-going letters sent between 1672 and 1677. An additional six pages at the rear of the volume were filled in 1695; these are copies of letters sent by Baret to Sir Josiah Child, the English merchant, economist, and politician. The volume passed into the hands of descendants of Baret's sister, Elizabeth Rayley, and was acquired with other Rayley papers and correspondence first by Norwich Public Library, and then by the Norfolk Record Office.

The text has been published here in full. Original spelling has been retained but common suspensions and contractions have been silently expanded and the modern use of 'i', 'j' and 'y' has been adopted. Names of people, places, and months are given in full where there is a simple contraction and no doubt about Baret's intention; where the author's intention is less clear the assumed expansion has been indicated in square brackets. The letters are virtually unpunctuated and have been left so, except where an occasional comma has been added to improve clarity. Capitalisation has been largely modernised. Sums of money have been rendered in £.s.d. form, as in the original manuscript, unless specified otherwise. Baret was inconsistent in his writing of numbers, sometimes using figures and sometimes letters. In this transcription, single digit numbers have been spelled out, but only when applied to quantities, i.e. 'one piece', 'two gravestones', 'three patterns', 'four years'; dimensions, weights, percentages and dates remain as digits. The aim throughout has been to produce a text with as few changes from the original as possible, but which is accurate, scholarly, and readable. Pagination refers to modern page numbers inserted by the Norfolk Record Office in 2019, and page references in the footnotes and the text of the introduction refer to pages of the original manuscript given in the transcripts, not of this publication. The pagination of the manuscript is included in the running header of the transcripts for ease of reference.

The definitions provided in the footnotes and glossary have been taken either from the *Fairchild Books Dictionary of Textiles* (8th edition) or the *Oxford English Dictionary* online unless otherwise stated.

A note on dates

In 1582 Pope Gregory XIII ordered the use of a reformed calendar to bring the calendar year in line with the solar year. This new Gregorian calendar was adopted by the Catholic countries in Europe but England continued to use the Julian calendar which was, by the seventeenth century, ten days behind the Gregorian, and was not abandoned until 1752. According to the Gregorian calendar the year began on 1 January, while in England it began on 25 March (Lady Day). Thus in England 24 March 1672 'old style' was followed by 25 March 1673, while in much of Europe it was already 4 April 1673 'new style'. It was therefore important for a merchant to make it clear, when dating a letter, which style he was using by adding NS or SN (style nouveau) to the date where applicable, and/or by using double dating, i.e. 24 March 1672/3, a practice adopted sporadically by Baret. Double dates have been added to the transcription where necessary for clarity.

Symbols and editorial conventions

* *	words which have been inserted in the original
< >	words deleted in the original
/ /	marginal entry or annotation
italics	editorial comment or elucidation outside the text, e.g. *in margin*
[*italics*]	editorial remarks within the text
[*illegible*]	word which cannot be read
[?]merchant	doubt about the transcription of a word
merch[ant]	words or letters omitted in the manuscript which have been supplied
[merchant]	word supplied
[?merchant]	doubt about word which has been supplied

Abbreviations

NRO	Norfolk Record Office
TNA	The National Archives

Glossary[1]

barakenes	barragan; barragon; barracan: a coarse cloth.
bratts	bratos: a wool fabric made in Norwich in the seventeenth century.
callamancoes	calamanco; calimanco: a woollen stuff patterned on one side only; originally manufactured in Flanders, later made in Yorkshire.
camblet	camlet: originally a costly eastern fabric, this probably refers to a substitute, a mixed fabric of wool and cotton.
drogett	drugget: a plain woollen cloth.
estamine	estamene; etamine: a worsted cloth manufactured in a wide range of qualities.
hartfords	possibly herford: a finer type of hammils cloth.[2]
hamells	hammils: a cloth used for shirts and sheets.[3]
lattin	latten: a mixed metal, usually yellow in colour, closely resembling or identical to brass.
lawn	a fine, plain cotton weave.

1 Entries are as rendered by Baret in the original text; variants are given in the definitions. Definitions are taken from *Fairchild Books Dictionary of Textiles* (8th edition) or the *Oxford English Dictionary* online, unless otherwise stated. I would like to thank Sally Tuckett, Lizzy Spencer and Michael Pearce for providing several of the definitions and references in this glossary.

2 J. F., *The merchant's ware-house laid open, or the plain dealing linnen-draper* (1696), p. 23.

3 *ibid.*

madder	a natural red dye.
crop madder	the best quality of madder.[4]
pipe madder	a coarser quality of madder.
gameene madder	a low-grade quality of madder sold in powdered form.
mascarado	a kind of 'say' cloth, made from worsted in Norwich in 1679 in imitation of silk 'mascades' from Canterbury; used for head-dresses.[5]
orr	ore: a fine grade of wool from Herefordshire.
Osnaburg	a course, plain weave cotton fabric, originating in Osnaburg, Germany.
peramides	Ursula Priestly identifies 'paramides' being manufactured in Norwich in the seventeenth century, though no definition has been found.[6]
perpetuana	a durable woollen twill fabric made in England.
Ravenburg/Rawenburg	Ravensburg: from a linen-producing town in Germany.
russells	a strong twilled woollen cloth.
saye	say: a fine quality fabric, originally made of wool, made from silk from the fifteenth century.
serge de boyce	serge de boys: a worsted fabric made in England in the seventeenth century.
serge de Nîmes	fabric produced in Nîmes, France; the original denim.
slezias	Slesia; silesia: an inexpensive lightweight linen fabric, made near Hamburg, Germany, in the historic province of Silesia.
tamel	tammel: a fine weave linen made in England in the seventeenth century.

4 For more on grades of madder *see* R. Chenciner, *Madder Red: A history of luxury and trade* (Abingdon, 2000).

5 E. Kerridge, *Textile Manufactures in Early Modern England* (Manchester, 1985), pp. 56, 128.

6 U. Priestly, 'The Fabric of Stuffs: the Norwich textile industry c. 1650–1750', *Textile History*, 16.2 (1985) pp. 204–5.

tamilens	possible variation of 'tamel'; possibly a variant of 'tamin' or 'taminy': a lightweight glazed woollen fabric.
tarras	a component for mortar or cement, commonly imported from Holland.
tekling	ticklenburg: a course fabric of hemp, linen, or linen mixed with cotton, named after the German town of Tecklenburg, where it was first made; similar to, but coarser than Osnaburg.
worsted	closely twisted wool yarn with parallel fibres.

The Transcripts

Letter-book of Thomas Baret, 1672–1677

Inside front cover

November the 26th 1672
Coppyes of all letters sent beyond seas[1]

[*p. 3*] Norwich the 27th of November 1672

Mr Rowland Cockey[2]

Sir, Yours of the 11th instant I received & am verry glad to heare that you & your good Lady are safely arrived at your owne habitation – where I wish you health & prosperity. I perceive you received mine of the 21 past but noe goods such as I wrott for can be sent & therfore I must be content to have my money remitted per exchange which please to doe per first conveniency for really I am in want for the ironmongers will force me at last to take theire owne price for I have offerd it to them at £17 per tonn & it will not doe but I am resolved to stay a litle longer. In your last you advise for some goods which I am providinge & doe intend to send away a case for London on Fryday next to be send per first shippinge when sent shall give you the invoyce which will conteyne some of every sort advised for but I can not understand you in No. 15 the darke greys shall come per next but I know not what you meane by haveing them with orrange mixture I never sent you such & therfore can not tell what will content. I would alwayse desire you to send me a patterne & then doubt not but I will humor the ware & collour to content. Inclosed I send you a patterne of such a collour as I thinke you <meane> intend if it be or be not lett me know per next I shall now send you one piece No. 4 of this collour but noe

1 Pen trials and squiggles on the first page and the inside of the back cover include the name of Samuel Rayley, a descendant of Baret's sister Elizabeth Rayley.

2 Rowland Cockey belonged to a Dutch family settled in Norwich. During the period covered by this letter-book, Cockey is based in Amsterdam.

more till you advise for them, accept tender of myne & wifes service to you and your good Lady whoe am

Your friend & servant
Tho: Baret

[*p. 4*] /No. RC2/5/ 27 pieces which amount to £106 12s 0d
per London to be shipt per Mr J[acomo] L[emo]

Norwich the 4th December 1672

Mr Rowland Cockey

Sir, Yours of the 2nd instant I received with the bill of sales & bill of exchange which I shall present as opportunity serves. The case of which the invoyce is above I sent last weeke for London to be sent per first which I wish safe with you what remaines to complete your advice shalbe sent soe soone as possible in this is six pieces of finer sort than No. 13 sent for tryall & soe are the two pieces No. 21 which I know will give content but yet I will send noe more till advise dus require these are pretty sad[3] greys but not soe sad as you wright for in No. 4 & 15 I have by me a parcell of No. 10 & five No. 19 but because you wright for none I forbeare to send them. Per your accompt of sales ending primo June you make resting then unsold 188 pieces in which you err one piece for it should be 189 & upon serch I find the error to be upon that piece sould to Symond Cox because upon the debet of charges you make one piece received back from him but doe not add it to the No. of pieces received whereby to charge your selfe with it I perceive you sell only for present money which coarse pray continue & remitt me more money as soone as possible you can lessen old debts as much as may be for I feare Holland hath an evill storme to undergoe next springe & soe I would be as cleare as I could pray by next give me accompt what the wares ware that were sent to Hamburg with the sorts & prices & to whome they are consigned that soe I may discharge them off your accompt & putt them to his. Pray lett me know what you have don in the debt of Founteyne. This butt service is all at present from

Your reall friend Tho: Baret

3 i.e. dark or deep.

[*p. 5*] Norwich the 11th of December Anno 1672

Mr Rowland Cockey

My last to you was of the 4th instant with the invoyce of the case No. 2/5 sent per port of London since which I have received none from you. The only occasion of this is to convey the inclosed in which I apprehend I have soe well humord your intended color as will give good <content> satisfaction but least I should err I send you this for approbation which if I receive I shall provide as desired. Spice dus beare a good price heere *vidz* nutmeggs cloves mace but especially the latter but much of that will not vend heere if you could send me some & direct me how to secure it from the enimies at home or abrode I should be glad but I leave it to you to doe as you think convenient for I must confess my ignorance. I heare there is two ships to come for Yarmouth. Pray my service to your lady & selfe whoe am

Yours at command
Tho: Baret

[*p. 6*] Norwich the 3rd January 1672/3

Mr Rowland Cockey

Sir, Yours of the 3 instant NS[4] per post I received & the newse therein dus verry much afflict me as well for the condition you are in as for my owne conserns with you all I can doe is to pray for you which I really both doe & shall, I have wrott to Mr John Langly[5] per this post to stopp the last case if not already gon & if sailed to stopp it at Oostend or elce wheare pray doe you the like if not already don, as for the getting goods hither I see noe likely hood & therfore must desire you to remitt what money you have by the most resonable exchange you can gett knowinge you will doe the best you can for me in that as alsoe in securing the debts & goods on hand which I shall wholly leave to you to act for the best security, if you can convey them away to Oostend Hamburg or some other place I thinke it will doe well for I thinke its not possible for you to withstand the forces against you butt I leave all to you yet should advise you to cleare that place as soone as possible you can for its possible you may have a brethinge time this winter if soe take the opportunity for I feare next spring if not sooner will have a dismall effect upon you, if Sweeds iron were cheape & you had the opportunity of any

4 Indicating use of the new style dating system, *see Editorial notes*, p. 24.

5 John Langly/Langley was a London merchant.

good conveyance to Yarmouth I wish you would send me some, heers lately an Oostender come from Rotterdam to Yarmouth but doe as you can see just cause my service to your lady as also wiffes to both I am

Your reall friend & servant
Tho: Baret

[*p. 7*] Norwich the 17th of January 1672/3

Mr Rowland Cockey

Sir, I have received none from you since yours of the 3d instant & have wrott none to you since mine of the same date. I have received advice from Mr John Langly that the last case wilbe stopd at Oostend & there remaine with Mr William Fitts till further order from you or my selfe soe I hope they wilbe lodged safe till we come to understand how things will goe, I shall at present give noe further order about them but leave you to doe as you shall see cause. I doe find heere all out land goods to beare noe price & therfore altho I formerly wrott to you to send some yet I now desire you to send me none neither momm[6] nor anythinge elce & what ever moneys you have of mine pray remitt it over to me per first because I have made a purchase heere which wilbe to be paid for by that time your bills can come due & to performe my agreement I must depend upon you for as much as possible you can helpe me with all pray by next lett me know what you can afford me towards it & give me some litle light into affaires how they now goe or are like in probability to goe with you, all our discourses heere are much to your disadvantage & therfore my feares doe make me to advise & request you to make what possible hast you cann to convey away my goods from Amsterdam to some more secure place & I hope you will doe the same with your selfe & concerns. Lidia[7] was well last weeke and gave my wife a visit, mine & wifes reall service to you and your lady & I pray god to preserve you amongst soe many dangers I am

Your reall friend & servant
Tho: Baret

6 Possibly 'mumm', a beer brewed in Brunswick, Germany.

7 Rowland Cockey's daughter.

[*p. 8*] Norwich the 10th of February 1672/3

Mr Rowland Cockey

Sir, Yours of the 3d instant S.N.[8] I received and have preserved it & by it doe perceive your apprehentions of safety in Amsterdam but really I can not be of your minde for its my owne thoughts & all my friends that there can be noe long safety in that place unless the discource of peace which you hint should take place which I see noe likelyhood of but all tendinge to the contrary & therfore I must desire your complyance with my positive order in this letter which is that by the verry first opportunityes you doe send all my goods to your correspondent Mr William Fitts at Oostend there to remaine till further order but I request you would not adventure above £2: or £300 vallue in one bottum unless you see safety in the conveyance & good convoy & then send as you thinke convenient if an occasion of relowning them should happen upon a conclution of peace they would be soe much the neerer to you but if you meete with convenience & safety for Yarmouth or London send them thither, in short my order is that by the first rationall conveyance of safety you send all my goods to Oostend London or Yarmouth which you can meete with all or if you doe thinke fitt send some to one place & some to another but I would have them out of Amsterdam which place I looke upon as not likely to continue in the safety that you doe imagine & for my debts pray use the utmost you can to draw them in. I perceive you had not received my last of the 17th past but hope its come to hand ere this although in ordinary cource of conveyance it might have beene with you before the date of your last, I have not as yet heard any thinge from Hamborough nor doe I know how to send thither & I beleive that Mr Jacomo Lemo is at same loss & therfore till I understand how to correspond with him I must trouble you pray be pleased per first opportunity to wright to him [*p. 9*] and tender my service to him & acquaint him that I should be glad to receive a letter from him with some advice conserninge the goods whether they will find a market there or if they will not to have an accompt wherein the defect lyeth its possible some others would helpe them if Mr Lemo dus wright to me desire him to direct his letters to me (for I suppose they come by shipping) to be left at Mr William Wilkinsons marchant in Abb Church Lane London to be conveyed: you complaine of searge de nîm[e]s[9] I am now come to a most perfect way of making of them that they shalbe gentle & not subject to spott but now as times goe I dare

8 Style nouveau (i.e. 'new style' dating; *see Editoral notes*, p. 24).

9 A fabric produced in Nîmes, France: the original denim.

not adventure farther till I doe understand better. I have acquainted your father of your good health they are all well & your daughter Lidia is verry well & chearly & I bless god wee doe injoy the same mercy my wife & selfe present our service & reall well wishes for the prosperity of your lady & selfe which is the needfull at present from

Your friend & servant
Tho: Baret

One thinge that causeth me to desire that my goods should be sent from Amsterdam is because there can be nothinge of trade wherby to dispose of them & then why should I leave them there to be exposed to the attempts of your adversaries I doe choose although with charge to have them elsewhere

[*p. 10*] Norwich the 10th of February 1672/3

Mr William Fitts

Sir, Altho hitherto I have requested & received favors from you by the meanes & assistance of others yet I hope future times may create a better knowledge & correspondency betwixt us. Tis not long since Mr John Langly of London advised me that he had sent you a case of mine marked No. RC2/5 intended for Mr Rowland Cockey of Amsterdam (which I hope is safe arived) with advice to lett it remaine with you till further order from Mr Cockey or my selfe. By late letters from Amsterdam I suspect Mr Cockey have ordered it to be sent forward which I shall not contradict but if noe orders be come to hand pray keepe it by you and per this poast I have ordered him to send severall other goods to you which when received pray advise me of them but keepe them by you till you have my order upon them unless Mr Cockey dus give you full advice how to dispose them & then please to follow it. This with tender of service & thanks for all former respects is the need full at present from him that is

Yours at command
Tho: Baret

[*p. 11*] Norwich the 19th of February 1672/3

Mr Rowland Cockey

Sir, Since my last to you of the 10th instant I received yours of the 14th instant with the bill of exchange inclosd in it which hath given me some occasion in part to alter my orders given to you therein which were for a totall withdrawinge my wholle conserns from Amsterdam butt since I perceive that you will still abide there & that there is some small trade to be driven there I will not totally desert you & that place but lett some small stock runn the fate of the place and therfore (in all other things performinge the contents of my last) pray keepe by you some of the most vendible wares to the vallue of about £100 sterlinge & send for that case from Ostend that soe I may have about 200 stock runing upon the place & truly that is all that I would have till I doe understand better the condition of the place & sell to none but for ready money downe for if sould for a month & any disturbance comes in the time none wilbe paid, pray keepe punctually to this advice & soe I will keepe a small trade goeinge as long as you stay there for I intend to send small cases of whatever you advise for & soe have them lay at Oostend ready for you to send for as you see occasion, this next weeke I shall send for London two or three serge de nîmes and 12 No. 4 which shalbe good wares & to content and observing this method betwixt us send for what you will & I shall order it in small parcells but never keepe above £100 worth of comodityes by you after your sale of goods upon a shipps arivall be over but if they should encrease upon your hands then reduce them to order by sending them back to Oostend there to lay till you have occasion to use them & packing them (as I suppose you will) the most vendible by them selves & the most unvendible by theirselves you can but wright to Mr William Fitts & he can refer me any to you [*p. 12*] as you shall desire & by this meanes the trade that will offer may be carried on with the hazard of but a small stock its truth the charges wilbe greate but that if possible must be helped by a raise of price which I suppose you may effect because few if any as the constitution of affairs now are will adventur to send any of these goods over & were it not upon the considerations before mentiond truly I should sett still my selfe but this designe I hope you will approve of if not I give full assent to have them all sent away if you thinke it convenient I looke upon Oostend as a safe place but if I should afterwards apprehend it otherwaise I would order my goods from thence to London. I perceive you drew my last bill per exchange at 34 per 4d I doe understand that others drew at same time at 2 usance[10] at 34 per 2d which is considerable I shall accordinge to your postscript draw upon you £100 from London if the exchange dus not run too high there if it doeth I shall refuse & soe stay till you remitt it to me although I borrow the money heere upon my occasion for I am for that way which will come chepest to me. I saw your litle daughter yesterday in good health as your other friends then were I wish you prosperity whoe am

Your reall friend to serve you
Tho: Baret

[*p. 13*] Norwich the 10th March 1672/3

Mr William Fittz

Sir, Both your letters of the 4th & 9th instant I received & am glad to heare of your welfare which god continue. The disaster befallen the shipp in which my goods were will proove much to my domage but I am much ingaged to you for the care you have taken about them which beeinge don in time I hope will render them saleable altho some abatement for domage will ensue but it cannot now be helped, it was a mercy it foundered in harbor, I must request you to procure what recompence is to be had from the shipp & as soone as occasion offers forward the goods for Amsterdam, your postcript that Flemish linings are desired heere I can not answer you to because that at present I am a perfect stranger to those comodityes. This with tender of service is all at present from

Yours at command
Tho: Baret

Pray give me your thoughts consearning warr or peace betwixt France and Spaine in Flanders this sommer and whether you doe thinke that any of my comodityes would sell in Antwerpe or not

10 Usance was the standard time given to pay a bill of exchange. This varied between countries and, in some cases, cities, though it was commonly 30 or 60 days. '2 usance' here means 'double usance', i.e. the usual time was doubled.

[*p. 14*] Norwich the 10th of March 1672/3

Mr Rowland Cockey

Sir, Yours of the 3[d] & 10th instant with the accompt of sales I received but perceive your leisure would not permitt you to finish the accompt currant but you intend to send it per a future poast with which pray send me ann accompt of what debts are standinge out. I tak notice of the mishapp befallen the case No. 2/5 of which I am hartily sorry but know thers as much care taken of them as can be & therfore I must be content but lett what care can be to make the shipp master allow for without all doubt he must be much to blame in the thinge, I am glad myne of the 19 cam to hand pray follow the contents of it & make them pay downe their money & that will prevent their retorning & cuttinge of wares at pleasure & then tellinge you you must take them againe or gett noe money. I shall examine your accompt of sales & accompt currant together when its received for I doe all ready see heere are errors past & soe I shall mention all together. I requested Mr John Langly to draw upon you £100 sterling which accordingly he hath don upon my accompt & therfore pray pay it according to his advice & pass it to my accompt for I have received the money its drawne at 34s 4d Flemish per £ sterling at 2 usance I suppose he advised you off it per post dated 25 Feb past & because that per last I did advise you I would cause such a some to be drawne I have till now defferred the advice of it because Mr Langly wrights me he had don it, if I have not carryed this marchant like lett me know & I will mend it for ever after. I perceive you have sent me 42 pieces per Andress Vanderling which I wish may arrive safe but at present noe accompt of him, when he dus retorne I shall send you a case most No. 4 & an other via Oostend in the latter of which I shall putt in some No. 18 or 19 which differ only in goodness & some No. 10 all which I have lay by me in the [*p. 15*] howse, I shall verry sodainely wright to Hamburgh to know how affaires doe stand there in the meane time if you have any newse conserning them pray impart it to me, at present you have not informed me at what rate of cash you sent them pray by next informe me that soe I may be able to charge my booke with them. In future never remitt me any money to be paid heere but at London for there it serveth my occasions as well as heere and the exchange ever runneth chep there then heere & I must looke for the most saving way for truly charges dus runn soe high as I am in doubt whether I gett or loose by what I doe. The cases 2/3 & 2/4 standeth me in neere £30 all charges & therfore unless you can raise prices soe as to answer <all> extraordinary charges it will make me wary in sendinge goods via Oostend pray lett me know if you thinke some of my goods would not sell at Antwerpe yet at present I should be cautious of sendinge thither till I better understoode the designes of the French least they should once more fall upon the Spanish Netherlands but however give me your thoughts about it that I may not be over tedious to you. Presenting myne & wives service to you & your good lady I rest

Your friend & servant
Tho: Baret

[*p. 16*] Norwich the 10th of March old stile 1672/3

Mr Jacomo Lemo

Sir and worthy friend salute. About October last past by the assistance of Mr Fittz of Amsterdam I ordered a pack of goods to be sent to Hamborough which by him were consigned to Mr Thomas Shephard butt he beeing ingaged with the English Hamborough Company[11] was not fre to sell stuffs in that place altho these are not comodityes which our English marchants or any others that I have heard off ever dealt in yett he refusing favord me soe far as to recommend my conserns to you which accordingly I ordered my friends at Amsterdam to performe beeinge destitute of all corresponding in that place butt hope sir by your assistance to be well provided in it, it was a noble favor in Mr Shephard which I doe and ever shall acknowledge & I begg the favor at your hands to present him with my service & thanks for it, hitherto I have beene ignorant of the way of conveyinge letters to you but hope if this come safe to your hand I shall setle a certaine correspondance with you. The sorts I ordered to you are but a few of the many that I deale in to the Court of England as well as forraine parts please to informe whether all or any of them wilbe vendible in your parts or what is objected against them if refused or what other comoditys would prove more vendible with you if the collors should prove not to content beeing informed what would I could alter them & per future letters I may send you patterns or samples of other sorts which might give better liking, pray give me a line or two in answer direct your letters to be left with Mr William [*p. 17*] Wilkinson in Abb Church Lane marchant in London & it wilbe safely conveyed to me or if you be accquainted with Mr Free an English marchant in your citty & can prevaile with him to inclose it to his brother Mr Arthur Remington

11 The Merchant Adventurers, a regulated trading company founded in London in 1407, were frequently referred to as the Hamburg Company due to the volume of their trade that took place there.

of London it wilbe conveyed to me with safety. This beeing the needfull at present with service tendred I remaine

Yours at command
Tho: Baret

Norwich the 19th of March 1672/3

Mr Nicholas Toll

Sir, per Mr Andress Vanderling the billander[12] from Yarmouth I have consigned to you a case of stuffs for the accompt of Mr Rowland Cockey marchant in Amsterdam marked No. RC2/6 which please to convey to him according to his order & if I may be any way serviceable to you please to command him that is

Yours to serve you
Tho: Baret

[*p. 18*] No. RC2/6 28 pieces which amount to the some of £112 10s 6d

Norwich the 19th March 1672/3

Mr Rowland Cockey

Sir, My last to you was of the 10th instant since which the billander Mr Andress Vanderling is arrived but not yet unladen soe have not received the pack No. TB[13]1 but expect it every day, I have sent to Yarmouth to Mr Officiall[14] the case above mentioned consigned to Mr Nicholas Toll of Rotterdam to follow your order it goeth with Mr Andress Vanderling when he retorneth I doe heare there is an other billinder intended from Rotterdam to Yarmouth by whome I will send you an other case which is allready packed & conteyneth 16 No. 4, eight No. 18, seven No. 10, the reason why I doe not send them now is because our newse runneth against you in respect of B[ran]d[en]burgs deserting you but if by a future poast any incouragin newse should come before the shipp saile, you may expect them by this the No. 4 in the case are all foulded two pieces in one & contented with double lengths & soe is the other case that is hinted to you I did intend

12 A small double-masted European trading vessel, *see illustration overleaf.*

13 Rendered as a merchant's mark, *see frontispiece.*

14 John or Anthony Officiall, Yarmouth merchants.

Bilander
Pearson Scott Foresman, Public domain, via Wikimedia Commons

them by Oostend & made them double to save charges the reason why I send No. 18 & No. 10 which you particularly advised not for is because I had them heere laying by me & by the goods you intend to keepe perceive them to be vendible with you all the No. 4 are darke greys to content. This is the needful at present from him that is

Yours to serve you
Tho: Baret

As soone as you receive this give advice to Mr Toll for I know whether any letters goe by shipp if they doe I shall advise him of it

[*p. 19*] Norwich the 26th of March 1673

Mr William Fittz

Sir, My last to you was of the 10th instant since which I have accompt of one pack of goods TB No. 2 which are to be shipt in Zealand for Oostend & soe for London to Mr John Langly for my accompt. The occasion of this is, as to salute you, soe to desire you that the pack above mentioned may not be sent for London but kept by you at Oostend till further order & if you should have TB No. 3 come to your hand pray keepe it by you alsoe & give me advice of it which will much oblige

Your friend to serve you
Tho: Baret

/No. RC2/7/ 31 pieces which amount to the some of £120 5s 0d

Norwich the 26 March 1673

Mr Rowland Cockey

Sir, Yours of the 17th instant with the inclosed from Hamburgh I received which I shall answer per this poast: my last to you was of the 19th instant wherein I gave you the invoyce of the case No. 2/6 the above is the invoice of the case No. 2/7 both which are shipt in Vanderlin and designe to sayle to morrow, I wish them safe at port, these with what are at Oostand No. 2/5 I suppose will fully supply your occasions but if you would have more give me timely notice for I must sett [*p. 20*] them anew to worke, this collor being now all off hand & off noe repute with us for we are for curious light yellowish collor & for No. 10 & 18 I have a greate percell neere 60 pieces which are not dresed up soe take noe harme but will quickly be ready if you should advise for them of which theirs not above 10 pieces of No. 18. I am hartily glad to heare the newse of a treaty I pray God it may succeede that soe wee may once more have fre traffick. The parcel No. 1 is gotten safe into the Kings store howse where it must lay till I retorne from London whither I am goeing to morrow as for the pack TB No. 2 I have written to Oostend to have it kept there till further order for if imported at London it will cost me a jorney thither to proove them retorne goods & therefore they shall lay there till an opportunity be for Yarmouth where they were shipt. I am at this time putt hard to it for money & therefore by this post I have given order to Mr John Langly to draw £200 upon you at 2 usance which please to answer upon my accompt if it should soe happen that you had not of myne to answer it then draw upon me heere and I shall performe your order but I hope you will not be putt to that trouble. The present discourse of peace or rather a treaty dus incourage me to request you to send away noe more goods (that is retorne goods) till further order. I have perused the inclosed accompt of iron & brass but truly doe not understand it in brass & copper & therefor at present shall not advise for any in the meane time I shall indevor to understand it better & may afterwards advise for it and for iron I can buy sweeds at £14 per ton at London which dus make our iron mongers offer noe considerable price for what I have by me I can not in large butt am

Yours at command
Tho: Baret

[*p. 21*] Norwich the 26 March 1673

Mr Thomas Shephard

/According to the English acco money
No. 1 cost 80 shillings
2 cost 78 shillings
3 cost 68 shillings
4 cost 78 shillings
5 cost 76 shillings
6 cost 72 shillings
7 cost 72 shillings
7 cost 72 shillings
8 cost 58 shillings
13 cost 78 shillings/

Sir, Yours of the ultimo February post I received & retorne you my most harty thanks for it that you will please to assist an unknowne according to the English person whoe yet hopeth in future to have a better correspondency with you for my intentions are to setle a trade there if I can possiable effect it, upon the perusall of your letter I find the court would not permitt you to act in it because I am an unffre man of that company which extends only to London I live 100 miles off from it nor are they comodityes ever before sent to that place or that the company dus deale in: truly I thinke it have but its not for me to give rules to them whoe are the rule givers in the case. Sir, I must & doe acknowledge your ingenious kindness to me & hope you will still be ready to give your assistance to that worthy person whome you have recommended Mr Jacomo Lemo whoe beeing a Dutch man may possibly be as farr from understanding my language as I should his. Pray Sir, favor me soe farr as to present my humble service to him & accquaint him that by a late post I wrott to him by the name of Mr Jacomo Lemo Marchant at Hamburg which mistake may occasion a miscarriage of the letter to prevent which I have sent you a coppy of it on the back heereof and underneath the true cost of the comodityes you have with you not adding the sevrall charges I have beene att abot them since they left England my request is to you that they may be sould to the best prices you [*p. 22*] can gett & if it be to any resonable advance that I can live of it I shalbe fre to send you what quantityes the place shall vend altho it be to the imployment of a considerable stock, if you incourage I will send you patterns of severall comodityes fitt to be worne by men by women by children for I deale in all sorts to the Court of England as well as to Amsterdam & I doubt not but to send you the best stuffs that ever you saw in England or out of it, if the place will afford profitt I doubt not but to afford comodityes to content & Sir to incourage the comodityes to the higher price if your selfe & Mr Lemo please to accept any pieces there is there to make you suits of for this somer I freely present it to you & place it to my accompt I request you to take the best stuff for the creddit & repute of the English manufactory. This beeing the needfull at present I remaine

Yours at command
Tho: Baret

Sir, Pray be cautious of giveing out any patterns & lett me know what they will afford.

London the 5th Aprill 1673

Mr Rowland Cockey

Sir, I hope the two cases by Vanderling wilbe safely arived before this cometh to hand because he intended to sayle 10 days since when I cam from Norwich, wee heere have remembed our friends all the world over & Holland in particular, in my last I wrott you I was in neede of money & I feared the exchange would rise & soe requested Mr J Langly to draw upon you £200 sterling upon my accompt which accordingly he hath don per last poast as you will understand per his advice which please to honor with acceptance & if you want any more wares advise of it to (altho in hast)

Your friend & servant
Tho: Baret

At 34s 4d Flemish money pray retorne me noe more goods till farther order & if any be sent since No. TB2 cause them to be stopt at Oostend.

[*p. 23*] Norwich the 11 Aprill 1673

Mr Rowland Cockey

Sir, My last to you was of the 5 instant from London to advise of what money Mr Langly had drawne upon my accompt. I am now just gotten home & find both your letters of the 7th & 14 instant & am truly glad that I have escaped the danger in the billander which truly I never understood till I see one at the key at London and in truth they are tooles indeed. I shall answer your letters by a future poast not now having leisure, the occasion of this is to send you some patterns of such stuffs as are the mode with us especially the three patterns with orrange collour the patterne of chamolett I cutt of a piece I this day sent for London & I think is the best piece that ever you see of Norwich make if you doe thinke it would sell with you I could if required turne that sparkling eye[15] of white into orrange which I thinke should doe incomparably if the peace should goe on, I have alsoe sent you a patterne of that my suite is off and alsoe a briske grey of the same sort but the silke in future may be made into orrange or any collour you order butt of theses sorts I have not one piece made but if per next you doe retorne me such patterns as you approove off I will sett closs to worke for I doe not vallue the making of 20 pieces in hopes of peace & I am also upon

15 'Eye' was used in the seventeenth century to mean 'a slight tinge or shade' of a colour.

an experiment with a No. 4 of which I send you two patterns <of> with white butt I doe intend to alter it to orrange & not permitt the sparkling to be above halfe so much as the one which I thinke may doe verry well much better then the piece with the yellow [*p. 24*] eye sent you in the sunke case, pray consider of these things & if you doe approove of them retorne me such patterns as you like with your advice upon them & I will to worke presently that I may be early to salute a peace in your contrey with prince collors & if you send me all the princes collours I will indeavour to mix them soe in a stuff as they shall give full content & I know noe better stuff to doe it in then that my suite was made of but I can not in larage,[16] I performed your commands to your freinds whoe are well, Mr Christ & Lydia & my selfe dyned together yesterday, pray accept my harty thanks for your freindly token whoe am

Your friend to command
Tho: Baret

[*p. 25*] Norwich the 16 Aprill 1673

Mr William Fitts

Sir, Yours of the 13th I have received & request you would send forward for London the pack No. TB2 in the same shipp you tooke it out off if it be in fitting condition for the voyage for I heare that ship is left behind & the rest arived at London the reason why I desire it in same shipp is because that beeing in London I did promise a bill of store for those goods & the masters name is putt into it but I leave it to you to send them in him or another as you shall soe best fitt consignd to Mr John Langly for

Yours at command
Tho: Baret

[*p. 26*] Norwich the 30th of Aprill 1673

Thomas Shephard

Sir, My last to you was of the 26th of March last this serveth only to inquire of your welfare & convey for your perusal the inclosed paper of patterns if any should give content upon advice I might send them to you these are but

16 i.e. enlarge.

some of the comodityes that I doe cause for to be made me for my severall occasions pray my service to Mr Jacomo Lemo I hope he received my letter to him of the 10th of March past I wish for peace to incourage fre tradinge this beeing the needfull at present I

Remaine yours to serve you
Tho: Baret

Norwich the 30th April 1673

Mr Nicholas Toll

Sir and worthy friend salute yours with out day this instant Aprill, I received & retorne you most harty thanks for your kindness in conveying my conserns to Amsterdam I begg the lik favour in the inclosed which please to speede I pray god send us peace that soe wee may trade free without those feares that attend & discourage adventurers, if in any thinge I may serve you please to command freely him that is

Yours to serve you
Tho: Baret

[*p. 27*] Norwich the 30th Aprill 1673

Mr Rowland Cockey

Sir, This serveth only to convey to you per shipping the inclosed letter for Hamborough and alsoe to aske your advice upon the two loose patterns inclosed which is a comodity that I doe expect should be the new stuff for our English weare, I am now againe full of feares conserning you for methinks the peace looke farther off us then we desire it should my intentions are to wright to you more at large per poast pray forward the letter for Hamborough, present my service to your Lady and accept the same from

Your reall friend
Tho: Baret

[*p. 28*] Norwich the 21st of May 1673

Mr Rowland Cockey

Sir, My last to you was of the 30th of Aprill past per shipping to Rotterdam which I hope you received with the inclosed for Hamborough, I have now before me both yours of the 21st Aprill past & 5th of this instant by which I take notice of the sales you mett withall which were very welcome in a deade time of trade I shall observe your advice in not sending any more No. 18 at present or any other sorts but what is advised for your letters especially the last have beene soe discouraging that truly I have don verry litle in providing any goods for you which otherwise I should have don yet in last you sent me some patterns & would have No. 4 made to those collours which is not to be don for No. 4 the warpe if good is soe coverd that it will not show throw & these patterns were of No. 3 a comodity which you have oft times forbidden and No. 1 in these <comodityes> collors show verry well a pattern of which is inclosed but I dare send none till advised if you would have of these verry sorts of which the patterns are inclosed give plaine advise & how many you would have of either & I will send them per first & for No. 4 & No. 15 I will cause some to be made to show as much on the orrange as they can but they wilbe sad collours for noe others can be made of them because its the orr[17] warpe which strikes throw & make our collour but in these the warpe is hid & we can never reach the collour upon the striking & therefore I shall advise with you upon [*p. 29*] patterns before I doe enter too farr for I have already lost too much by drugg wares[18] I have neare 20 pieces of darke grey No. 4 by me which I shall send as soone as I can & then I shall have don with that collour till further order & could I but hope peace I should be briskly ingaged in the yellow or any other collour for dull trade make me as dull at it. Inclosed I send you a pattern of the nearest that I can come in No. 4 & the mischeife is its verry difficult to gett them even for these light warpes will make wares seeme ready when they would not in other collours, I see you have agreed with Ch. Fountaine its hard but what can not be helped must be indured & I shall pray hartily for his honesty in future for I shall give him a noate of expectation in my booke. I am sorry my naighbours are such under sellers but I can not helpe it I thinke you might agree there

17 Ore, a fine grade of wool from Herefordshire (thanks to Sally Tuckett for this definition).

18 i.e. goods that were unsaleable, generally because the market was flooded with similar merchandise.

not to undersell each other. But lett them doe their pleasure for either my ware or collour or somethinge elce dus exceede theirs or elce I should have noe trade truly charges & hazards are greate now & therfore doe require a good price when peace dus come if I can I will abate but if I should they will still sell lower. They heere complaine that you doe undersell & soe their correspondents wright that they are forced to sell low to keepe pace with you, the truth is I beleive your custom[ers] play slim with you both when they goe to others then they pretend you sell low & soe worke upon them & when they come to you they say others sell low to catch you if they could but lett them [*p. 30*] say what they will I care not soe long as they buy & pay for them chamolets will doe here altho it seemes they will not with you but when I have made one with a gold eye I will send it you & am almost of the mind it will tempt you for it dus far exceede any haire-chamolet pattern that ever you sent me No. 4 with an eye of silke orr & brode I shall by next send you patterns and alsoe all your prince collour with a darke browne which dus predominate mixt in No. 3 or No. 1 which will give content for they doe well but these collours can not be humored in No. 4 or No. 15 for the reasons given before, I doe now give you my full thoughts pray give me a cleare & full advice upon it & then I will sett close to worke to answer your orders I am now desirous to have an accompt currant for I have had none since primo June & therfore lett me have it per first you say the goods sent are much too short which I doe not understand for I cause the true lengths to be putt upon them & therfore I suppose they doe not fall short of what they are marked altho they may if they expect all should hould full 30 yards, the working them in the mill will differ the lengths & bredths & is not to be helped. My service to your Lady & selfe whoe am

Your friend to serve you
Tho: Baret

[*p. 31*] Norwich the 11th of June 1673

Mr Rowland Cockey

Sir, Your letters of the 26 of May last & 13th of June instant I received & shall now answer them, my last to you was of 21 May last in which I was large & doe much admire that its not come to your hand before your last to me Mr Langly conveyd it for me I wish it be not miscarried but as yet hope it is not because I now understand Mr Chr[istian] Langly kept it a weeke by him before he sent it, as to newse I know none but wee cry a victory in the first ingagement[19] as well as you I pray God grant us peace if it be his blessed will that soe the occasion of effusion of blood may cease as to trade I see you have but little nor are you like to have much this beeing the time of action, I must confess I am some what unwilling to adventure any more goods as yet for I feare your condition is not soe safe as you may imagine yet I doe intend to be providinge some No. 4 & No. 15 to the patterns you sent me that soe I may be ready to supply you as future advices shall direct, I shall next weeke if not sooner send a pack to London to goe by way off Oostend & another to Yarmouth for the first oppertunity to send from thence I will have them lay ready for your incouragement in advice butt as yet I know of noe oppertunity to send them you say that my goods are not soe good as formerley which shall be amended, the truth is the cessation of my Holland trade hath caused me to employ those workemen in English comodityes which I use to employ in Hollands comodityes which is the true occasion of your complaint, if we had peace I should be verry ready to crave the advice & assistance of your freind Mr [*p. 32*] Davall in Hamborough to whome pray my service when you wright. I have not as yet received any advice letters from Mr Shephard or Mr Lemo soe know not whether they have received any of my letters or disposed of any of my comodityes which with the danger of the present warr dus make me at present unwilling to enter farther into the Hamborough trade could your freinds give me any incouragement I might send him a pack of goods for a beginninge, Mr J[ohn] Langly adviseth me that he hath drawne £100 upon you for my accompt at 2 usance which please to honor with acceptance & payment in my last I requested you to send me an accompt currant not having had any since primo June 1672, as to the old No. 15 bad collors pray retorne them by way of Yarmouth by first oppertunity for if I had them heere I question not but to make them saleable againe. Please to accept the retorne of my thanks to you and your good Lady for your presents the first I have received & experrimented its goods the other per Mr Devel I shall expect & give it a serious perusall sutable to the goodness of a booke which hath your commendation I wish I had oppertunity to make you requitall & hope that I shall in future. Your friends & daughter are all in good health my service to you & your Lady whoe<re> am

Your reall friend to command
[Tho: Baret]

19 The first engagement between the Dutch and the English at the Battle of Schooneveld, 7 and 14 June 1673.

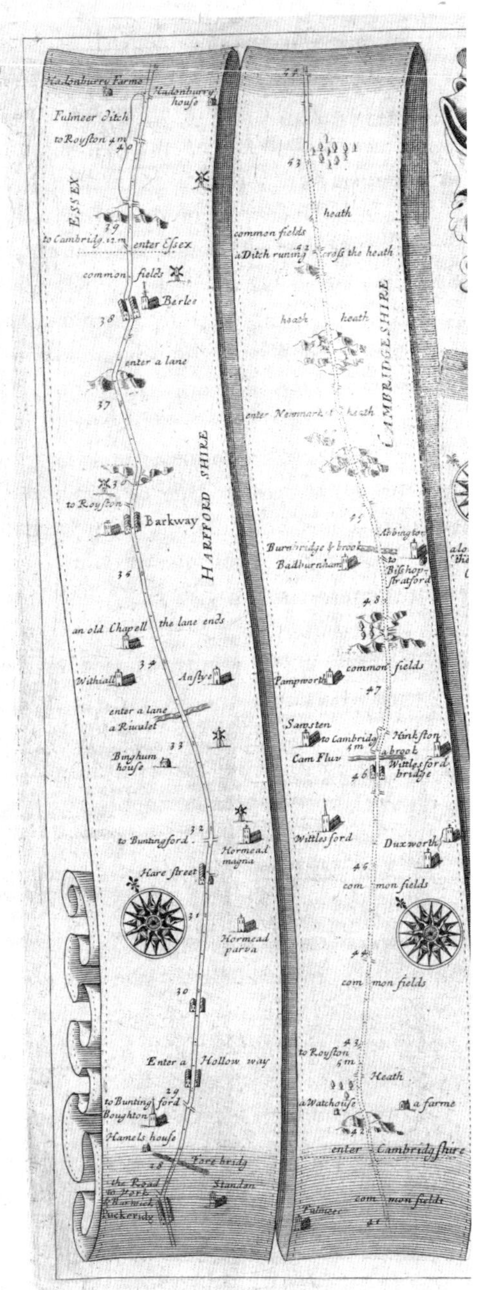

A Route Map: the road from London to Norwich in Norfolk. John Ogilby, 1675 © The British Library Board. Maps.C.6.d.8, plate 46

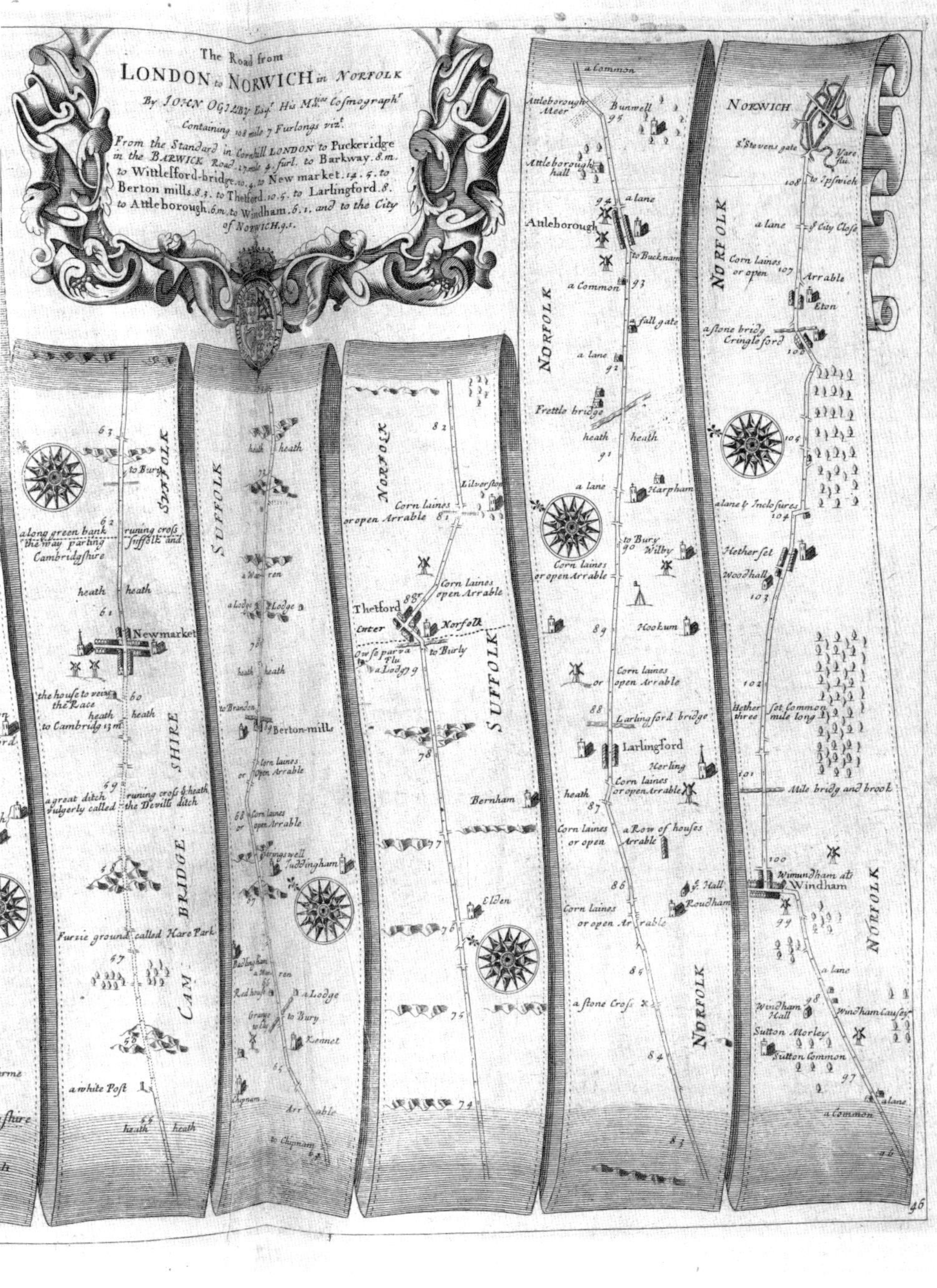
The Road from
LONDON to NORWICH in NORFOLK
By JOHN OGILBY Esqr His Maties Cosmograph^r
Containing 108 mile 7 Furlongs vizt.
From the Standard in Cornhill LONDON to Puckeridge in the BARWICK Road .27.mile 4.furl. to Barkway. 8.m. to Wittlesford-bridge.10.4. to New market.14.5. to Berton mills.8.3. to Thetford.10.5. to Larlingford.8. to Attleborough.6.m. to Windham.6.1. and to the City of NORWICH.9.1.
SUFFOLK
CAM BRIDGE SHIRE
Newmarket
along green bank the way parting Cambridgshire
runing cross Suffolk and
the house to veiw the Race
to Cambridg 13 m
a great ditch vulgerly called the Devills ditch
Furzie ground called Hare Park
a white Post
heath
to Bury
to Brandon
Berton-mills
Corn laines or open Arrable
Chipnam
to Chipnam
a Lodge
Kennet
NORFOLK
Lilverston
Corn laines or open Arrable
Thetford
Enter Norfolk
Owse parva Flu
to Burly
Bernham
Elden
Attleborough Meer
Bunwell
Attleborough hall
Attleborough
a lane
to Bucknam
a Common
fall gate
Frettle bridge
Harpham
to Bury
Wilby
Hookum
Larlingford bridge
Larlingford
Herling
a Row of houses
Roudham
a stone Cross
NORWICH
St Stevens gate
Yare flu
to Ipswich
a lane
Corn laines or open
Arrable
Eton
a stone bridg
Cringleford
alane & Inclosures
Hetherset
Woodhall
Hetherset Common three mile long
Mile bridg and brook
Wimundham als Windham
Windham Hall
Windham Causey
Sutton Morley
Sutton Common
a Common

[*p. 33*] Norwich the 27 of June 1673

Mr Rowland Cockey[20]

Sir, My last to you was of the 11th instant since which I have received none from you, the above is a coppy of a letter sent you which I feare is miscarryed I have sent to Yarmouth a pack to be sent to you per first oppertunity which conteyneth as follow 18 pieces No. 4 cost 76s per piece *£68 8s 0d* and I have provided for an other in which shalbe a percell of No. 15 which will come to you per first oppertunity which I suppose will not be long because wee are in dayly expectation of a billander from Rotterdam having received advice of him from Mr Toll by whome you may expect the goods, I have made a piece or two to the inclosed patterns which are to come in that I am providing for if they doe content you in the patterns I will if advised make some more. I pray God send us peace my service to your Lady & selfe whoe am

Your friend to serve you
Tho: Baret

[*p. 34*] Norwich the 4th of July 1673

Mr Thomas Shepard This letter was not sent[21]

Sir, Yours of the 2d June I received and by it perceive that my former letters & said patterns cam safe to hand but I perceive I meete with a greate infortunity by not being permitted to have my goods exposed to sale by a person fitted for the imployment nor am I like to have leave granted by the Court that any should act for me I must acknowledge my selfe not to be free of the Hamborough Company neither doe I know how to procure it & therefore I must totally defit trading to your ports & steere my coarse of trade some other way yet I doe thinke it some what hard in soe generous a Company as yours is to discourage the new inventions of our English manufactory which amongst others would prove to the bennifit & repute of our nation, if I did know how to procure leave I would attempt it but since I am ignorant I must acquiess not without my thankfull acknowledgements to you of your kindness in beeing willing to assist me if you could. Sir, it beeing in vaine to have the goods lay any longer in the condition they now are under I have ordered my friend Mr Rowland Cockey of Amsterdam by whose advice they

20 Merchant's mark in margin, *see frontispiece*.

21 This letter is crossed through.

were sent to you to appoint some persons to call to you for the goods & alsoe the paper with the patterns to whose order be pleased to dilliver both & the same person that received them shall reimburse you of what charges you have beene at about them. I am truly sorry that I am not in a capacity to correspond with you I wish I were, in the meane time if I may be any way serviceable to you please to command him whome you shall ever finde

Your friend & servant
Tho: Baret

[*p. 35*] Norwich the 7th of Julie 1673

Mr Thomas Shepard

Sir, Yours of the 2nd June I received and by it take notice you have received all mine with the patterns therewith sent & that you were willing to dispose my goods & doubted not but that you might sell them to accompt but because I was not free of the Company & that the Court would not give you leave therfore you could not undertake the disposing of my goods yourselfe or incourage me to send any more into your parts, this is the contents of your letter in answer to which I retorne you my most harty thanks for your willingnes to deale for me in case the Court would give you leave & alsoe acquaint you that your Court are verry hard with you & me in not permitting you to vend the new invented comodities of our English manufacture for a subject of England whereby not only profitt but repute may be gained to our native contry, its possiable your Court may not have taken notice of the late Act of Parliament by which the King and parliament have given incouragement to marchants to trade frely into any countryes or places about you and therfore I shall heere give you a coppy of the late Act of Incouragement which passe the royall assent about three months since *viz*

> *Anno vicessimo quinto Caroli Regis* &c[22]
>
> for incouragement of the Eastland Traders be it enacted by the Kings most Excellent Majestie by & with the advice and consent of the Lords Spirituall & Temporall and Commons in this present parliament assembled & by the authority of the same thatt it shall & may be lawfull to & for every person & persons native or forrainer from & after the 1st day of May which shalbe in the [*p. 36*] yeare of our Lord 1673 at all times

22 In the twenty-fifth year [of the reign] of King Charles, i.e. 1673/4.

to have free liberty to trade into & from Sweden Denmark & Norway anything in the Charter of the Governor Assistants & fellowshipp of marchants of Eastland or any other charter grant act or any thingc elce heertofore made don or heerafter to be done to the contrary in any wise notwithstandinge.

Sir, this is a true & faithfull transcript of the Act of Parliament & by it you see that you may correspond with me & act for me whither the Court gives leave or not if you be willing to undertake the imployment & therfore I request that by first oppertunity you would please to lett me know what you will doe in it that soe if it be your pleasure to refuse I may consigne my goods to some other person least that by their long layinge by they should take domage by not beeing timely exposed to sale. Sir, give me leave to desire you to give me your speedy answer that soe if you refuse I may supply my selfe with an other correspondent whome I shall request to receive the goods & patterns & repay you such charges as you are out off, this with the tender of service is the needfull at present from him that is Sir

Your reall friend & servant
Tho: Baret

[*p. 37*] Norwich the 9 of July 1673

Mr Rowland Cockey

Sir, Yours of the 7th instant I received with the inclosed patterne to which I have ordered severall to be made both of No. 4 & 15 of which I hope to send you some by the next shipp for Rotterdam having the greter part of a pack already by me but as yet I doe not heare of any arrived from your parts altho dayly expected in which I hope to recive the retorned No. 15 upon which I shall exercise my skill to make them vendible againe, by last I sent you a patterne of a new invention upon the stuff No. 4 but it proving some what rewey[23] I have made an other experriment a patterne of which is inclosed & doeth prove free from rewes and I thinke will give soe good content as you may adventure to advise upon it but that I leave to your judgment, I have only made one piece which shall come per next but I desire that by the verry next poast you would please to give me as large advise as possible you can upon any patterns or goods sent because by that time your letter come to my

23 i.e. uneven or ribbed.

hand we shall have but 14 dayes to make any wares in for that upon the 14 of August next wee shall shall have all our loombs sealed up from working any more till Michelmass next by the fixeed law of this place & therfore pray forget not by next post to give me your thoughts of all vendible goods & what quantityes you desire & alsoe pray remember me with an accompt currant not having had any since primo June 1672, our imbargo is now off as is discoursed soe hope for sodaine oppertunity for Rotterdam which way I choose that by Ostend beeing soe chargeable that wares will not alow it, as to Hamborough I have lately received a letter from Mr Thomas Shephard the contents of which are that in regard the Court there [*p. 38*] will not give him leave to vend any goods for me he hath putt them into the hand of an honest man to dispose for me but he tells me plainely he is not skilled in the way soe feares they may lay long by & discourageth me in sending any more but with all tells me that if he could gett leave himselfe to receive & dispose my goods for me he did not doubt but many of them would turne to accompt. I have by this post informed him that by a late Act of Parliament in March last free liberty is granted to all persons to trade into those parts & soe by next request his answer whether he will correspond with me or not & if he will not I will order Mr Davall to receive my goods of him but whether he will or will not present my service to Mr Davall & lett him know that iff he can any way incourage my comodityes I will consinge some goods to him but request him to have noe discoarse with Mr Shephard about me & alsoe send him the inclosed coppy of the Act of Parliament wherby he may freely deale for me without any leave to be asked of the Court there, in hast I rest

Your friend & servant
Tho: Baret

[*p. 39*] Norwich the 16 of July 1673

Mr Rowland Cockey

Sir, I have at at present none of yours before me to answer, my last to you was of the 9th instant which I hope is come safe to your hand in which I did mention some patterns that I had sent but it fell out soe that I could not then send them to you but have now inclosed them, that pattern which hath noe paper affixed to the back of it I have made a wholl piece to it of 53 yards which shall come in the next, that pattern which hath a paper affixed to it is only a yard of stuff that I made for tryall, I send them to you for your opinion if you like any or both you may have some made to it of these or any other collour you shall thinke fitt. I pray god send us peace but truly I feare wee shall not have it sodainely my thoughts are many times conserning you & could wish you & you wholl conserns heere till the action of this sommer were over these patterns are not hot prest[24] whereby you may see them at worst & hot prest them if you please, I am considering with my selfe whether I should desire you to buy me a shipp or two that are good of about 60 tonns a peice conceiving you might buy good penniworths[25] in Holland but I would have none but late built shipps, lett me know your thoughts per first about it & at whatt rate such shipps may be bought. My service to your Lady in hast I rest

Your friend to serve you
Tho: Baret

[*p. 40*] /No. RC2/8/

6 pieces No. 15 that 31 yards per piece at 4s 2d per yard cost	£38 15 0
1 piece No. 22 that 52 yards at 3 shillings per yard cost	£7 16s 0d
4 piece No. 23 cost 90 shillings per piece	£107 0s 0d
8 piece No. 4 cost 76 shillings per piece	£30 8s 0d
19 pieces	£94 19s 0d

shipt at London per Mr John Langley

Norwich the 6th of August 1673

Mr Rowland Cockey

Sir, Yours of the 25 past & 4th instant I received. I have by the port of London sent you the case above mentioned which I hope will come safe to your hand the No. 15 beeing the new collour to content & fine wares cost more per yard then last did & I hope you will gett it answered the piece No. 22 is not hott pressed if gives you as good content as it did me whoe see it from end to end it will proove a commodity, No. 23 showeth well but its verry difficult to make them free from rewes, No. 8 are good collour but now I have noe more of the sad darke gray collour & therefore if you would have any of that collour you must give time for making the yarne for now I am altogether upon the orrange mixtures and have neere 50 pieces of that collour in No. 15 & No. 4 which wilbe all finished in 10 dayes time when we shall cease farther making till Michaelmas, as soone as finished I shall send them for London for conveyance unless an opportunity by the billanders retorne which we have

24 Hot-pressing: a technique for finishing cloth.

25 i.e. a bargain, or good value for money.

soe long expected should give conveyance from Yarmouth the pack RAC[26] in canvace dus lay still at Yarmouth through the neglect of J[ohn] Official elce might have beene with you by a billander that cam through the roade the master landed & cam to him and I was in Yarmouth & prayed him to shipp it that afternoone least he should be gon & he deferred it till next morning & the shipp sayled for Rotterdam by break of [*p. 41*] of day which neglect I shall hartily chide him for the billanders from Rotterdam not yet come, when the No. 15 come I shall use my skill about them and doubt not but to make them saleable againe I much wonder at the No. 4 potted but I doe not know what accident hath befallen it its a mild piece & soe can not possiably be greasy, when you have an opportunity send it over & its possiable I may amend it but if you can sell it with an abatement pray doe when your rundelet[27] dus arrive if drinking to you will make you briske you shall not be mellencolly. Sir, I doe thanke you for your prints which I hope to receive, pray my service to your Lady litle Ledia was well yesterday I am

Yours to command
Tho: Baret

[*p. 42*] Norwich the 6th of August 1673

Mr Thomas Shepard

Sir, Yours of 21st July past is now before me I have perused the contents of it, as for your respects in it and former actions to my advantage I must & doe acknowledge my thankfulness to you & if ever it layes in my power to make any retaliation you may frely command it butt the contents of your letter in short is this that if I were a member of the Hamborough Company you would afford me the utmost of your assistance which I doe acknowledge to be a favor with much ingenuity as to the some you mention the fredome will cost I stick not much at it but had rather alowe it to your court for permission then to give it heere upon reasons following, yet the Act that giveth dispensation which I formerly gave you hath this following clause alsoe *videlicet* and it is heerby farther enacted by the authority afforesaid that whatsoever person or persons subjects of this realme shal desire to be admitted into the said fellowshipp of marchants of Eastland that every such person shalbe admitted into the said followshipp paying for his admission the sum of forty shillings & noe more. This and the former clause are by all marchants heere

26 Rendered as a merchant's mark.
27 Rundlet: a measure for wine or spirits; also a cask or vessel containing liquid.

taken to have relations to your Company butt I am not ignorant that it dus dislike your court there & therefore amongst your selves you have made a resolution not to deale for any butt such as are of the Company, tis truth the parliaments dispensation dus not voide your charter & goods of a subject of England can not now be seized yet I am informed you will make them pay citizens [*p. 43*] duty but that is but small, the success that hitherto I have had would discourage a younge man from sending any more but I must confess I have a minde to try to setle a trade in your parts & to doe it by our contrymens hands but to be out of money for a fredome before ever I can trye my experiment or be in a probable way to gett soe much by the trade seemeth a litle hard I must confess I have beene informed the Hamborough marchants are men of able estates & ingenious men butt the Company as a Company are much indebt and if soe this might be an argument against my beeing of it but I have other reasons which follow, I am informed that your Charter extends only to London & certaine limitts there about which can not reach to me whoe live 100 miles from it this *secondly* City of Norwich hath always had Hamborough marchants & Eastland traders till within these last 40 yeares I must confess I am too young to remember any but *thirdly* my father dus remember severall & soe I claime the previlidge as a cittizen of Norwich for me liveing heere to be free of a company in London might bringe severall charges of the place upon me for its not above three yeares since they forced my father in law[28] to fine in London I never expect to be guilty of an ald mans estate but beeing an out lyer if they should thinke soe it twere to noe purpose to me to say the contrary. Sir, upon the wholle I hope you wilbe permitted to correspond with me with out beeing free, please to give mee your thoughts per next & direct your letter to me in London to be left at Mr William Wilkinsons marchant in Abb Church Lane for by that time your answer can gett England I expect to be in London, [*p. 44*] this with service is the needful at present from

Your friend & servant
Tho: Baret

	£ s d
/No. RC2/9/ 11 pieces at shipt from Yarmouth by J[ohn] Official	63 17 0

28 John Mann of Norwich, father of Baret's first wife Hester. He was mayor of Norwich in 1653, and subsequently sheriff of London and high sheriff of Norfolk: *see* B. Cozens-Hardy and E.A. Kent, *The Mayors of Norwich, 1403–1835: Being Biographical Notes on the Mayors of the Old Corporation* (Norwich, 1938), p. 87.

Norwich the 28th of August 1673

Mr Rowland Cockey

Sir, Yours of the 25 instant received with the Bill of Exchange upon Mr Andr[e]w[s] which I shall present tomorrow he not beeing at home this day, I am glad No. RC2/8 is safely arrived the above with that formerly sent to Yarmouth wilbe shippt in Riscott[29] whoe intend to sayle godwilling next weeke if not this I wish him a good voyage & this day I shall send for London another case of stuffs all No. 4 & then I can send no more till new made except you should want six or eight pieces No. 15 more butt yet lett me have advice what is wanting both for stuff & collour because although I can not make wares yet I can provide meterialls to bring off wares by the verry first & if sales should incourage I wold worke now in private corners wher I [s]hould not be found out, underneath I will give you the invoice [*p. 45*] of the pack sent for London I perceive you are coming over I wish you a prosperous jorney & shall be most hartyly glad to see you at London where I shall over 14 days and abide there some tyme, my harty thanks for your prints which with the retorned stuffs & books I reid and am sorry the author had such fate, pray my service to your lady this night I saw Lidia well & soe are the rest of your relations I am

Your reall friend & servant
Tho: Baret

/No. RC3/0/ 22 pieces of No. 4 at 76s £83 12s 0d
I can not tell but that I may send this per Yarmouth with the other two.

Norwich the 19th of November 1673[30]

Mr Rowland Cockey

Sir, Yours of the 14th instant I received, I am truly glad that you & your Lady & family are in good health I bless god I am at last gotten safe home to my owne habbitation where now I find all friends in good health and doe present you with their service but wee have lost our good friend my co[u]s[in] Cock[31]

29 Probably Jacques van Reyschott: *see p. 47*. This is in a different hand, and the name is rendered differently, indicating use of a clerk/apprentice to copy outgoing letters.

30 The date here appears to be a mistake given where this letter appears in the volume. It seems that the month should be September.

31 Possibly the Revd George Cock, rector of St Peter Mancroft, Norwich, died 28 Oct. 1673.

whoe departed this life about a month since to the greate greife of all his friends & to this citty in generall, now I am come home I doe find that my workemen have made me since my departure about 40 pieces of No. 4 good wares & good sortment in collour which doe waite your advice for transportation I am sorry for the prohibition of our manufactory but shall waite your advice how to mannage my affaires in future if we can not sell them for English then wee must sell them for Spanish [*p. 46*] Antwerpe Bruxells or any other place & if you doe resolve of any place to beare the name then gett the armes of the place or any other marke that you thinke fit cutt in iron or steele & send them over to me & then what ever I send in future I will seale with those stamps & send them over to Oostend & soe you may deceive the prohibition that way & alter the No. I propose this to you if you thinke fitt it may at least deceive the rest of the traders in those comodityes from these parts when I cam from London I requested Mr Langly to draw £100 upon you for truly I am now in streights I must now request you to send me my accompt currant for I have had none since primo June 1672 but in future I must oblige you to send me one every six months for for want of it I doe not understand my selfe in the mannagement of my affaires which gives me noe content, pray lett me have it as soone as you can for I must for London againe at Christmas, accept the tender of service from him that is

Your reall friend
Tho: Baret

[*p. 47*] London the 23rd of September 1673

Mr John Fitts

Sir, Yours for Mr Rowland Cockey of the 19th instant new stile I received & am glad to heare that Jaques van Reyschott is safely arrived at Rotterdam in him was two cases & one pack marked No. 2/9 3/0 & 3/1 the invoyce of the last I suppose is come to hand ere now but if the letter should miscarry I can not rectifie it till my retorne to Norwich not havinge my books heere with me, since my cuminge to London Mr Langly has shipped of for me one pack which by mistake is No. 3/1 but should have beene No. 3/2 but as under that mistake mistake [*sic*] take the contents as follow:

No. RC3/1 that	5 pieces No. 15	cost as formerly
	12 pieces No. 4	
	17 pieces	

Mr Langly hath advised of this pack to Mr Nicholas Toll of Rotterdam which I wish may come in salvo[32] the £150 sterling by him drawne is passed to accompt & verry sodainely if exchange favor I shall either draw myselfe or order him to draw as much more which please to give acceptance to. Mr Rowland Cockey is gon from hence to Colchester and tomorrow intends for Norwich & was in health on Satterday last & left his orders with me to acquaint his Lady that he was well & saluted her with love & service pray doe the same for me, this is the needfull at present from him that is

Your reall friend to serve you
Tho: Baret

[*p. 48*] London the 24th of October 1673

Mr Rowland Cockey

Sir, Yours of the 20th instant I receive & am verry glad that you are safely arrived & have had so good success as to have a young sonn brought forth I should like it well to meete such news but I am heere tyed by the legge for 14 days longer but I have finished my busines & am now once againe free from partnership, I hope when I retorne to Norwich to finde a parcell of wares fitt for you which I shall send hither for first safe passage in this ensuinge troublesome season what I wrott about 3/1 I perceive was a mistake beeing heere without my bookes it was the RC16 putt me out I shall at my retorne be mindfull of the No. 23. Mr Langly Mr Devet & selfe wished you & your good Ladys good health in a glass of van de blanke or in English white wine I thanke you for seeinge my wife, were I in Amsterdam I would not long be your debtor, I thanke you for the acceptance of Mr Langlys bills upon my accompt when the exchange is to my minde which at present it is not yet much lower than what I last drew at I shall draw or cause to be drawne £100 if not more but I shall stay some while yet because I doe expect that after the East India sales are over & wee have discovered our resolves concerning Spaine the exchange will much fall or rise & soe I shall watch my opportunity. This with service to your selfe & Lady is all at present from

Your reall friend
Tho: Baret

32 i.e. in safety.

[*p. 49*] Norwich the 5th of December 1673

Mr Abraham Hoorne

Sir, Yours of the 10th of November past I received & am glad to heare of your good health and safe arrivall at your owne habitation. I have now received the Edams cheese out of Jan Maijart <the cost of which please to informe & I shall most thankfully repay it> *and am sorry you should putt your selfe to so much trouble & charge but I hope in future I shall have an opportunity to /express my thankfullness to you/* and *for* the charge of the coate when I doe understand what it is & acknowledge my selfe ever obliged to you for your care & trouble in it if it should happen that the coate is not made nor the buttons bought then I desire you would only send me over cloath enough to make a coate without buttons & I would make it heere accordinge to our English manner but if it be already don then I will weare it as its made & if it doeth please god to send peace its possible I may see Holland in it. Inclosed I send you a paper of *patterne of* such stuffs as I make heere if any will vend with you at Rotterdam please to advise & I will send you over a pack of them for tryall, this is the needfull at present from

Yours at command
Tho: Baret

You may please to shew the patterns but doe not discover they come from hence but from what other place you thinke convenient and if any of the patternes give content send a piece of them over & how many pieces you would have to each patterne you doe retorne me & they shalbe sent to you per first shippe for triall

[*p. 50*] London the 12th of January 1673/4

Mr Rowland Cockey

Sir, Yours of the 2nd & 16th instant I received since I cam hither, the first beeing inclosed, I could not stopp heere which made it of the older date ere it cam to my hand in it was the bill of exchange for £312 12s with the addition of exchange & banke money the vallue of £30 sterlinge which I shall get accepted upon my retorne to Norwich my jorney to which place I shall begin next Thursday, the accompt of sales to primo January instant I received and am much troubled at the domaged pieces notwithstandinge my great care butt lett the abuse be to my selfe abate the marchant what is reason for it & for your advice I shall answer it per verry first as soone as I retorne whether it be by the way of London or Yarmouth, havinge at present a supply by me of both sorts if my memory faile me not & should be glad of future advice to imploy my loombs in which at present are almost at a stand, the coppy of the states letter did not proove authentique heere for it was never delivered what newse this last trumpater did bringe I can not yet learne, I suppose you will receive his majesties & L[or]d Keepers[33] speech to the parliament by some other hand they beeinge long would proove chargeable in postage. I wish you a happy new yeare & more happy by a good & lasting peace, my service to your lady & accept the same from

Your friend & servant
Tho: Baret

[*p. 51*] Norwich the 23rd of January 1673/4

Mr Thomas Shephard

Sir, I received yours of the 12th instant & am truly thankfull to you for that paynes you have taken & arguments you have given to the honourable court of your Society in my behalf, althought it hath not attained the end desired I perceive they are resolved in their way & because I am loath to have my goods lay & perish there they will force me to steere an other coarce then ever I intended & I wish it may not turne to ill consequence to them in future butt if it doeth I am not to be blamed for I have sought all wayes to prevent it they are all worthy understandinge marchants & if ever they did see any of the comodityes must acknowledge them to be of new invention & differinge materialls from what comodityes they ever had before butt I shall cease these arguments & request you to secure the goods from their seizure in case they would doe it upon any distast of my actions heere because I doe intend to indeavor to procure a liberty heere & as I have found you my faithfull friend soe I shall freely communicate my intentions to you. The parliament of England are greate incouragers of the trade of the nation as is manifest by the liberty granted for the Eastland trade, whale fishinge & other such like trades which were societyes as well as the Merchant Adventurers and therfore I am now drawinge up reasons & statinge the case to severall members in parliament & cravinge their advice upon it with directions how I shall steere my coarse to effect a generall liberty of trade in your parts in all comodityes not particulerly mentioned in your pattent or by you

33 Sir Heneage Finch, Lord Keeper of the Great Seal of England.

accustomed to be sould & pray the parliament to declare what comodityes are & what are not under your <regulation> *Society* [*p. 52*] that soe the promoters of trade by new experiments & inventions upon the manufacture of the nation may not be discouraged to the hindringe of his majestie in his customes increase of shipping vendinge of our manufactures &c. I am much incouraged by understandinge persons that the reasons which I give will prevaile with the parliament to setle a free trade upon new experiments & inventions. To assist me in this I have now all the papers reasons answers & petitions which were used in the same case to the parliament in 1656 butt my friends to discourage me tell me they feare that if the parliament dus looke into this business its possible they may goe farther in it then I would willingly have them I must confess I am loath to doe the company any injury, but if they will force me to extremity that I must either have my goods rott upon the place or elce seeke a remedy which possibly may proove injurious to them. I am not to be blamed if any evill ensue butt yet really I am loath to doe anything that might be injurious to them because till now I never received any discourtesy from them & in refference to my selfe should I make it publique & procure a generall liberty others might stepp into the trade to my particuler domage, the reason why I doe wave your proposall of gettinge it under the hand of the Secretary of State that these comodityes are not conteyned in your Companyes charter is because that at the present the parliament are severely lookinge into the actions of the publique ministers which will make them wary of determininge anythinge against a society of their owne heads fearinge they might call them to answer it before the parliament whoe although they might doe the thinge themselvs yet might blame him for determininge it singly & the attemptinge to effect it this way may insence them against the motion when it cometh before them [*p. 53*] soe that could I procure this from a Secretary it would only serve the [?]turne for the present & to procure it would take more tendance paynes & money by servants fees then it would to attend a committe of trade in parliament and therfore my friends advise me to the parliament I am now providinge my reasons to offer them & alsoe possessinge severall members of the parliament with the justness of the cause whoe doe assure me they will promote it butt I shall not act anythinge more then preparatorye till I receive your answer to this which pray lett be by the first & if you will putt your selfe to the trouble of it pray motion them once more & in your answer be pleased fully to informe me in those two particulars 1) whether in probability theire would be a market for my comodityes worthy to be called to me if I were permitted freely to expose them to sale & 2nd what are theire reasons which make them soe resolved against givinge liberty to expose them to sale when I desire to receive noe bennifitt by the privilidges of the company butt to pay the charges of the place as Dutch men & other nations doe for what comodityes they there sell discorses of this nature proove tedious in their relation pray excuse it whoe am

Your servant to command
Tho: Baret

Sir, Since the finishinge of my letter my thoughts have beene busyed about this affaire & its come into my minde that if a letter from the Secretary of State would doe any thinge subtly the sight of an Act of Parliament which concludes them & all Norwich stuffs to be worsteds[34] or made of worsted yarne or worsted & other materialls & there upon a peculier government setled upon it, reade the act throw & you will finde it setlinge them a worsted company I say surely this will [*p. 54*] give them satisfaction for this is an act of parliament & theirs but a charter if they should say these are not Norwich stuffs or worsteds because all such by the act are obliged to be sealed by the company in answer to which it neede dus require I will send you affidavits that those verry stuffs are made under the regulation of the worsted company in Norwich or Norffolke & the reason why those are not sealed is because they were made particularly for the sale of Amsterdam & after they were made to that perfection that the Company requires I gave them a new manufacturinge which did alter both their lengths & bredths & if the seales had beene on whilst this was doeinge it would have torne the stuffs soe as to have quite spoyled them

Yours
Tho: Baret

Observe this act was made Anno 1662 since all former disputes were

Norwich the 24th of January 1673/4

Mr Abraham Hoorne

Sir, By a letter dated the 5th of December last past which was sent by shippinge from Yarmouth I saluted you & retorned you my thanks for the Edams cheese which I received out of John Maijart which letter I hope cam safe to your hand although I have not since heard from you, in the letter I sent you severall patterns of our English manufactures which I deale in that

34 Closely twisted wool yarn with parallel fibres.

soe if any of them would sell with you in your parts I might send you some over for an experriment beeinge desirous to setle a correspondency with you not knowinge but some of your comodityes might be vendible in this place & soe fitt to make retorns in them, not havinge heard from you make me to suspect that my letter did miscarry if soe I would send you over some more patterns which is the needfull at present butt tender of service from him that is

Your reall friend to serve you
Tho: Baret

[*p. 55*] /No. RC3/2/
11 pieces No. 15, 30 yards per piece cost 4 shillings per the yard
10 pieces No. 29, *alius* No. 4 ffff[35] cost 76
21 pieces shipt per Mr John Officiall or order

Norwich the 26th January 1673/4

Mr Rowland Cockey

Sir, Yours of the 26th instant I received & my last to you was from London of the 12th instant the pack conteyninge as above I hope you will receive in due time by some of the billanders from Yarmouth. These No. 15 are much better than the last sent you or indeede then any you have had & did really cost me 10s per piece more than formerly because I would have good that you might have noe cause to complayne the same coarce I have taken in the No. 29 which is noe other then No. 4 made to a better goodness & really these doe stand me in 7 or 8s per piece more than ordinary, I shall prefix noe price to you to sell at butt leave you to gett as good a price as the wares deserve when you see them but if these No. 15 will not afford 37 sterling at least per ell I will send noe more soe good indeede I hope they will yeild more, you wright to know if I can afford No. 15 such as last at 33 sterling

35 This notation appears on five pages of this manuscript, both within accounts and within prose (*see also pp. 57, 84, 119, 171*). It appears in letters to Rowland Cockey, John Fittz and Robert Pease, suggesting that it was widely understood within Baret's network. The meaning of this notation is unclear, but it could possibly be a rendering of the Latin abbreviation for 'in integrum', to mean 'complete' or 'whole'. *See* A. Cappelli, *Lexicon Abbreviaturarum* (Leipzig, 1928), p. 244. Thanks to Dr Chris Joby for this suggestion and reference.

per ell the truth is its a verry low and neere price & can not welbe afforded soe or under 35 sterling which price is pretty well butt as times now are trade deade exchange low & the like I would sell at 34 sterling as good as those you mention but if they tye you to 33 sterling I must pinch it in goodness which I would not. I hope these No. 29 will afford 45 guilders I am sure they deserve it these are darke greys darke brown & orrange & light greys & orrange & I have about 20 pieces more of same goodness & collor which lay at London to come to you from thence by the first opportunity I am in hand with No. 23 & have some ready to come off this comodity I am a litle suspitious of because with all the art & <care> paynes that I can take yet it will prove a litle rewey for if the yarne or silke dos proove any thinge uneven as the best in plotts will it makes a rew but to prevent that I worke them all with two shutles which is both charge & trouble but that I matter not if the comodity would take & if it doeth if their be even yarne or silke to be purchased for money I will have it but to make them both sides alike is imposible for then it turns to an other comodity [*p. 56*] a patterne of which I will ere it be long send to you but this I can doe that whereas in last I made the warpes of skey & gold that soe those colors might peepe thorough I can make them only of a darke collour the same to the strikinge & then they wilbe both sides alike as to color exceptinge the eye of silke butt to make them both sides alike as to wares can not be butt I can turne it into No. 1, No. 14, No. 18 & they wilbe both sides alike & make the warpes fine worsted & keepe skey & gold warpes & strike them as No. 23 are but they will proove verry deere if made good the suite which I had at the assize was No. 18 strooke off with mixt wooll upon silke warpe, any of these stuffs would doe mighty well if they would goe to the price of them & if you can incourage I will make some for tryall could I but see any appearance of peace I would adventure to make two or three pieces to each of these sorts although I lost by some of them & I would make those that sell pay for the adventure but this warr damps me but yet if you will incourage I will adventure it. This pack of goods are consigned to Mr Antho[ny] Officiall his brother John I feare is dyinge if not deade[36] as to the accompt currant if it wanteth nothinge but the Rotterdam Zealand or Ostend charges which are of late contracted send it away without them its only under wrightinge that the charge of such place or places upon these goods are not heere included but must be added to the next. I have a phantacy that yet before summer you wilbe glad to make peace for now the parliament will take you to taske

36 For John Official of Great Yarmouth, merchant, see probate papers, 2 June 1674, TNA, PROB 4/1575

Mr Langly have received the old hock & hath either drunk it out alone or elce keepe it to drinke your good health when peace comes but *he* sayes he will tapp next weeke when I come at it I doe assure you shall not be forgotten & accept my thanks, in the meane time my service to you and Lady I am

Yours to serve you
Tho: Baret

[*p. 57*] This is a postscript to last letter

Mr Cockey

I would faine be havinge some goods from Holland for I could dispose of some madders[37] at London therfore give me an accompt of their prices. Cropp, No. 0, pipe, gameene,[38] are fittest for that place, mull madder & the two latter sorts are fittest for this but heers two much dirty madder heer already & therfore if I bringe any hither I would bringe good, lett me know how spice dus rule & wyer & brass ketles I suppose these comoditys may be brought over but alsoe lett me know what the fraight is & whether that will not eate out the profitt for I am ignorant in them & alsoe of the danger if any be in them to land them lett me know how iron dus rule with you & if there be noe good to be don in buyinge a prise ship or two in Zealand for I would faine buy one if a penniworth were to be had in one elce I may play the foole & adventure to build one but I would not exceed 60 tunns or thereabouts.

Yours
Tho: Baret

Inclosed I send you a new patterne which is almost both sides alike. I am now in greate hopes wee shall have a peace & therfore if there be any comodityes fitt for my sale heere which would rise if a peace dus come I should be willinge that you lay out 2 or 3 hundred pounds for me & therfore give me your advice for if there were noe good to be don in these ways I would take the opportunity to draw before the exchange dus rise

37 Madder is a herbacious plant, the roots of which are a source of red dyes.

38 Crop madder, the best quality of madder, a red natural dye; pipe madder, a coarser quality of madder; gamene madder, a low-grade quality of madder sold in powdered form. For more on grades of madder *see* R. Chenciner, *Madder Red: A history of luxury and trade* (Abingdon, 2000).

No. RC3/3 19 pieces No. 29 cost 76s per piece
3 pieces No. 4 cost 68s per piece
2 pieces fff[39] No. 15 cost 4s per yards at 30 yards
2 pieces No. 15 cost 3s per yard at 30 yards
26 pieces shipt at London per Mr John Langley

Norwich the 11th of February 1673/4

Mr Rowland Cockey

Sir, My last to yow was of the 26th past since which I have received none from you. The above is the invoyve of one pack of goods to come to you from London which Mr Langly takes care of to shipp it. The wares are the same to them sent you laste which I hope are saffely arrived having beene sayled from hence since fryday last, in this pack are two pieces of No. 15 which are [*p. 58*] good wares & as good as I can afforde to sell at 33s per ell if this ware dus give your customers content then I will make only such & leave off the finer & higher prised ware, inclosed I send you a patterne to have your advice upon it which I should thinke might sell for No. 15 the price wilbe about 33s per ell its a verry good stuff made fine thick & even it differs from a searge de Nîme[s] only in that the back is a plaine stuff, I have only at present made a small remnant for tryall if you can incourage I shall goe on with them or elce cease them. I did order Mr John Langly by last poast to draw £100 upon you for my accompt which I suppose he hath don although as yet not advised me off it which pray accept & performe my intentions were to have charged noe money as yet butt the truth of it is that my necessity at London through disappointments there obliged me to it, I now am in perfect hopes that there wilbe a peace & cessation of armes sodainely which makes me to bethinke my selfe for trade I have within these 10 days bought 1000lb weight of combed yarne in mixtures to my content & now in the same hands its risen 3d per lb & the apprehention of a peace doth make comodityes rise heere wooll especially & I suppose it will doe the same with you there & therfore if iron be cheape with you as I am informed that it is at 6 guilders right sweeds I could be content that you did buy me a parcell and lett it lay by till an opportunity to gett it over I should accompt 20 tunn noe burthen but I would have almost half squares for they are verry scarce heere & soe is narrow brode which is 2 *inch* & ½ brode. Sir, I shall leave you to doe

39 *See* note 35.

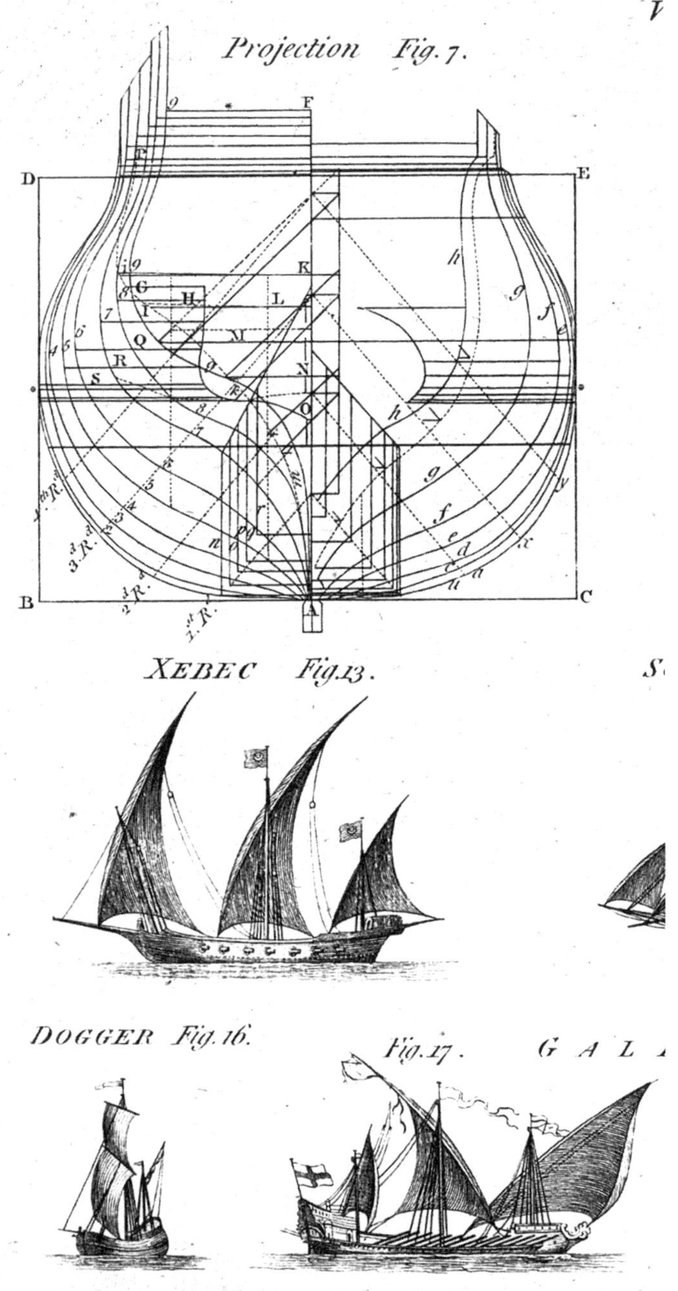

Ship-building: detail showing various types of ship, Brig, Billander, Dogger, Galley, Galliot, Ketch, Schooner, Sloop, Snow, Xebec. Engraving by J. Taylor. Wellcome Collection.

V E S S E L

KETCH Fig. 10.

SNOW Fig. 9.

BRIG Fig. 11.

BILANDER Fig. 12.

GALLIOT Fig. 15

SCHOONER Fig. 14.

SLOOP Fig. 19.

L L E Y

Fig. 18.

for me as you conveniently can butt truly I doe looke upon this juncture of time to be fitt to buy comodityes in, pray Sir my service to your Lady & accept that same from

Your reall friend
Tho: Baret

[*p. 59*] Norwich the 13th of February 1673/4

Mr Rowland Cockey

Sir, My last to you was of the 11th instant & I hope before this cometh to hand you will have hearde of the good newse of a peace[40] betwixt England & Holland although I have long wished for it yet now really it is come sooner then I could expect it butt not any thinge the less welcome be for that it doeth revive my spiritts & I hope it will revive trade that soe you may be in a more certainty of advisinge for wares which advice I am now ready for & hope your next wilbe an incourageinge letter. By last poast Mr John Langely advised me that he had drawn accordinge to my order £100 upon you which I now wish had not beene don because the exchange did rise soe much upon the discovery of the peace concluded butt for that as soone as the exchange is risen a litle higher I will remitt £100 to you in leiu of it if your next letter in answer to this dus advise me soe to doe, because that in regard I understand that iron is cheape with you as I did hinte to you in my last I would have a parcell bought for me & sent over by the first shipps that come 20 tonn if cheape would not be two bigg a parcell for me if you can not effect this out of my effects in your hands upon advice I will remitt you money from London for the raise of the exchange will much helpe me, by last I advised you that I would have half square or thereabouts & some narrow brode that is 2 *inch* ½ the rest narrow flatt I would alsoe desire you to send for me to London five or six bales of madder *vidz* two of cropp, two No. 0 & 21 of pipe or gameene madder if they be good & to be bought cheape & send them by the first shipps thither as to all other things which I wrott for before if you have don nothinge in them lett them alone if you have I shall accept it butt if they be now to be don I feare the time is over slipt butt I shall leave you to act in these things for me as you would doe for your selfe but the sooner I can have these things

40 The Treaty of Westminster ended the Third Anglo-Dutch War. It was signed by Charles II on 9/19 February 1674.

over it wilbe the more to my advantage. [*p. 60*] This with service is all at present from

Your friend to serve you
Tho: Baret

Norwich the 25th of February 1673/4

Mr Rowland Cockey

Sir, Yours of the 16th & 23rd instant I received & have since heard of the safe arrivall of the pack RC3/2 at Rotterdam by a shipp yesterday arrived at Yarmouth from same place I hope ere this time its come safe to you I wish as good success to that from London. I have this day received advice from Mr Ferrier (whome at present I imploy although I thinke it not soe convenient because he hath all other mens imployment upon his hands) that there is a shipp sett in for Rotterdam which is obliged to goe the first by which I intend to send you a pack which will conteyne severall new stuffs & the white callimancoes[41] advised for with some No. 15 No. 29 & No. 23 which pack shalbe marked RC3/4 lett your orders be with Mr A[nthony] O[fficial] about it what you wright about wares shalbe observed and performed with as much speede as possible. I am glad you sent me over the cloath marke of the pieces No. 15 sould to Arrant de Young for now I will not loose one penny by it had you done soe by the pieces held short I would have had recompence. I have by me a parcell of No. 10 which are of the old stock when you would have them over please to advise & they shalbe sent since the certaine newse of peace all materialls & manufacturs are strangly risen in price some materialls are risen 4s in the £ sterlinge but the lowest is neere 3s the person of whome I bought my callimancees cam this day & tould me that if he had them now to sell he would have 8s per piece more & yet I gave him then 4s per piece more than I gave him for the last I sent to London & mixt wooll yarne is risen 8d in every pound weight with in 14 days & I expect it will yet rise higher for wooll is risen a third penny for it is a most terrible rott for sheepe & therfore how in future I can afford wares or you sell them time must discover butt truly I thinke you should doe well to raise your customers by degrees that soe [*p. 61*] when I come to send my deere made wares I may not loose by them but the actinge of this I leave to your selfe. I had noe intentions that what I wrott merrily about

41 Calamanco i.e. calimanco: a woollen stuff patterned on one side only, originally manufactured in Flanders, later made in Yorkshire.

Mr Langly & the Old Hock should make you chide him for lett him assure himselfe I wilbe quitt with him although he should have given his mistris it for a present but I doe not know that he did soe. By your accompt spice is verry deere & therfore I shall not medle with any & madders are not cheape yett you may send me a bale of each *vidz* of cropp No. 0 & gameene to London per first shipps after peace for tryall butt because its a comodity that I understand not I leave you to doe as you thinke most convenient for me but I suppose such a quantity my dyers in London would take off my hands & I have reserved to my selfe in London a dry celler under my ware howse for such occasions, butt as for iron I hope you have bought some for me upon my former letters & because I must understand all things by degrees pray for tryall send me a fatt[42] of ketles *those* of three or four fulls to the fatt are most vendible lett them come by the first shipps least the Wiggetts fill mens hands before myne come over. Pray my service to your Lady and accept the same from

Your loving friend to serve you
Tho: Baret

[*p. 62*] Norwich the 25 of March 1673/4

Mr Rowland Cockey

Sir, I have now three of your letters before me *vidz* of the 6th, 20, & 27th inistant the extremity of the wether & my other occasions & my beeing absant from Norwich hath hindred me in answering them & my intentions were fully to have answred them now but that I am soe ill & full of paine by a defluxion of rhune[43] upon my eare neck and shoulders that I am not in a capacity to right large I have sent you a case of goods as follows which Mr Ferrier takes care of & although I know not of it assuaredly yet hope they are sayled

/No. RC3/4/
2 pieces No. 24 cost 72s
2 pieces No. 25 cost 70s
10 pieces No. 20 cost 85s white callimancoes
2 pieces No. 23 cost 87s
1 pieces No. 26 cost 87s

42 i.e. a vat or container.
43 i.e. rhume or rheum, a rheumatic disorder.

2 pieces No. 27 cost 82s
2 pieces No. 28 cost 100s
7 pieces No. 29 cost 76s
6 pieces No. 15 cost 4s per yard 30 yards
4 pieces No. 30 cost 98s
38 pieces

Whatever advise your letters conteyne I shall be mindfull of & in futer I shall make small packes to content & putt up two or three togeth[er] but your advise came to late for theise inclosed I have sent you some patterns of the new stuffs pray send two bales of madder for this place one of each sort the rest for London & because I must be tryinge sevrell small things to make returne [?]in pray send me a fatt of Nuremburge toyes[44] that soe I may trey if there be any good to be dun in them pray be mindfull of my account now the wather is open for I am very solicitous to know how my affeares stand, the darke pieces No. 29 which you like soe well was only ane experiment but it proves to deare to continue unles your customers will advance £4 per piece extra ordinary for its all pure wadded black which cost 6d per lb in the yarne [?]dyngen extraordinary & that coller doeth [*p. 63*] soe tender the woll above others that theres above 2d per lb lost in combinge of it above others & the springe for collour and tendernes is 2d per pound above others soe that I can not comput less then 8s per piece difference if youer *<illegible>* costomers will give it I will ca[u]se yarne to be made elce I can not but he that weaves it will find the benifit for it will not chang the collour as others the pieces of black grey you complayne of I knew of them before there was six pieces in all in which my comber did abuse me but he beggeth pardon & blame his servants for delivren it by a mistake for it was not intended for me but truly a man may be mistaken of a collour when in the grese. I am sorry the searge de nîmes did not give content for fines they exceds the French & as for the barenes of woll it was my owne fault or rather it is our humour here to have noe more woll then the milling cause had I then heare in one howers since with a fine carde strooke first one way & then the pieces turned & stroke the other way yould have woll enough pray doe but get one of those persons that dres your cloaths at ther dyinge & he will sone geett you woll enough but he must doe it by gentell strockes for that stufe will not endure much force because the striking will drave up in heaps I doe realy see that your yarne are to small for that stufe

44 Toys were small manufactured items for ornament or amusement rather than any practical use.

& therefore I have sen[t] to others parts to have yarne spun on purpose for that comodity for I will give you content if it be possible, your cosen Marke[45] is an ingenious man & proposeth high things & if he douth fayle in his expectations he will not be the first that have erred if he weare here to assist his father that soe I had two heads against one I wold adventure to provide wares with him he hath bought callimancoes very reasonable before the raise but how ever sell with him if his weares be as good as mine althou I geet not by them if he dus by all weares that I by he must find a marked not in Holland. I perceve iron is deare with you & cheap heare but I think it must rise by noue unles you gett *a good* partener & a good quanti[t]y of squares & narrow brode for them I want s[q]uuares especially other iorn is to be had /pray turn over/ [*p. 64*] plentifull at London for £14 per ton or verry litle more but squares & narrow brode are derrer. You[r] d[a]ughter & frinds heare are in good helth I shall be mindfull of the beere my serves to youer self & Lady I am

Yours to searve you
Tho: Baret

Norwich the 8 of Aprill 1674

Mr Rowland Cockey

Sir, My last to you *was* upon the 3rd instant which was written in soe much hast that I could not take the contents of it fore a memorand but as I remember it gave you the accompt of my goods beeing left behind & a slight account of a small packe then sent which with the others is shipped in Carver & nowe layeth ready for the first wind the invoyce of the last is as followth

2 ¾ brode pieces No. 31 cost 88s	No. RC3/5
4 pieces No. 30 cost 98s	
7 pieces No. 29 cost 76s	
1 pieces No. 4 cost 68s	
14 pieces	

The wares are all good & to content but the No. 29 are most greys with gold but now I have altered them into the collour to your patterns sent me which gave content of which I shall sodainely have an other parcell for you

45 Mark Cockey.

but can not send them till I retorne frome London wether I am goeing upon Monday next & shall retorne againe for Norwich that daye fortnight with out fayle & therfore send all my letters loose by the post & I can stopp them at London whilst I ame theare, yarnes doe rise heare much although at present I ame not verry sensible of it having a good parcell by me & I would hope you might [*p. 65*] raise them there to ansure the advance heere which is 6s upon evry piece of No. 29 & proportionable in all others according to their prise. I have this day frome Mr Richard Huntington received your present for which I retorne you my harty thanks & shall indeavor to understand them & alsoe dilliver one to Mr Langly fore his mistris. I have now gotten the beere brewed for you & when it be convenient to send it shall doe it but it will not be fitt till I retorne from London, I have don my best Kitt have taste of it & thinks it will give content but your advice cam in an ill time for mault is now risen with us to 12s per combe which is neere halfe advance but I would not scant it altho it runns the deerer, I wish I had knowne your minde a month sooner at which time I had provided for two barrells the one for your Lady from my selfe & the other from my wife to you butt of this more when I send them. Sir, I have consigned this case & truss of goods to Mr John Fitts to send forward to you & if he could putt off any of my goods at Rotterdam I would send him some therfore if you thinke it convenient may hint soe much to him I suppose since his goeinge from you you may be destitute of a servant I have a young lad that I would gett you to take but at present he is not above 13 yeares ould when he is fitt I shall persuade you to take him or dispose of him but of this more when the time cometh, lett me know what quantity of No. 23 I might make for I have ordered but six more then is allready sent, Mr Rich Huntington have accepted of Mr Langlyes imployment & I doe intend to make use of him if he please to accept it, when I come from London I shall goe downe & speake with him butt if you consigne my goods to him I must request his care of them by letters before I doe wish a safe arivall to what is cuminge & shall gett Mr Langly to take care of them in my absence. [*p. 66*] I wish I had 2 or 3 toun of sqares that were good altho they cost 7 guilders or 7½ to sort out the rest of my iron with but if they be not soe to be had must be content without them but truly now square iron is the most wanted pray remember my accompt for till it cometh I shall minde you of it in every letter. My service to your Lady & accept the same from

Your friend to serve you
Tho: Baret

Norwich the 15 of Aprill 1674

Mr Rowland Cockey

Sir, I have now three letters of youres before me *vids* the 10th 13th & 17th instant which I shall ansure, my last to you wase of the 8th instant & this day I have advice that Carver in which wase 3/4 & 3/5 gott well to Rotterdam upon Satterday last by the arrivall of which I soppose you are pretty well supplyed in most sorts but least you should want I doe intend this weeke to send you 12 or 14 pieces more of No. 29 & No. 31 which you may expe[c]t by the first shipps, you seme to be two full supplyed with light collors upon which accompt I have for the present turned quite out of that collour & am wholly upon the darke greys & whit for a piece or two & darke browne & gold & shall follow these collors till I have sorted out what you have by you, as to No. 15 I ame at present quite out of them for when you receaved the 11 pieces you did dislike bothe stuffs & collors & told me you feared you should not sell them upon which accompt & having soe many upon hand as I than had I turned all my loombs into other things but now I have altred agayne & after next weeke shall have two pieces cume of every weeke I have heare inquired to buy some but can finde none that are good there was a good parcell in one manes hands which I had a minde to have bought & tryed an experriment with them for they weare all hott pressed upon which accompt I have refused them for a long time but it [*p. 67*] soe fell out that your brother Cockey had bought them the night before as I doe heere there is 26 pieces all good wares & good collors butt stoutly hott pressed & as I heare he gave soe good a prise for them as 35d per ell will be noe extravaggant profit to bragg of, I wish I had bought them but you forbad all hott pressed I will supply you as soone as possible I can but mixt wooll yarnes are now soe intollerably deere as I can not afford them under 38 sterling or 40 sterling per ell of the goodnes that I send you & really you must advance No. 29 to 46 or 48 guilders per piece for I profest I have offerd to severall men 76 & 78 shillings per piece to make them for me & can not gett them to doe it when they come to know what goods are in them. W Cubit hath small reason to thanke his friend for sellinge you his No. 4 at 35 guilders for he can not now make a piece but dus stand stand [*sic*] him in a greate deale more money. I have perused the invoyce of the ketles & iron but at present have not time to doe it fully butt I finde you putt me downe more provition then I ought to alow its truth I did agree to give you 3 per cento for sellinge whilst others give but two because you obliged to sell for noe others in my comodityes but for buyinge there I can give but the comon rate therfore pray alter it, you should doe well to lett me know how much madder is risen & what price I shall sell it heere at if I can gett more then you sett I will for in regard you goe halfe part I would have your instructions in it least I should mistake not beeinge well versed in the comodity, I shall wright to Mr Langly at London about the madders & have allready prepared warehouse roome for them. I had thought to have beene this day at London but my father fallinge sicke hath hindered me but I hope he is upon the mendinge hand[46] however I intend not for London now till whitsontide. All your friends are well & litle Lidia my service to your Lady & accept the same from

Your friend to serve you
Tho: Baret

pray Sir remember to send my accompt

[*p. 68*] Norwich the 17 of Aprill 1674

Mr Rowland Cockey

Sir, This servse only to lett you know that this night I have sent downe to goe by the shipps now redy to sayle the truse[47] under mentioned the invoyce per next beeing beinge in hast

Yours to serve you
Tho: Baret

/No. RC3/6/
1 piece No. 50
2 pieces No. 31
9 pieces No. 29
2 pieces No. 4
3 pieces No. 28
17

In this pack is three darke greys which are wadded black for which you must have 2 or 3 guilders extraordinary for they cost as much

46 He lived for another ten years and was buried in St Andrew's church, Norwich, on 6 November 1684.

47 i.e. bundle or collection.

[*p. 69*] Norwich the 11 of May 1674

Mr John Fittz

Sir, Yours of the 30th past I receved & all soe the fatt of ketles & madders & the iron out of the sever[a]l shipes as advised only I want one barr of iron out of Bateman as I am informed whoe sayth that he had one ditt[o] short at Rotterdam but for certain heers one short in the generall number I have heer with per Bateman sent you two small bundles of stuffs No. RC3/6 & No. RC3/7 which pleased to forward for Amsterdam to Mr Rowland Cockey and if any of my comodityes that I doe deale in will serve for the sale of your place please to advise me off it but I must lay this obligation upon you that you sell none for any but my selfe & then I shall assure all advices you shall give me, this with servise is the nedfull at present frome

Your loving friend to serve you
Tho: Baret

Norwich the 11 of May 1674

Mr Rowland Cockey

Sir, I have severall of yours letters before me all which I shall fully ansure by next post. This per shipp to accompany two bundles of stufes as follows

No. RC3/6 17 pieces – £69 14s 0, No. RC3/7 13 pieces £53 6s

the more full invoyced & accompt of them I shall give per post only in generall I thinke you your selfe will see a greate reason to advance their prises accept service I am

Yours to serve you
Tho: Baret

[*p. 70*] London the 24th of Aprill 1674

Mr Rowland Cockey

Sir, Yours of the 24th & 27th instant I have receved whilst I am heare in London but I have not received yours by shipps nor doe heare of the arrivall of any of the shipps but hope they are all in safety & shall confeare with Mr Langly abought the madders now I have the envoysed butt truly

I feare wee are likely to come to a loosing marked heere notwithstandinge they doe rise with you for I doe not understand they will offer above 70 pieces cropp & proportionable for No. 0 soe that I doe not know what to say whether to keepe or sell, my jorney heither was in shuch hast that I could not give you the invoyce of a small packe No. RC3/6 which was sent for Yarmouth last fryday night but must defer it till I retorne againe yet I gave you shuch an accompt of the particulers in a letter per same shipp that will direct you in theire disposall, I doe intend god willinge to begin my jorney for Norwich this day sennitt & doe hope to finde a good parcell of No. 29 which are all darke collour to your mind & now I shall make noe [o]ther till your greyes be gleaned away, in the last weare some bright darke No. 29 which weare all wadded blacke & did cost me extraordinary which I hope you will gett ansured to me otherwise I shall make no more shuch but content my self with the best of the other sort that I can gett, No. 15 will rise very high now & therfore I feare I shall be able to gett very few but some I will have which shall lay by till your costomers come up to my prise. As to what you advise for I shall take care to supply you as sone as I returne I have six callamankoes laying by me which weare bought with the other which shall send per first but for the mixt callamankoes I doe not understand you but could wich I had yours thoughts more perfectly if you mean to have them strooke with mixt woll as No. 31 are the prises would be incredible at [*p. 71*] that breadth but if your next doth advise me to it I will make one piece for trial I believe it might give content but the prise would not be admitted, as to No. 28 I could make them to be afforded at 55 guilders but then I must use small silk instead of great silk & keep out a pound of stricking but then the wares wold not content you for they wold be skinlike raggs & have a broad loose wale. I am sorry No. 30, 24, 25 15 will not take but I can not helpet & therfore must be content pray put them of as well as you can I shall make no more but the loss by shuch as these doe take of my profitt in other things which makes the pro[cee]des of trade to be indifferent, if Mr Marke dos sell his great parcell of No. 15 prest at 30 as you sould mine it will be a good stepp to spoyle his stuf trade, this is the nedfull at present from

Yours to serve you
Tho: Baret

London the 29th of Aprill 1674

Mr Thomas Shepard

Sir, Yours of the 16 of February I received and should have ansured it before had not the siknes of some neere relations hindered my cominge sooner to London to effect the inclosed which is attested by Judge Turner,[48] as soone as I retorne to Norwich which may be in three weeks time I shall there procure some others testimonialls in the case which will prove somewhat troble some in regarde they can not see the goods for there is not one piece of them but should any receiver see if he wold [*p. 72*] freely & willingly sweare them to be worsted stufes & maide under their regulation but because I can not produse the stufes to them it will be the more difficult & therfore my intentions are to make oath before a master in chanse[ry] that I bought the stuffs of shuch & shuch mean & <that> then those menn to make oath that they had sould to me such stuffs & that those stufes & all others wich they had sould to me at any time whatsoever were Norwich worsteds stufs make in the County of the City of Norwich or County of Norfolke & weare under the regulation & according to the bylaws &c of the Society of Weavers in Norwich & Norfolke &c if this will not satify I think I shall procure the attestation of the governors of the Worsted Company that such stufs as thes are represented to them are under their regulation & are worsted stuffs. Sir, if theise will not doe it I wich that I knew what wold for I am desirous to setle a trade in Hamburge as well as Amsterdam & your Company as well hinder the one as the other. Sir, I am now determined to goe towards Norwich this very afternone therfore be pleased to excuse my hast who am

Your humble servant
Tho: Baret

[*p. 73*] Norwich the 13 of May 1674

Mr Rowland Cockey

Sir, My last to you was of the 11 instant per shipps to accompany the two small bundles of stufs sent per Bateman with two teirces & two hogsheads of beere which I forgott to advise of in that letter, I have one teirce of beere yet behind which mett with an accident of leaking that I must alter the caske wich may come per next if I can gett it redy tyme enough for it must be filled, when that cometh I shall give you a further accompt of them you

48 Possibly Sir Christopher Turnor (1607–1675), baron of the exchequer.

must give them full age or you spoyle them, next year will be the soonest you can use them. I have received yours of the 4th & 15th instant & per shipps the iorn [*sic*], fatt of kitles & four bales of madder but theirs one barr of iorn wanting of which I have given notis to Mr John Fitts because that Bateman dus pretend he received no more at Rotterdam but all things come to a bad marked heare but I must waight for a better. I am glad to heare that the pack No. RC3/6 is safely arrived but by mistake I have now marked another of the same the invoyces of both are as follows

/No. RC3/6/ 8 pieces No. 20 cost 85s
3 pieces No. 15 cost 4s per yard at 30 yards
1 ¾ piece No. 31 cost 85s
5 pieces No. 29 cost 76s
17 pieces

/No. RC3/7/ 6 pieces No. 20 cost 85s
2 ¾ pieces No. 31 cost 88s
5 pieces No. 29 cost 76s
13 pieces

[*p. 74*] I can as yet heare nothing of the arrivall of the madders at London but hope they are in saftey but when they come they will meete with a bad markets these No. 20 cost us formerly havinge the most of them layinge by me old bought the fox collour No. 15 cost me 15s extraordinary & the darke grey the same I have perused your accompt of prises & truly if you cannot advance your prices I must make the wares worse for I can not afford No. 15 at 35 per cento nor 29 at 43 guilders, mixt wooll yarnes are soe very much advanced in the price that I can not sell at old rates No. 29 must be 46 guilders & others accordingly but if you will lett me debace the wares I can make to the old price if others will sell to loss I am not willinge to doe it those are all darke collour to content & now all my loombs are in none but such I perceive some comodityes noe note soe vendible as was expected particularly No. 30 &c my rule for all such as you doe sell them of at the best price you can gett although it proveth loss & I shall make no more of such comodityes & the first loss is generally the least, Mr Claytons No. 15 are all old dyed wares & prest or elce I had bought them heere your co[u]s[in] M[ark] C[ockey] are all prest wares whereby it is likly the marchant will not like them, when suite in law is over I desire the iron wich you have bought for my accompt may com over per first & with it if reasnoble sende me over two tunn of [?]bej Lukes[49]

49 Iron rods from Liège (Luik in Dutch).

Dyer's madder, rubia tinctorum. Handcoloured zincograph by C. Chabot drawn by Miss M. A. Burnett from her *Plantae Utiliores: or Illustrations of Useful Plants* (Whittaker, London, 1842). Miss Burnett drew the botanical illustrations, but the text was chiefly by her late brother, British botanist Gilbert Thomas Burnett (1800–1835). Florilegius / Alamy Stock Photo rods and three tunn of right sueeds rods but I wold have one tunn of them to be large rods for shipps nayles & rivets & with them send me halfe a tunn of right sweeds palmes for anchors the anchorsmiths doe much want squares & yet could not goe to the prise of them if I had for them but they tell me that if I had any very thick narrow flatt iorn that we are good at this extremity they wold make shift with it instead of squares but it must be very thick [*p. 75*] which is a [s]cantling fitt for no use that I know of theire & that at this time if you can meete with such send over a tunn for tryall, this is the needfull as to trade at present, my next is to complayne to you & of you for not sending me my accompt currant of now two yeares cum the primo June not with standinge you have soe often promised it to me you can not thinke that I can take it well to be kept soe long in ignorance how my affaires doe goe whether to profitt or loss I must confes my self to be a young marchant & pardon me if in a litle anger I tell you you deale with me as such as I shall make out to you in sevrall particulers, upon the last accompt currant that yow sent me I gave you my exceptions with as yet you never ansured to me but now in this I expect those & all others to be rectified, I latley gave you my exception aganst 1½ per cento for buyinge & I find you have mad me no alowance for good weight in the kitle fatt wich I accompt as an error & in the last accompt of sales ended the last of February 1673 you put dou[n] provition for the sales of wares to be twixt 2 to 300 guilders which was returned agayne, you alsoe put down brokeridge which upon 3 per cento provition is not to be aloued, you alsoe putt downe packhous hire for the wares sent to Hambrough London & Yarmouth but that amount to no considerable matter they are all upon my particular accompt, the next is upon the madders sent in company where the 1 per cento for good weight in the whole parsell sent to London is omitted & you have allsoe put doun provision at 2 per cento when as they come in company but this last I suppose you expect I should make good to my self by putting an over provition to my self for disposinge them I ame over tedious & truly in a [?]subject that doeth not please me & therfore I shall end in a requst that thes things may be all rectified & that I may have my accompt currant sent me bye very next for I shall not be sattified till I have it that soe I may comput [*p. 76*] how squares doe stand if you did constant[l]y which I desired give me an exact accompt once every month of all wares sould mony received & payd upon my accompt then I weare able to keepe to contra accompt & wold give my self some sattisfaction which corce I must requst you to doe when we doe begin the new accompt. I bles god we are all well & soe is your daughter pray accept servis to you & your Lady from him that is

Your reall frend to serve you
Tho: Baret

/No. RC3/8/
3 pieces No. 31 cost 88s
2 pieces No. 15 cost 4s per yard
2 pieces No. 23 cost 87s
12 pieces No. 29 cost 76s
7 pieces No. 28 cost 200
2 pieces No. 32 cost 72s
26 pieces to be shipt in Edmond Smith

Norwich the 29 of May 1674

Mr Rowland Cockey

Sir, Yours of the 29th instant & primo June I received yesterday I have seriously perused the content & what doeth conserne trade shall be mindfull of & per next post give full ansure to them which I could not now doe by reason its my busy day for London. [*p. 77*] I hope this will finde you with helth restored which is the desires & prayers of him that is

Your loving friend to serve you
Tho: Baret

Sir, by the shipp above cometh ovre Mr Thomas Larwood of this place by whome I have sent you a token I know you doe not much like his company for he is a pryinge person but I had noe other freind cuming over to send it by

Norwich the 3rd of June 1674

Mr Rowland Cockey

Sir, My last to you was on the 29th past per Smith in which I gave you notice of the receipt of yours of the 29th past & primo instant wich I shall now give ansure to begininge w[it]h what dus conserne trade in all which I have taken care to provide for you as wel as the tyme will permitt which shall be sent per next shipp Thomas Kipper about 14 days hence the white narrow russells[50] & paramiles[51] are bespoken & wold it prove a constant trade I wold keepe some

50 A strong twilled woollen cloth.

51 Paramides: Ursula Priestly identifies 'paramides' being manufactured in Norwich in the seventeeth century, though no definition has been found: U. Priestly, 'The Fabric of Stuffs: the Norwich textile industry c. 1650–1750', *Textile History*, 16.2 (1985), pp. 204–5.

constantly goeinge, as to No. 15 & No. 29 I can not gett yarne enough to supply my occasions that is of shuch collor as give you content & yet I use the utmost of my industry, as to No. 23 I am dishertned in it for its soe difficult to make them even that my workemen will leave rather than goe on the most I can gett is but one piece per weeke but I will doe the best I can to increase the number & in those & all others things I shall doe the best I can to ansure advise. I am much troblet [*p. 78*] at the madders cropp yelds but 76 shillings to 80 shillings & omber 61 shillings to 64 shillings which is great loss I have given Mr Langly your advise to keep them two to three months which I hope he will comply with, all my iron & ketles are in the same condition very neare but I am determined to keepe lett whose will sell, the truth is heers litle trade but I hope for better this is all as to trade at the present, my next should be a large reply to your ansure to myne of the 13th past which giveth me noe satisfaction at all for there is noe objection there <is noe> made but is playne & evident by your accompts & invoyces the discovrey of which is noe such examininge of nicetyes as to be reflected upon but will by all be accompted as errors to be amended in an accompt currant & therefore till I see wether they be or not amended in your accompts which I dayly expect I shall be silent. Sir, I doe thanke you for undertaking my commission which I hope neither have nor will be lost to you although I can not say but that the extremity of the late tymes have beene injurious to me but I hope for better, as to the prises & goodnes of No. 4 & No. 29 I doe assure you that either your self or my self are very much in a mistake conserning them but to undiscover it I m[u]st comm[an]d the next you see of M[ark] C[ockey] doe but compare the back of the wares of the same collour as well as the foreside & see wich is finest there may be 8s difference in that & doble the mony to the weaver I am sure Mr Wrench hath not made soe good by 6s in the pieces as as my No. 29 are for these two yeares last but if caorce warpes will give content I can turne to them & save mony by it & besides many of Mr C[ockey] were never milled wich saveths length bredth & the charges of workinge & he that [*p. 79*] weares them will give small thanks for his purchis although at present you can not resolve to take les than 1½ for buying & yet I expect but one to be putt to accompt but more of this as I find my accompt, as to my informers which you suppose weake marchant &c I must acknowledge it for I had no other then myself & the reasonableness of the things that I wrott to induce me to wright what I did. I shall noe longer insist upon this subject but presentinge service to you & your Lady remaine

Your reall friend & servant
Tho: Baret

Norwich the 12th of June 1674

Mr John Fitts, Norwich

Sir, I received yours of the 5th instant since which Carver is arrived but not Bateman I wish him a safe passage. I observe what you wright about the barr of iron mistaken as alsoe that you will undertake to sell stuffs for me & no other person, upon which I have per Kipper sent you over a small bundle for tryall as these goe of I shall send you more the invoyce is under written I doe No. them anew to you at Amsterdam. No. 1 dus yeld 43 & 44 guilders No. 2 yelds 38 sterling per ell of the place & No. 3 of which but few have beene as yet sent dus yeld 55 & 60 guilders, I could not spare a greater parcell at this tyme but if you [*p. 80*] incourage shall send more per next shippe I suppose you doe mistake in No. 23 for I have made but few of them & are very hard to be made even & doe rise very deare. I have per ditto Kipper sent one teirce of beere & one bundle of stufes which please to forward to Mr R[owland] Cockey not elce at present but that I am

Your loving friend to command
Tho: Baret

I shall in future wright per post least letters per shipps may meete with some miscarrage

Invoyce of a bundle of stufes shipped in Thomas Kipper

/No. JF1/	10 pieces No. 1 cost 72s per piece
	1 piece No. 2 cost 4s per yards at 30 yards
	2 pieces No. 3 cost 92s per piece
	13 pieces

Sir, If you could procure me a barrill of tarras[52] & tuo or thre westphalia hambs to be sent me by Mr Kipper when he doeth retorne it wold be a great kindnes to me

52 A kind of rock commonly imported from Holland; a component for mortar or cement.

[*p. 81*] Invoyce of one pack of stuffs sent per Thomas Kipper marked & nombered as in margent contents follows

/No. RC3/9/

18	pieces No. 29 cost 76s
1	piece No. 4 cost 68s
2	pieces No. 31 cost 88s
1	piece No. 23 cost 87s
3	pieces No. 28 cost 100s
3	pieces No. 32 cost 72s
2	pieces No. 15 cost 4s per yard
30	pieces

Norwich the 15th of June 1674

Mr Rowland Cockey

Sir, Yours of the 8 & 15th instant I received & shall ansure them per post. This day I have advice that Bateman is arrived at Yarmouth the above goeth per Kipper in whome alsoe is the remaining teirce of beere which if it be to content will much please me butt it wilbe much better to drinke if you give it 12 months age before you broach it, two of the teirces I doe intend as a present one to your selfe & the other to your Ladey & of the other I shall give you an accompt of cost as sone as I doe know it which I hope will be within a day or two. Pray send me over six fagotts of the best flemmish steele I am tould that marked with the brake or pole is the best, I have disposed of a parcel of iron where by I shall be redy for more narrow flatt & brode as sone as it will be purchased resonable but till then I will stay for I have 2 or 300 barrs by me but what I have sould is very low for markets are very bad [*p. 82*] heare, if No. 28 will not yeld 60 guilders sell at 55 guilders & 54 guilders rather then keepe them I have but one piece more & shall make noe more till advised the same I desire for any other wares that drugg sell them off at the best rate you can gett & I will send no more of those sorts I doe see the first lose is generally the least, this is all at present from

Your reall frient &c
Tho: Baret

Norwich the 17th of June 1674

Mr Rowland Cockey

Sir, My last to you was of the 15th instant per shipp with an envoyce of a small pack sent per Mr Thomas Kipper No. RC3/9 which I wish safe with you for I suppose he doeth sett saile this day I received both yours of the 8th & 15th instant & in ansure to the first I have sett close to the making of No. 29, 15 & 23 & have cast of all other sorts at present I shall against next shippes have a piece to the scarlett & white pattern of callimancoe that you sent me which I doubt not but will give content yet I dare not goe too deepe till I see how this will please for experiments of this nature when they fayle doe doe [*sic*] prove soe extreme chargeable that it eates out the profitt of the other. By next shipps you shall have [*p. 83*] some paramides & I shall have the narrow white russells at worke & over a litle tyme shall send some I have now frome a farr contry although in England procured such yarnes for serge de nîmes as will make as good wares if not better than the French of which you shall have some per next, your brother Cockey doeth complayne heere of his over buyinge himelf in callimancoes & that his sonn was catched to loss in his serge de nîmes that hee sould before he had them & as I am informed he hath sent such a parcell of No. 4 or 29 that what for bad wares & bad collour he will complayne agayne verry sodainely butt I doe soe the humors of the father & sonn soe well that I dare adventure a good wager that eare it be long they will be soe confounded as they will give it over, I see they have attempted No. 23 but can not as yet affect any thinge nor doe I thinke they will be able to prevent its rewynes for I doe finde it one of the most difficult stufs that ever I did undertake, the Luke rods are arrived but they will rise soe deere as I shall never make my mony of them, the madders I have ordered to be kept till wee doe understand how the next cropp will prove, the highest that is offered is 83 for the cropp & 63 for omber which is loss in both accordinge to the best computation that I can make, I have written to know the dimentions of anchor iron but as yet have noe accompt retournd me, as to Mr Langlyes marryinge[53] I heare nothinge at all he [?]it <I believe> doeth carry it as if theare *were* nothinge at all in it I beleve he thinks the greatest plesure is in courtinge, I have only two pieces No. 32 more but they are good wares & thicker then any yet sent but I shall make no more till advised for becase they rise deere, as to No. 28 if you can gett no more sell them for

53 Possibly Christian Langley, who married Elizabeth Cockey of Norwich on 28 July 1674 at St Helen's Church, Bishopsgate, London.

50 guilders but I will not make one piece more to sell soe for theres loss in them but since they are made & with you its better to sell them than keepe for the first loss doth generally prove the lest. I retorne you thanks for your [*p. 84*] invitation to Holland but my London occasions will not permitt me to leave England this sommer. Praye my serves to your Lady & accept the same from

Your reall friend & servant
Tho: Baret

/No. RC4/0/
6 doll[54] paramides made up two togetther No. 335 cost 28s
2 single narrow russells No. 34 cost 40s
2 pieces No. 32 cost 72s
2 pieces No. 29 cost 76s
2 pieces No. 15 cost 4s per yard 30 yards
3 pieces ditto nomber 35 fff fff[55] cost 4s 6d per yard 30 yards
1 pieces ditto nomber 35 fff fff[56] cost 4s 6d per yard 25 yards
18 pieces

Norwich the primo July 1674

Mr Rowland Cockey

Sir, Yours of the 3rd instant I receved, my last to you was with the above dated the 27 last past per shipps which I thought had sayled last Monday but now I am informed it doeth not sayle till tomorrow & therefore I ame designed to pack this night & send it away to come with the other per Carver for heare is noe other at present ready to sayle, if there had I should have forborne I can not give you the contents per this post but it will be most No. 29 & a piece or [*p. 85*] two No. 23, I hope they will come to you before any advise but if they doe the No. will direct you which is all at present conserni[n]g them, in ansure to yours of the 3rd instant I wonder mine of the 15 past per shipps is not come to hand but I suppose it is with the goods come to you before this time but least it should miscarry take the contents as follows

54 i.e. double.
55 *See* note 35.
56 *See* note 35.

/No. RC3/9/
18 No. 29 cost 76s
1 No. 4 cost 68s
2 No. 31 cost 88s
1 No. 23 cost 87s
3 No. 28 cost 100s
3 No. 32 cost 72s
2 No. 15 cost 4s per yard 30 yards
30 pieces

I see that Mr Andrewes & others stepp in to my way of trade which may spoyle it although it doeth not setle a trade to them selves for there is & shall be a difference in goodnes betwixt what I shall send you & what they bringe or send, I shall now give over experrimts & keep close to No. 29, 23 & 15 for hitherto it hath proved to my loss, white is now sent will prettey well supply your occasions for 29 as for No. 15 I can meete with none that gives me content like to my owne & I wold sett more on<e> worke but truly I find it difficult to geet good mixt wool yarnes to <collour which> keepe those lombs that I have in worke bad yarnes & collours which contente them will not me or you & therefore I doe the lest because I will keepe up the <*illegible*> reputation of my goods that soe my trade may last when others faile, I have now sett on for six or eight pieces No. 15 every fornight if my mean worke & as many No. 23 & if I can meete by the by with any No. 15 that are good I will by them but this is a very teedous comodity to make it swallows a vast deele of yarne & is 14 days to worke a piece but I shall doe the best I can to supply you, I must confes your tediousnes in my accompt & some other things the which I have given you accompt off have made me but dall in my busines for I did verryly juge by those things that you had a minde to tyre me out of the of the inployment for such long accompt [*p. 86*] I can not fancey & therefore praye put them to an isue that soe I maye goe on againe with plesure last night I sould one bale of crapp madder No. 14 for 86s per lb which I thinke is prettey well sould I ame truly sorry that Mr Langleys knowlige of yours part in the madders should cause any difference had you given me the lest hint that you wold have had it as a sea[c]ret neither he nor any livinge although never soe much my friends should have knowne one worde of it & therefore praye pardon my ignorante error. I have beene with your father & acquainted him as you desired they all & your daughter Lidia are in good helth Mr Langly & the widdow & her family are all gone for London together I suppose gat thither last night. My serves to you & your Lady who am

Your loving friend & servant
Tho: Baret

Pray send me over eight pieces of cloath for packcloths for I can get none of Mr Langly or Ald[erman] Cockey & I am in want

The pack now sent conteynes
/No. RC4/1/
27 pieces No. 29 cost 76s per piece
1 pieces No. 23 cost 87s per piece
28 pieces

[*p. 87*] Norwich the 15 of July 1674

Mr Rowland Cockey

Sir, Yours of the 9th instant per shipps & 17th per post I received, my last to you was last night to goe by Bateman with two packes the invoice of which shall be inclosed, I perceve that my letter per Kipper was broken open which I wonder at for I sent it inclosed to Mr Fitts & I dare say neither of them wold doe it. It was missing some tyme if you doe remember the person that brought it examin him about it for I suspect that M[ark] C[ockey] have taken it up to see my wrightinge in it pray doe the best you can to finde it out, I have written to Mr Fitts about it & shall examin Kipper when he retorne for I wold willingly finde it out. I perceive you finde fault with some No. 29 becaue they are not soe good as the greye which I doe beleve for they ware made under expectation of 47 guilders per piece & when yarnes ware 8d in the lb weight cheaper & 4d per lb better for heare is your brother & the Wiggetts & others doe hunt & teare for wares that the combers will have what they lift & make as bad yarns as they list & therefore I doe expect that in one months tyme wheare you have one trash peice in your citty you will have ten for I see you will be clogged sufficently which will leave our jehu drivers[57] the art of loosing & making them more tam[e] in future I doe really expet to see them in a short tyme knock off as fast as they now fall on, I shall goe on in my old way & make good wares the best I can make to afforde at the prices they

57 i.e. the driver of a coach or cab, usually reckless: 'the driving is like the driving of Jehu the son of Nimshi; for he driveth furiously', II Kings 9:20.

will give if they will advance theire prices then I will advance my goodnes but if they lowre soe must I for truly I will not trade only to be reputed a marchant but I will have some living & fitt in what I doe ore elce I will sett still, I must confece that I have of late mixt No. 29 & good No. 4 since you sould them at 42 guilders otherwaise I wold not have borne up under the charge & losses which I meete with in selling old goods & I have none to helpe me but these & butt that I will beare low selling a while ine hopes to baffle [*p. 88*] out those interlopers I wold not make one piece that is truly No. 29 unlese I warre sure of 45 guilders for it, I have in these packs now sent divided them and putt No. 29 <as [*illegible*] guilders which price> No. 4 upon what are soe areally I perceive you sell No. 28 at 55 guilders which price if you will hold to I will make to the full goo[d]nes as these were when you have occasion to wright for any but if you shall lower I must abate which I can doe for 3 or 4s & not much diserned, as to No. 15 I doe make them soe good as I can not well afford them under 40 sterling at which rate others tell me they sell & I know not better wares if I can juge they are worse, No. 35 cost me about 5d per yard more than the others & doe deserve it if that prise or at least 43 sterling per ell will not be given for them I shall make noe more of that sort but content my selef with the ordinary, if that prise would be given I would gladly know because then I would give order for moore yarnes against Michaelmas which will take time for it cometh neare 300 miles by land carrage, as for No. 31 I see they have brought the price doune to 49 guilders & 50 guilders & soe I strooke the loombs about a month since that soe I can send you noe more till I gooe to worke a fresh & then if materialls doe not fall I can not sell under 53 and for No. 23 I must give them quite over for they cost me 90s heeare soe the last cost me to a farthing & they yeld with you 50 guilders, lett your customoers buy wheare they please they shall have none of me soe I have now sent you one piece in the pack 4/2 which I made for a rarity in goodnes if they will not give 58 guilders for it sell if not I will have it sent back for my owne use rather then loose by good wares & those of this sort you complayne of did not really desearve it, as to the goodness of wares if you would have pitch on the silke I can make them to content but the more the silke shows the dearer the wares are, as to No. 32 the ware is not bad but the truth is our yarnes are too small for that comodity but I have some one making of the same materialls 35 are of & those will give you full content & be but a letle dearer per next shipps you shall have some come, I received the packcloathes & which theare had ben more of them doble canvase dus prove too chargeable, I received alsoe the ham & doe retorne you *my* thanks for it & when I doe eated it I will remember you in a glase of clarrite as to the beare I hope it is good [*p. 89*] and will prove good if I weare to use it my selfe I wold keepe it till winter although it will take noe hurt if it were kept two winters this will prove good nogg[58] I assure you it is too mighty for me for I did not scent it, as to steele & iron I suppose the prise will yet be lower when more shipps come in & therefore I thinke it best to forbeare a while till more shipps come in for I would be loath to buy now but at the verey louest price for it was sould heere by a Yarmouth man last weeke for £13 15s 10d per tonn & I have yet by me 2 or 300 barrs well sorted & therefore can well stay but I shall desire that when you can meete with a good penniworth iron that I can afford to sell at £14 per tonn heeare at four months time that is good iron send me what parcell you think convenient but I must have brode & square & narrow to sell all at one price theise are the best termes I can geet our iron mongers to, when you can meete with good steele that is cheape send me halfe a dozen or 10 fagotts but be sure it be pure good or send none & take your convenent time to procure it & the iron, this with tender of service is all at present from

Your loving friend
Tho: Baret

[*p. 90*] Norwich the 18 of July 1674

Mr William Peacock

Sir and lovinge friend salute, yours of the 20th instant NS I received & thank you for it beeing desirous to heare of your happy arrivall amongst your friends whome altho unknowne salute for me, Sir I have perused your letter & pattornes which are good & the same I have befor me although as yet I have made none of those collors these patternes I see are not of English make & whether owers would please you or not I am ignorant butt Sir as you are my friend soe I shall deale plainely with you at the present, you know I am ingaged upon my owne accompt in Amsterdam & doe not make more goods then serve my perticuler occasion should I inlarge and accept your proposall it might not be long before it might be suspected that I should send the best upon my owne accompt (altho it ware not truly soe) & furnich you with the worst, to avoide which I thinke it to be prudence to refuse your proposall although otherwayse I should be redy to serve you

58 A strong variety of beer, brewed especially in Norfolk.

in any thing which doeth not interfeare with my single consernes as this would doe both in the goods you advise for & alsoe the retornes & the truth is that comodityes are soe high heere & with you for retornes & the markets for sales soe low in either place that I can finde litle good to be done in either place, I have perused the price currant of comodityes with you & can observe noe comodityes that I doe understand which would turne to accompt weare it heare by me at those prices, this with service is the nedfull at present from

Your loving friend to command
Tho: Baret

[*p. 91*] Norwich the 18 July 1674

Mr Rowland Cockey

Sir, Yours of the 20th instant I received my last was to you on the 15th instant I have perused yours in its severall particulers and although I doe not thinke that every complainte which your costomers make is worth the mindinge yet when there dus come soe many it doth make me begine to examine whether I bee not part of the occasion, what is in me I shall cause to be altered but really times doe runn soe hard & I have lost soe much as may have occasioned me to buy some lower priced russells then what my owne loombs use to make, the truth is I was forced to turne them in No. 15 & 35 because I would have good & sett others to make me No. 29 to whome I did alow as much materialls as ever to any butt it seemeth they doe not give content & therefore I shall turne them out altho I make the fewer of that sort all men can not make a like yet lett me tell you in that parcell of 27 pieces No. RC4/1 there was 12 pieces which were as they should be & gave noe just occasion of complaint, as to the grey No. 29 giving better content than these now I gave you the reason in my last beside which its observable that a grey upon gold shall shew better in the ware than a sad collour by 3 to 4s in the piece altho they bee both alike in meterialls in evrey respect I have tried it severall times and finde it true & hath inquired into the reson of it which is this the light collour passinge but litle dyes are not made tender by it & soe are made of the finest wooll which will not worke in sad collour & then the next is the spinster can not indure to worke sad collour but doe it with all the slight & cheate in lenth & goodnes imaginable whereby three pounds of lite grey yarne will goe as farre as 3½ of sad mixtures & this we can not remedy whereby I am [?] tryed with single mixt wooll yarnes but complainte will doe no good, as to the holes you mention in the millinge the wares I doe assure you its the best artist in towne that doeth them & its soe small a thing that occasions it that truly I admire that any piece scapes without some hurt for the least sand that scapes in the thinge [*p. 92*] they use or the dirt that comes along with the water or a piece of stick where ever it lighteth makes a hole or a garle[59] in the thick stuffs & more damage in the thin & therefore they must not be two curious in such things, I see them before they were made up & thought they might pass, as to the coarcenes of the piece No. 28 in the midle I am ignorant of it I wish I had its cloath marke & would finde where the fault layes. Sir, I have noe reason to be angry for your finding faults where justly they are I like it the better for by it I know what will give content, I had sould a bale of madder but before dillivery heare ill words of the person & soe it hangs in suspence a present till he give me security for I would be loath to make a bad debt, I see you have sould No. 35 at 41 sterling but you must advance or I can not hold there goodness, I am glad this sort doeth please you I shall againest goeinge to worke provide more of that yarne altho it be difficult to procuare & chargeable for I fetch it almost 300 mile by land carrage, as to some wares provinge narrow its only the mill working upon them for they are made all of one bredth but some times throw the millers neglect they goe too long but the ware is the better for it, the white piece in No. 4/3 which I could not give you the price of in last cost 74s I hope it will give content, I observe what you doe write about the white russells & shall cause them to be strooke up better which will make them looke finer if it doeth not make them rise some what deere, as to paramiles[60] of that goodnes I can not geet them cheaper than 28 but shall trye some other makers, I have now given order to have six pieces of 31 made which will come off before leavinge worke. Lidia is well was with me on Satterday & talkes of cominge over to see you. I shall pack this night to be redey for next shipps in which wilbe some white russells No. 15 & 35 & 23 & some 29 which wilbe to content I have spent a letletime in casting up the hempinge cloath now sent & doe finde that it wilbe to my los for I have bought it 1d per ell English cheaper then this wilbe stand me in [*p. 93*] and therfore I shall now pay a litle for experience, pray turne over, as to iron I wrott to you in my last if you could buy it for 6¼d all sorts I could be content to have a good parcell & if squares doe hold still deere send none of them at present but make up your parcell of narrow & brode the last brode you sent were of a good scantlin & I would

59 Marked or spoiled (thanks to Lizzy Spencer for the definition).

60 Paramides; *see* note 51.

willingly have ⅓ brode to two of narrow that is the sortment which gives best content, I would allsoe adventure upon one tonn of iron potts for a tryall & halfe as many iron ketles I perceive they doe not care to have any of these which weigh above 30 to 35lb a piece for the biggest but the lesser sorts are most desired, I have inquired what they will yeld heere & they tell me about £16 per tonn but you know if they be reasonable with you & if they be send me this parcell for a tryall, heere are some persons which aske me for cropp ketles I know not what they are but if you doe I would adventure upon a small parcell for tryall if they be reasonable I suppose some persons call these blackarse ketles but I am ignorant in both I would gladly have a litle of evrey thinge of these hard wares where by to gett into some trade for my retornes but at present all things sell low & the Wiggetts sell at any rates I thinke for they sell kitles lower then I can afford mine, this with tender of service is the nedfull at present from

Your loving friend to command
Tho: Baret

[*p. 94*] Norwich the 31st July 1674

Mr John Fitts

Sir, I received yours of the 27th instant & shall insure it per post not having time now I can not mach your patterns sent but have heere with sent you one pack containing as followeth

/No. JF2/ 10 pieces serge de nîmes No. 15 cost as formerly if the collour please not shall order them elce where these deserve 40 sterling per ell & I hope yow will not sell them under heere *with* comes two packs No. RC4/4 & No. RC4/5 cont[aining] 45 pieces but some are soe thin stuffs as three pieces hardly make one, speed these to Mr Cockey with the inclosed which pray for safety inclosed to him not elce at present beeing in hast I rest

Yours to serve you
Tho: Baret

Norwich the 31st July 1674

Mr Rowland Cockey

Sir, I received yours of the 26 instant per shipps & 31st instant per post & shall answer them per next poast not having time now I have sent you twoo packs heerwith the contents follows

/No. RC4/4/	2 pieces No. 15
	6 pieces No. 33
	14 pieces No. 34
	22 pieces

[*p. 95*]

/No. RC4/5/	5 pieces No. 29
	4 pieces No. 32
	7 pieces No. 23
	5 pieces No. 35
	2 pieces No. 15
	23 pieces

The invoyce shall come per next post, I doe now want iron of all sorts both brode narrow & square send me a small parcell of each per first & one or two fagots best steele if iron be cheape as formerly advised I shall not accompt 20 tonn well sorted too much but of this & other things I shall advise more per next, I hope your distemper is removed I rest

Your loving friend & servant
Tho: Baret

[*p. 96*] Norwich the 5th of August 1674

Mr John Fittz

Sir, My last was to you of the 31st past per shipps since which none from you in it I advised of one small pack sent per Smith as follows

/No. JF2/ 10 pieces serge de nîmes No. 15 30 yards per piece cost 4s per yards. The collours are not suitable to your patterns nor can I get any to them and now owre time of leavinge worke is soe neere as I can gett none made till after Michaelmas, these are such collours as the time afford & I thinke verry good but if they will not suite the fancyes of your place pray keepe them fairely by you & I will order them with the others you have remaininge to some other place in fut*u*er for abought a month hence I may want them, I have received the hambs & doe dayly expect the tarrass in which I suppose you have made a mistake calling it 3¾ ton which I am informed is but soe many lb. The hambs mett with a mischance by ratts which lettbe prevented in future by puttinge them up in such covers as the ratts will not eate through, I shall have occasion for more tarras & hambs & therfore by next please to send me three vessells of tarras more & by every shipp that cometh till I order the contrary pray send me three or four hambs of right Westphalia bacon lett them be pretty large ones of abougt 12 or 13lb weight but lett them not be too fatt or ould whereby they may be resty[61] for these twoo things are accompted defects, gett the shipp masters to take care of them for me Bateman Smith or Kipper will under take it for me, I wright for noe more at one time because they may be privately gotten on shore for if they be taken they are lost & must be compounded for, consigne all for me to Captain Huntington. This is the needfull at present from

Your lovinge friend
Tho: Baret

[*p. 97*] Norwich the 5th of August 1674

Mr Rowland Cockey

Sir, Yours of the 3rd instant I received which conteyneth the said accompt of the late & dismall strorme in your parts which was pretty smart heere in lightning & thunder which destroyed two or three barnes in the contry pretty distant from us, I pray god sanctify these afflictions to us all & to divert such in future, my last to you was of the 31st past per Smith in whome was two packs the invoyce of which followeth

/No. RC4/4/	2 pieces No. 15. 30 yards cost 4s per yard
	6 pieces No. 33 cost 27s
	14 pieces No. 34 cost 40s
	22 pieces
/No. RC4/5/	5 pieces No. 29 cost
	4 pieces No. 32 cost
	7 pieces No. 23 cost
	5 pieces No. 35 cost 30 yards
	2 pieces No. 15 30 yards cost 4s per yard
	23 pieces

61 i.e. rancid.

of which take this followinge accompt No. 15 soe good as these are with the charges upon them doe not cost me less then I putt them, No. 33 & 34 are as good as the prices you order will procure I can make them to what goodnes will be desired if the price wilbe ansured I would have bought some of your father but he would not take under 45 or 46, as to sealinge them I did not know it was requisitie but all shall be soe in future & had your letter come one post sooner all these had beene [*p. 98*] sealed but they were gone the day before the first, No. 34 were to brode & the next were a litle too narrow because I did not know theire exact bredth but since that they are all as they should be for length and bredth & now I have ordered all to have 2s worth of yarne more to be putt into them which I hope will give content, the No. 29 are of the best some darke greys others sad brownes I have now only of the best but I keepe them by me till you have sould off what you have by you, these No. 32 are verry handsome wares two of them are made of my best yarne which you will know by their thickness, I must confess these No. 23 are not soe good as I would have had I putt new persons upon them whoe could not hitt right at first but you shall have better in future therfore putt them off as well as you can, to sell No. 35 at 41 sterling is really too low but I must leave you to sell as well as you can & I hope that I shall get some abatement in yarnes at Michaelmas to helpe me if your co[u]s[in] Ma[rk] C[ockey] hath 40 pieces No. 15 I dare say half are trash I am offered such as he doth buy & I dare not medle with them & now upon your hint I shalbe cautious not to buy too many fearinge the market may be glutted & then I may buy cheap heere to afford soe with you I have now taken care that noe more wares shalbe torne in the millinge for I have found out what it was that caused the miscarriage, you doe wright that the No. 29 are not vendible collours to prevent which you should send me over patterns for collours which are good & which are not <good> for truly I thought there had beene none bad except two old collours which are pale collour and yellowish which layd heere by me & I thought they might humor some collors you had sent me, its now owre time to leave workinge upon the 14th nigt & truly I will see some better sales then I doe at present meete with before I goe to worke againe, what you have by you gett the best price you can for tis to noe purpose to keepe them & I have severall more heere [*p. 99*] to come off & when I goe to worke againe I shall then consider how I like the prises then given & steer accordingly, I have now beene inquiring into some comodityes for retornes & am advised to send for a small parcell of the comodityes under written & therfore if they be reasonable pray send them per next shipps or what you can gett of them that are reasonable for I leave it to you to send or forbeare accordinge as the price incourageth, I have now quite sould my selfe out of all sorts of iron but the Luke rods which are soe deere as I can not make my money if there by any Sueeds rods good & reasonable send me some. This is the needfull at present from him that is

Your loving friend to serve you
Tho: Baret

200lb weight of brass black bottums from 14 *inch* to 20 *inch* they must be strong ones 20 *inch* will weigh 3lb
200lb weight of Guinney panns[62] for warming *alius.* Warming pann bottums if these be good & cheape send 300lb weight
100lb weight of warming pann covers
two or three cropps of ketles of about 100lb weight to the cropp of these lett some be better then others for they mix slight & best together
send a small parcell of blackmores from five pints downwards two or three fatts or what they call them wilbe enough
300lb weight of copper sheets from 40lb to 30lb the sheete
send me a small parcell of large iron wyer the best & tuffest to make combs teeth with all & another small parcell of large wyer for the rimms of fryinge panns & skillets
I would alsoe buy three or four gravestones for tryall from 5½ *foot* long to 6½ *foot* & from 2½ *foot* brode to 3¼ but the midling stones are the most vendible

[*p. 100*] Norwich the 19 of August 1674

Mr John Fitts

This serveth to convey the inclosed which forward to Mr Rowland Cockey with the severall packs marked as in the margent[63] in a former letter I requested you to send me some hambs of right Westphalia bacon send me but 12 in all when that quantity is sent then stopp till further order, I alsoe then sent for some tarras make up the nomber then advised for six & sent them per first with four of your best Holland payles & four caggs of the best east contry sturgion lett two of them be rands & two of jowles but I would have the best, when your occasions give leave I should be glad to heare how

62 Brass pots produced for the Guinea trade.
63 There is nothing in the margin here.

the last goods sent you give content. In what I can serve you please to advise him that is

Your loving friend
Tho: Baret

The tarras is received

[*p. 101*] Norwich the 19th of August 1674

Mr Rowland Cockey

Sir, Both your letters of the 10th & 17th instant I received & have perused them, I am glad that I have some iron shipt I wish it saffe heere for I have litle square or narrow by me & not much brode but I bought that at London, butt conserninge iron & other comodityes I wrott sufficient per my last of the 5th instant to which I refer you, I have now sent you three packs per Kipper the invoyce of which shall come per next poast for I am soe busy with reckoninge & packinge that I can not wright per poast this night therfore shall only give you a particuler of the contents underneath, I am much trobled at what you wright conserninge No. 15 & 35 with your fingers I know the reason of it its because the warpe is made *a litle* thinn on purpose to receive in such a quantity of strikinge I can easily prevent its slippinge under your fingers but then the wares wilbe much thinner & will weare more greasy & shininge then this will. You may accompt it a disparragement to the ware but it wilbe advantage to the weares except wrastlers this is the same way that I have ever made them I wonder it should be disliked noe sooner had I knowne it I could have altered my loombs in 14 days time butt now wee have don makinge till after Michaelmas, if you try any wares made heere you will finde them shipp as these doe butt if they give not content when I goe to worke againe I shall alter them but then they wilbe thinner, if these No. 29 in generall give not content I despaire of ever doeing of it & I hope No. 34 will doe the like these No. 23 are of the best especiall six pieces, I can not inlarge but rest

Yours to serve you
Tho: Baret

The contents of No. RC4/6 4/7 4/8

[*p. 102*] /No. RC4/6/ containing 39 pieces marked as in the margent
/No. RC4/7/ containing 30 pieces marked as in the margent
/No. RC4/8/ containing 21 pieces marked as in the margent

Norwich the 21 of August 1674

Mr Rowland Cockey

Sir, My last to you was per Thomas Kipper of the 19th instant with the above said goods which I hope will give content. I observe what you doe wright aboute the certaine Inglish man profferinge No. 29 at £3 &c lett the person be Mr John Wiggett or home soever if he wil but make me the proffer heere to be dillivered I will accept it & doe assure you mine doe cost considerably more but there is wares in No. 4/7 that all the Wiggetts in the nation can not make such butt in short I must leave you to gett the best price you can for the wares I send you I have enough for two packs more & then I shall sett still till goinge to worke againe & then I shall be very slow unles prices give incouragement, lett M[ark] C[ockey] sell his fathers wares like a childe & leett his father heere tell evrey body of the proffitt if he please lett them but alone for a while & you will finde them to clogg them selves soe much with a taile of wares that it will tyer them at last & theire conceited profitt will vanish, if they doe ruine the trade it can not be helped when its at worst twill mend. I hope Lidia wilbe well with you before this come to hand, pray my service to your Lady & accept the same from

Your loving freind to command
Tho: Baret

[*p. 103*] Norwich the 27th August 1674

Mr Rowland Cockey

Sir, Yours of the 31st past per post & of the 25th instant & primo September per shipps cam this day to hand. I have perused the contents of them all to which I shall give ansuer per poast this serveth only for a short answer to them which is that I perceive trade is soe abused that there is noe good to be don in it, what you wright conserninge serge de nîmes & No. 29 is a greate mistake for its not possible they can be bought soe if as good as mine which you say they are I shall not contradict you in it but give me leave to assert that

Ald[erman] Cockey[64] heere buyes none soe good as I send you & therfore I know not how M[ark] C[ockey] should sell as good I doe not say every peice I have seene Mr Cubitts & the Ald[erman] & others & I will prove it to all juditious men in the makinge of those wares that they are not soe good as my best by 8 or 10s per piece, I speake in reference to wares if the collour of his be better then mine its your fault you doe not send me patterns & then I would turne to any collour you would order if they aprove of darke warpes the same wares in darke warpes would shew 6s per piece better then upon gold or gold & skey which I have followed as conceavinge it best approoved because elce you would have ordered an alteration which I should have complyed with presently butt in short the case is thuss you have a greate many of No. 29 on hand & of serge de nîmes & more are cominge to you & I have 20 to 30 more but I will not send them as yet which in all is a verry greate parcell its to noe purpose to keepe them but to take the first market be it loss as it is & therfore pray sell them as well as you can & lett it be as litle to my loss as you can, I have now don makinge & will not make one piece more till you advise me what wares what collours [*p. 104*] & what price & then I will suite the market price or make none & therfore against Michaelmas pray lett me know what I shall goe about or whether I shall sett still & this is all at present from

Your loving friend
Tho: Baret

I have ordered Mr Langly to draw some money upon you haveinge occasion at this time more then ordinary to recon with my worke men I have sould only one bale of madder of the wholle parcell & therfore lett me have your advice whether to sell or keepe & I will doe accordingly

Norwich the 27th of August 1674

Mr John Fittz

Yours of the 3[d] September NS by R Downinge I received & have perused the contents of it & wish Smith a good voyage when I heare you have sould

64 Alderman Mark Cockey is later identified as Rowland Cockey's brother, *see p. 140*, also referred to on *pp. 67, 82* and *87*. Alderman Cockey had a son, also called Mark, *see p. 142*, who is referred to as Rowland Cockey's cousin, *see p. 63*. Alderman Mark Cockey stood for Norwich in the parliamentary election of 1678 and was heavily defeated. He was in a debtors' prison in 1686 and died on 4 Dec 1697. historyofparliamentonline.org: will of Abraham Cockey, 1686 (TNA, PROB 11/388), register of the Dutch church in Norwich (NRO, MS 21490).

the serge de nîmes & if I doe like the price I have such an other parcell of excellent wares & collours which I may send you per next shipp pray speede the inclosed & you will oblige

Your friend to serve you
Tho: Baret

[*p. 105*] Norwich the 28th of August 1674

Mr Rowland Cockey

Sir, My last to you was last night which I sent downe to Yarmouth to goe by Thomas Kipper whoe at present layth redy but wind bownd in it, I gave an accompt of the receipt of yours of the 25th & 31st instant & primo September NS which I shall now fully ansure you now & formerley complayne that wares are worse & worse I doe not nor have I reason to complaine at your wrighting soe, butt truly you are soe short in your advise that I cannot understand it for to say generally wares are bad & not to say where in is but to leade me into a wood & not to informe soe as I may amend it & although I have alwayse desired you to send me patterns of what you like & what you doe not yet you doe it not, there are severall thingh to be considered in wares the collour of the strickinge the collour of the warpe & the well makinge of the ware its possible one of these may faille & yet the other not & to complaine in generall termes that ware is bad & not to be particuler in what is noe sollid advise to better my understanding, if you had saide that the collour of the warpe ore the collour of the strikinge had not given content & then by patterns or description have ordered what would it should have beene amended or if you had said the making of the ware had beene only falted & sent patterns of such as would please I would in 14 days time have turned all my loombs to give content but for want of this particuler advise I have gon on till I have filled both you & myself with wares called bad wares & for my hart to this moment can not conceive where the fault particulery layeth which I can not but impute to be an omission of your side for you can noe sooner complaine soe as I can understand but I am both readey & willinge to amend it, the fault you found in the serge de nîmes is & shall in all I make in future be amended & soe should any thing in any other comodity, the next thing complained of is that the prise is too high & that others have as good as my best at for cheaper rates & for ansure I deny it assuredly that any have soe good as my best for I have seene of all there wares & have dilligently inquired what they allow for them & my alowance is greter than any mans & it is honestly putt into it wares I have examined the worke mene whoe drese theire wares & they tell me faithfuly that noe [*p. 106*] mans ware is soe good as mine by 2 or 4s per piece in the generall sorte but to my best none have to compare, I must confes that comodityes of late by reason of our trade heere beeinge over are somwhat fallen for I did give for No. 15 £5 16s 0d money per piece & now I doe give £5 8s 0d per piece raw and understand as they come of the lombe & cannot have them cheper but I doe cause a greate deale of yarne to be putt in to myne more then others doe allow which you may distinguish by the weight, for experriment weigh a piece of mine againe a piece of theires & see what the difference is & compute it pro rato of the whole although that be to disadvantage because the diference is in the chargeable mixt wool although they be now at the cheapest yet I can not reckon that any No. 15 cost me less then £5 11s 0d first peney out of pockett & the No. 35 cost me 8 to 9s per piece more, this is the neerest computation of the true cost as they now are that I can make & for No. 29 I have now bene reckoning with my worckmen upon the neerest computatione that I can make as things now stand they cost me 64s per piece raw of the loombs & the charge of millinge tantering raising presinge &c is 3s shillings per piece soe if by shillings per piece one with the other some may be 1 or 2s better then an other but I cast them at this rate all together pray weig some of these with othere mens ware the difference here is in the mixt wooll yarnes & doe but observe the closnes and finenese of the backsides for there warpes be corse there is a greate disadvantage in weighinge, as for No. 4 some cost 58s some 56s first penny this is the most particuler accompt that I can give you whereby you may know how to sell whether to profitt or loss my last adviseth you to take the first markett & for these that now come by Kipper I thinke its best to keepe them by you unopened till you have cleered your hands pretty well of what is upon hand, I am much discouraged with the trade that now is & give me leave to tell you that I doe verry much suspect that you doe graspe at two much imployment indeade more than you can mannage to your owne content, my reasons are that in all this time & not withstandinge soe many letters w[r]itten for it yet I can git noe accompt from you & besides if you were not two much incombred with business [*p. 107*] I am sure I should have had more particuler advice about wares & collors & alsoe patternes for direction, pray Sir by next lett me have my accompt sent me for truly I shall wright nothinge but angry letters till I have it. In your last invoyce of iron there is 1½ *provition* putt downe which I can not admitt of the trade will not beare it & noe man but your selfe demands it, pray Sir give me occasion to wright none of these discontented letters but doe those things which are frindly & right tuixt marchants those persons whoe are noe friends to us altho seemingly such would be glad to heare of those discontents betuixt us I am willinge to supply you as long as I can & to the utmost of my power but should I pass by theise things the world would chronicle me for a foole & not a marchant, butt enough of this & give me noe occasion in future, accept tender of service to you & your lady from him that is

Your loving friend to serve you
Tho: Baret

[*p. 108*] Norwich the 16 of October 1674

Captain Clarke & lovinge friend

My occasions drew me from London in a litle hast whearby I could not see you before I cam downe, I hope this will finde you in good health as I blesse god I am at the wrightinge of it, inclosed I have sent you an invoyce of the case of goods which I desire you to dispose of for me to the best advantage & to bringe me such retornes for the proceeds as you shall judge will turne to best accompt in England, I leave the wholle to you to doe for me as you would for your selfe what retornes you can possibly make bring home with you & for the rest I leave them to your discretion & orderinge because I am a stranger to the Barbados & trade therefore its possible I may now have sent some things which are not soe propper for the place, if it doeth prove soe I desire you to sell them at the lower rates which is better than to bringe them back againe. I shall not neede to advise you that the profite had needs to be greate outwards because of the charges & loss in the retornes homewards I know you understand that better than my selfe & therefore I shall truly & wholly leave it to your mannagement & whish you a happy & prosperous voiage boath out & hom & shall alwayse be ready to shew my selfe

Your lovinge friend
Tho: Baret

If you bringe me any sugars home for retones lett them be the best & dryest for I desinge them for this place [*p. 109*] /October 6th 1674/

The invoyce of a case of Norwich stuff marked TB No. 1 q[uan]t[ity] three small packs marked No. 1 2 3 sent to the Barbados in the Samuell per Captain John Clarke <to dispose of for> consigned to the said Captain John Clarke to dispose of for the accompt of Thomas Baret of Norwich as followeth

TB No. 1 22 pieces comes to	£61 1s 0d
TB No. 2 22 pieces comes to	£59 11s 0d
TB No. 3 23 pieces comes to	£42 09s 0d
67 pieces cost in the whole besids all charges	£163 01s 0d

Errors excepted

Tho: Baret

[*p. 110*] Norwich the 16 of October 1674

Mr John Fittz

Sir, Yours of the 19th instant per post SN I received & take notice of the contents of it. Kipper is arrived & I yesterday went downe to Yarmouth but could not come at the tarras & iron the other things I have received I perceive its your custom to abate for measure which is not at Amsterdam but the customes of places must be submitted to which ought to be considered some other way but that I have leave to you those that sell as good No. 15 as mine at 33 sterling per ell will not supply the markett againe if they understand themselves, I am now retorned & as yet have noe wares come off to supply your advice but shall have in 14 days & as soone as possible shall send to you, I doe take the best care that possible I can to have good collours & doe hope that mine are better then others, I shall alwayse indeavore to send good lett others clogg them selves with bad, I shall observe your patterns & come as neare the collour as possible but it will take some time because its a collour not to be gotten at present. I have sent per Edmond Smith one pack marked No. RC4/9 which forroward for Amsterdam pray in futer what evre goods you evre send ovre whether it be those from Amsterdam or from yer selvfe send me with them an accompt of the charges that you are out of for them at Rotterdam for want of which I can not tell the true cost of the goods that come from Amsterdam where by I am forced to sell my goods heere with not understanding the true cost of them which doeth not give me content for I cannot tell wether I geete or loose by them therefore pray omitt if not in future if you put the charges of the goods from Amsterdam to my accompt & give it me per letter, you shall not neede to give any accompt for them to Mr Cockey & I had rather it should be soe & then I shall give creditt for those charges here & by soe doeing [*p. 111*] I shall the better know the true cost of my goods heere havinge the Amsterdam charges per envoysed from thence, I suppose Smith may be arrived before this come to your hand I spake to him to desire you to send me some grave stones which I shall now wright againe *vidz* send me eight grave stones lett two be 8 foote longe & 4 foo[t] brode three lette be 6 fo[ot] 8 inches longe & 3 fo[ot] 4 inches brode & the other three betwixt those sizes provide them as soone as you can & lett them come by first opportunity. This is the nedfull at present from

Your lovinge friend
Tho: Baret

Norwich the 16th of October 1674
/No. RC4/9/
15 pieces No. 29 cost 63s per piece
11 pieces No. 23 cost 85s per piece
4 pieces No. 31 cost 80s per piece
3 pieces No. 34 cost 42s per piece
1 piece No. 32 cost 70s per piece
34 pieces

Mr Rowland Cockey

Sir, Upon my arrivall heere I finde both your letters of the 6 & 16th instant SN but have not time now to ansure them or right any thinge conserning the pack above but in short it cometh by Smith whoe I suppose is this day sayled for he tould me yesterday at Yarmouth that he would sayle with [*p. 112*] the first faire winde which serveth this day, the No. 29 are all darke collours & I hope will give content altho the prices they are sould at doeth not content me, I have received both your kinde presents *vidz* the turtles & the quinces which will give me many an oppertunity to remember your kindnes for which be pleased to accept the retorne of mine & my wives thanks to you & your Lady for them I doe expect the <next> weeke after next to have a pack of No. 34 very good which I shall send per next, pray lett me have my accompt for I shall never be satisfyed without it, accept the tender of serves to you & to your Lady & Lidia from

Your lovinge freinde
Tho: Baret

[*p. 113*] London the 8 of September 1674

Mr Rowland Cockey

Sir, I am this eveing come to London & last night Mr Langley & my selvfe remembred you at Cambridge he desired me to lett you know they ware all well & likely to finde a good faire for sales but they sould low and were upon the vye one with other an accompt of which he would give you afterwards not not [*sic*] having received any letters from you since my last to you I thought now to have been silent but that I have reckoned with my weavers & concluded with all since then & doe finde that whereas then I advised No. 29 cost 67 I doe find that all my last being putt together they doe arise but to 64s per piece which I thought fitt to hinte to you & also that since M[ark] C[ockey] is such as he is in what comodities he has the same with you as to collour & goodne[ss] for a while to learne him witt or to beate him out of trade sell as he sell altho it be to no profit, send me some more iron as sone as you can but for bras or copper of all sorts its a drugg & therefore if my last order be not ansured lett it alone. This is the needfull at present with serves I rest

Your reall friend
Tho: Baret

[*p. 114*] London the 15th of September 1674

Mr John Fitts

Being now in London I cannot give you date of your last letter or mine but I doe remember that I have any before me unansuered as to those wares you have of mine to sell be not to high in price especially if any other person have of the same comodity & doe labor to undersell you for I have mett with some persons whose indiscretion is to apprent that have sett them selves to beate me out of trade but I resolve I will not be soe & therefore if Mr M[ark] C[ockey] doth you any inconveniency sell as he sell if the comodities be alike altho I save nothing by them but yett I am so much a lover of my selvfe that I request you to sell to my best advantage unless you meete with some opposition upon the accompt above but I hope you are out of his reach for I heare he doeth only play his trickes in Amsterdam which I will beare no further than necessity doth oblige being at Yarmouth I understand that you doe require a certificate of all iron to be sent to you & that you doe oblige soe greate a quantity to be certified of by wayte that you much injure me heare in the entring of it & there fore for future lett your certificate be only for soe many barres in such a shipp with mentioning the waight but if you must mentioning the waight lett it not be above half the waight or as low as possible I had chose you should be exact in the number of barrs then to extreame in the waight for its much to my domiage in passing them heare & therefore for future pray study in this case to helpe me who am altho in hast

Your reall friend
Tho: Baret

[*p. 115*] London the 29th of September 1674

Mr Thomas Shephard

Sir, Yours of the 19th of May last I received whilst heare in London & by misfortune laid it aside wheare I could not come at it till now, I begg your pardon for my delay of ansuering it which I shall now performe. I am very thankfull to your court for admitting the sale of my goods butt I perceive I must send noe more unless that I shall take up my freedome of the Company which I shall not doe upon the uncertanty of a new trade & alsoe I have seen the oath of freedom of the Company which dos particularly expre[ss] Holland Zealand & the rest of the Low Contres with so large an obligation to the Company that I can not take this oath & continue the trade which I now have in the Low Contry without breaking of it & I have so greate a reverence to an oath that rather than incurre the necessity of breaking of it I shall for the present desist in the Hambrough trade till some better expedient can be found out & then Sir I shall be ready to serve you my uttermost, in the meanetime I know many others who trade constantly & are noe more free than my selfe. Sir, I make it my best request to you that you would be pleased to dispose of my goods as well as you can whether it bee to profitt or loss they have laid long by & I am loth to have them lay longer, Mr John Dey of Hamburgh was with me in Norwich not long since & sett saile that very day I went to Yarmouth to have seen him he writes me word that he inte[n]d to send a shipp for Yarmouth & will spare me freight wher if so be you can make me any returnes upon those comodities you have by you, pray omitt not this opportunity & lett it be in the best sweeds iron 1/3 square & the other 2/3 narrow flatt which I think is the cheapest sortment but if not 1/3 of each narrow flatt brode of 3 inches & square, had I more consernes in your hands I should be for whale finns Ossinbrigges[65] but I must content my selfe as I can but truly it greives mee that I can not cont[i]nue my [trade] which I plainly perceive I could make to be advantageous [*p. 116*] to the trade of the nation & possibly not disadvantagious to my selfe but I will loose both rather than I will breake an oath. Sir, I most humbly thanke you for your assistance & in any thing in my power you shall find me to be

Your reall friend & humble servant
Tho: Baret

London the 29th of September 1674

Mr John Dey

Sir, Yours of the 16th instant I received per last post from Norwich. I am hartily glad to heare of your safe arrievall at Hamburgh. Hearing that your occasions detained you longer at Yarmouth than you first intended I went downe thither to see you but it soe happenned that you sett sayle the morning of that day I cam thither to, by last post I sent downe the inclosed to Mr Christian Langly of which I doubt not but he will give you ansure, I take notice that you doe intend to lade a shipp for Yarmouth next mounth & will spare me lading in her I was sorry that you staid so long at Yarmouth where by to hinder your i[n]tended voyage to have been performed before this time because the Act of Navigation[66] taking plai[c]e the dutyes heare will be much advanced upon a forraigne bottom but the particular difference I can not as yett understand, besides the time you give me notice is soe short that I can not tell how to remitt you any money to buy me comodities with all for as I would have them bought in at the cheapest price so I would have my money drawne or remitted which would proove most to my advantage but the shortnes of the [*p. 117*] time disables mee from the putting those desines in exeation & therefore I shall now adventure upon the less parcell which I shall be only in iron which lett be of the best spruce or Swedish iron that can be gotten, by no meanes send me any spall[67] iron & in that comodity lay me out for a trayall £150 sterl lett it be half narrow flatt quarter square quarter brode of 3 inch lett it be as thinne & clever drawn iron as possibly you can gett for that giveth it

65 Osnaburg, a coarse, plain weave cotton fabric, originating in Osnaburg, Germany (thanks to Sally Tuckett for this reference).

66 Probably referring to the Navigation Act of 1673.

67 i.e. a shard or splinter of iron.

a great comendations heere as for the mony I can not tell how to remitt it to you for to serve this occasion & therefore please to draw it upon my selfe at Norwich or upon John Burton at Mr Barets warehouse in Abb Church Lane in London or upon Mr Rowland Cockey of Amsterdam for my accompt & your bills shall be duly complyed withall if you draw upon Mr Rowland Cockey Mr Thomas Shepard can soe assist you that he shall give you creditt to your writing altho he never did see your hand upon paper or if you give me order I will remitt the mony to you from this place or from Amsterdam doe which is most to my advantage & as this doth succed soe I shall in large further but pray keep [*illegible*][68] what pass betwen you & my selfe. I have advised Mr Thomas Sheppard that you have spared me freight for a parcell of iron which I have requested him to send me as retornes for <my> goods hee hath of mine so dispose & therefore pray present my service to Mr Shippard & ask him what tonnage you shall reserve for him upon my accompt. This with tender of serves is all at present from

Your lovinge friend
Tho: Baret

[*p. 118*] London the 30th of September 1674

Mr Rowland Cockey

Sir, Yours of the 14th per <poa[st]> shipps I received since which I have had none, my last to you was of the 8th instant from hence which I hope is come safe to hand. Next week I shall returne to Norwich I hope to go from hence on Mond[a]y but Thursday shall be the longest, upon my returne I shall finde ready a parcell of No. 29 all dark brown collour & darke warpes as also a parcell of white russells all which shall be ready for your order. I doe understand that there is a parcell of iron coming per Kipper for me although I doe not as yett understand if per your advice or invoyce I wish it safe pasage, pray send me no more comodities of one sort or other till further order for at present my hands are full & the markett is glutted as also because I have ordered one Mr John Dey marchant in Hamburgh to draw £150 sterling upon you for my accompt, I suppose you may know him for he came from Yarmouth with Thomas Kipper last voyage he is now freighting a shipp from Hamburgh to Yarmouth & I have ordered him to

68 From the context the meaning appears to be 'private' or similar.

send me in itt a parcell of comodities to that value I have sold in Norwich to Mr Asten[69] a dyer a bale of [?]overoft madder No. 12 for [?]69s per cento to pay at six months which is most miserable mistaken in the weight for you doe charge it at 157lb 0= & it weighs but 11st 2lb 14oz in the scale bare weight I stood & see it weighed my selfe its above 40lb 0= shortt as neare as I can compute it unless some other bagg have it over it will be a cruell loss, since my coming to London I find that madders do rise a lettell I have ordered Mr Langly that if they come to 70s per cento en [?]beroft to sell he offred 66s if you doe not like this price then advise per next what price they shall be <*illegible*> sold att & I will compute with you in it, if the cropp dos prove naught they will rise high for heares but little in hand yet Mr Langly advise as things now stant to sell if they come to 70s on [?]beroft advise as you think best but defere not to ansure per first, Smith is safley arrived I hope to finde all my consernes safly received at my returne. Sir, I am [*sic*] you have received your daughter in saftey & that yourself & Lady are in good helth as my selfe & wife are, heare accept the tender of our service [*p. 119*] to you both I am

Your reall friend & servant
Tho: Baret

Sir, I pray remember & send my accompt for I shall never be satsfied till I have itt

London the 30th of September 1674

Mr John Fittz

Yours of the 25th instant I received heare in London from which place I shall returne next week. I perceive you have sold some searge de nîens [*sic*] at 30 sterling with a yard allowance which allowance was more then ever I knew of before for we make none such at Amsterdam but if it be the custome of the place it can be helped no other way then by the price sould at for this rebats 1 sterling per ell, I take notice of the returnes you have made which I hope to finde safe when I com to Norwich for I heare the shipp is safly arrived, what advise is before you not ansured please to send per Kipper per whome you advize is a parcell of iron from R[owland] C[ockey] which I wish safely arrived, lett your certificate be for as small a parcell as possibly you can for the resons formerly hinted to you by my

69 Possibly Henry Austen, dyer, who became a freeman of Norwich in 1651.

last of the 5th instant, if you have occasions for any more weares pray give advise to him that is

Your reall friend to serve you
Tho: Baret

/No. JF3/
4 ffff[70] serge de nîmes No. 35 30 yards cost 4s 2d per yard
3 serge de nîmes No. 15 30 yards cost 3s 10d per yard
4 white narrow russells No. 34 26½ yards cost 42s per piece
11

[*p. 120*] Norwich the 4th of November 1674

Mr John Fittz

Yours of the 19th past I received, my last to you was of the 16 of last month since then none from you, above is the invoyce of a small pack this night sent downe to Yarmouth to go per first shipps, the No. 35 are better wares then any you have had as yet & I hope will ansure the diffrence that is in price betwixt them & No. 15, I must desire you to raise your price for 34 sterling per ell is no living price for wares of that goodnes these are of, if your costomers will hold to a good price I will make them as good as they desire but if they lowre the price I must debuce[71] the wares which I will not doe till by soe doeinge they oblige me the four pieces of No. 34 are such as I sell at Amsterdam for 26 to 27 guilders per piece I sent you these for tryall if they doe not sell lett them lay by till further order, in my last I wrott for some graves stones which take your best time for them that soe you may gett those which are good & at reasonable rates & in that comodity observe this order lett the stone be to the scantlings[72] that are ordered & of the thickest to be gott & free from flints bedds & crickes for all these are very injurious to them & mak them sell at under rates, the last stones sent me were verry meane and I had much to doe to put them of[f] to a savinge bargaine and therfore you had better take time then be too forward to buy bad, I am informed that tarres is bought cheaper then you bought <mine> & yet as good, I am now full of all comodityes that I know of & therfore shall wright for none if you have any mony mony of mine by you as I presume you have

70 *See* note 35.
71 Variant of debase.
72 i.e. measurements.

pray remitt it to me per bill for at present I am some what streightned, this with tender of servic is all at present from

Your lovinge friend
Tho: Baret

Abought 14 days hence I shall have such an other parcell for you

[*p. 121*] Norwich the 13th of November 1674

Mr Thomas Shepard

Sir, Yours of the 26th of October I received & by it doe understand that you have written two letters to me which never cam to my hand which I much wonder at for I doe not remember that I ever had one miscarry before I am truly sorry for this accident because it will loose time. Sir, I am of your minde its pittye the wares should lay & decaye & therefore please to send them upon my accompt to Danzig or any other place where you thinke a market may be obteyned & order them to be sould to the best advantage they can but lett them be sould to noe profitt or to loss rather then keepe them longer I have brave serge de nîmes & other comodityes by me which I know would turne to accompt butt your company is injurious to me but its in vaine to complaine. I am sorry that I have noe other affaires to request your assistance in then the puttinge of a parcell of good stuffs made bad for your companyes pleasure & injustly two for I doe verryly beleive they are noe more under theire charter then any comodity of England which is free, all that I have farther is to retorne you my thanks for what you have already don & to request you would use your skill to helpe me in the disposall of what is allready there if you could propose any thinge to me about a future trade I should accept it & ever shew myself to be

Your reall friend & servant
Tho: Baret

There is one Mr John Dey of your place pray favor me to convey the inclosed to him as soone as it cometh to hand it requiringe speede.

[*p. 122*] Norwich the 13th of November 1674

Mr John Dye

My last to you was of the 29th of September from London since which none from you, in it I did advise you to draw £150 upon Mr Cockey Mr Burton or my selfe to be sent me in iron in the ship you advised should sayle from Hamburgh the midle of last month but hearinge nothing from you I suppose your project for sending the shipp doe faile butt if it doth not you have now driven it soe late as I am not willinge to adventure this winter & therfore if not done before this come to hand pray send nothinge on my accompt nor draw any mony altho formerly advised I shall now defer all to a new safe time & shall then be willinge to adventure with you whoe am

Your loving friend
Tho: Baret

Norwich the 13th of November 1674

Mr Rowland Cockey

Sir, Since my last to you of the 4th instant I received both yours of the 6 & 9 instant & am glad Smith is in salvo hopinge the goods are come safe to hand before this & will give content. I see trade is bad soe shall doe the less but that would be adventuringe in some comodityes ware my accompt first passed which I expect by every post & pray faile me not, by a former letter I wrott you word that I had ordered Mr John Dye to draw £150 upon you & to send me goods for it but I have not heard from him since & he hath delayed the time soe long as I am now not willinge to adventure & therfore by this poast have wrott to him that if not done before myne cometh to hand he shall forbeare which order doe you alsoe comply with. All this is the nedfull at present from

Your lovinge friend
Tho: Baret

[*p. 123*] Norwich the 4th of November 1674

Mr Rowland Cockey

Sir, My last to you was of the 16th past which had the invoyce of a pack No. RC4/9 since which none from you which makes me a litle wonder at it consideringe with what ernestnes I have often wrott to you for my accompt currant butt now I plainely see you slight me & my imployment, the one is not worth wrightinge nor is the other worth wrightinge about, I have severall times given you complaints concerninge 1½ per cento for buyinge in & other things of that nature but you give me noe other answer but that you will have it, I have now for many months beene desiringe an accompt from you after two yeares standinge but can not be answered nay more then that since I have beene thus ernest for an accompt currant you now will not soe much as give me an accompt of sales if this be marchant like dealinge I doe not understand it I have beene all a long hither to persuadinge of you by all wayes of kindnes that I possibly could invent to draw you to doe me reason but I see it will not worke with you & therfore it hath now brought me to my serious resolve that I will send noe more goods to you till that I have my accompt currant stated & have satisfaction about those severall things which I have soe long & often complayned to you off, these recentments havinge beene long & you have heard of them sufficiently from my selfe & others which doe make me resolve if possible to come to some understandinge how things doe stand betwixt you & me, I have severall times desired you that as my money cometh in you would remitt it to me butt I can not gett you to doe it but you putt me upon drawinge which is 2 per cento verry neare to my loss & all to comode your selfe by keepinge my money in in your hands for your private occasions, this I am & [*p. 124*] have beene sencible of for a long time although I have beene patient under it by these things I plainely see you are not that kinde friend which you would seeme to be but will make use of a friend to the uttmost of your private advantage, these things have made me looke into the accompt betwixt us which I can not state perfectly because you have kept me in soe much ignorance but yet I am sure I am pretty neare it & by this accompt you have about £1,400 or £1,500 of myne in your hands besides all wares retorned & sent to Hamborough besides all moneys drawne or remitted upon my accompt & besides all comodities whatsoever that I have received from you as neare as I can guess this is the least butt that I may trye whether I have made any mistakes or not pray by the next poast lett me have my accompt currant that soe if possible the breach may be made up againe & the correspondency renewed betwixt us for I am resolved to cease all tradinge till our accompts are setled & then I may begin againe. Mr Cockey I have a verry considerable some of money to pay at Christmas neere £1,000 & I can not conceive but that you have money of mine in hand to a good vallue & therfore I depend upon you for £500 which pray remitt to me per first send me some bills per next for I have noe minde to draw upon you from London because I finde it to be too much to my charge & truly the trade will not beare it. Mr Cockey I am verry desirous our friendshipp may remaine & therfore I entreate you to doe me reason & not delay it for if you doe I must correspond with others which if you force me to lett the blame lay at your owne doore for I can noe longer admitt of these actions & delayes without complaininge, pray lett me heare from you by next poast which will oblige me to be

Your truly loving friend
Tho: Baret

[*p. 125*] Invoyce of one pack of Norwich stuffs shipped in the Biscay Marchant Lucke Roath Master consigned to Mr G[e]orge Richards of Bilb[a]o for the accompt of Thomas Baret of Norwich marked as in the margent contents as followes

/No. TB1/

10 pieces of stuffs No. 1 cost 65s per piece	£32 10s 0d
10 pieces of stuffs No. 2 cost 65s per piece	£32 10s 0d
10 pieces of stuffs No. 3 cost 60s per piece	£30 0s 0d
2 pieces of stuffs No. 4 cost 50s per piece	£5 0s 0d
2 pieces of stuffs No. 5 cost 45s per piece	£4 10s 0d
34 pieces	prime cost £104 10s 0d

Norwich the 19th of November 1674

Mr George Richards

Sir, Havinge a parcell of very fine wares by me which I thought proper for some parts of Spaine I was inquiringe of my good friend Mr John Langly if he could recommend me to a friend of his that would assist me in setlinge a trade for some comodityes of the new invention of this place upon which he did recomend your selfe to me upon which although I am a stranger to you yet I have presumed to consigne a small pack of wares as above to you for a tryall & should & should [*sic*] be glad they might prove fitt for the place to occasion farther adventure that which in incouraged me to trye this experriment was the trade which Bibbo[73] hath which[74] Madrid these beeing stuffs which I concevd fitt for the <place> expence of that place I could have sent many sorts more but was loath to adventure to deepe till I had some understanding of the place whether they would vend & turne to accompt, I take pleasure only in dealinge in the best comodityes & upon such an attempt as this is in Amsterdam have setled soe good a correspondency there as that my wares sell equally with the French whoe have the <good> requite of good markets. If your ansure to this should incourage I would send you over a many patterns of those stuffs which I cause to be made for my perticular occasions if any stufes would doe with you you could send me over no patterns although of other contreys makes if made as well or mixt with silck [*p. 126*] but I could make it I have had good success in other parts of this nature alredy lett the stuffs be thick or thin its the same I am now makinge some for Holland as thick is cloath but they are very fine which makes them deare & soe I suppose not fitt for your parts, if the clergy of Spaine weare black & would accept of stufes I doubted not but to send what would give content the wares above are fine wares closse strooke yett thinn & light beeinge half silke half worsted especially No. 1, 2, 3 the other are putt in by the by for experiment if the collour should not please I would alter to any collour advised I have only given you the first cost but can not appoint you any price but shall fully & freely leave to you to doe fore me as you would for your selfe you know what is profitt or loss in them I should be glad they might returne soe good an accompt as may give further incouragement to trade in them or any other comodityes of these parts for its my ambition to promote our manufacture, what comodityes your place doeth afford for retorne I cannot tell but would request you by a letter to informe that soe I might inquire what would be proper for this place, iron is a comoditye which I much deale in from other parts & I finde iron to be made with you but how it will take heare I know not yet, for experriment I would adventure upon 4 or 6 tonn as wee call heere & therfore if my wares have the good happ to come to a good marked with you I would request you as soone as you have effects of mine to ansure it that you would send me such a parcell of iron for tryall lett it be very good & sorted as is usally sent to London & consigned to Mr John Langly to follow my order [?]& bought it please to send my letters to him also this with tender of servies is the nedfull at present from him that is

Your reall friend & servant
Tho: Baret

73 Bilbao.
74 Likely 'with'.

[*p. 127*] Norwich the 20th of November 1674

Mr William Peacocke

Sir, My last to you was of the 18th of July past since which time I have beene co[n]sideringe of your kinde profer to dispose of some goods for me in commission, its truth I am & have beene conserned with my good friend Mr Rowland Cockey but I am not ingaged to send goods to noe other person & therfore if I should enter into a correspondency with you I make it my request that it may be kept priavet & not discovered for what nede any person know from whome or whence you have your comodityes & therfore Sir if you be still of the same minde & shall intimate it to me by letters with your advice upon it I shall be ready to serve you in what I may, this with tender of serves is the needfull at present from

Your reall friend & servant
Tho: Baret

[*p. 128*] Norwich the 9th of December 1674

Mr Rowland Cockey

Sir, Yours of the 23rd past I received & have seriously perused every part of it which I shall fully answer, you begin with a confession that I have cause to be displeased for want of my accompt & yet your leter is 26 days ould & noe accompt cum although letters of the 11th instant are arrived is this to deale like a marchant or friend with me I thinke its neither, as to the phrase of answeringe me as my servant I looke on it as a complaint may I finde you dealinge with me as a friend its all I doe expect, as to your faithfullnes in refusinge all imployments but mine I beleive in some sence its true but you have sould other persons wares which have beene lodged in others hands by your order. That I wrott I would send noe more goods to you till I had my accompt stated I doe acknowledge & am firmely resolved to stand to it come of it what will I doe not in the least doubt but you wilbe supplied by others which please to accept of with all my hart for I will noe longer deale wheare my accompt must be standinge out two yeares & halfe wheare I must pay 1½ per cento provition for buyinge wheare others pay but one wheare I must pay 3 per cento for sellinge & others but 2 per cento & in comodityes where I loose 10 per cento by them where I can have noe accompt when wares are sould nor when money is received nor can I have any money remitted to me butt all kept in hand and myselfe kept in ignorance as if I were only to send over goods & never to know what become of them if this be honest just or faire dealinges then I doe not understand what is & therfore I say it againe till you do me reason in these things I will not send over one piece, you say that if goods cost as I advise the trade will cease of it selfe to which I shall make noe reply but this that those goods cost me to a farthinge of what I gave you accompt of & therfore [*p. 129*] you have small reason to deale soe severely with me where my loss is soe greate, lett your kinsman sell No. 29 or No. 4 at 34 guilders for I nor can nor will supply to sell soe but for what I have must doe as well as I can but were I to goe on in trade (which I will not till you deale better by me) they should want the comodity or give a better price ere I would make soe good wares againe what ever opinion you or they have of them yet as bad as the trade is I did not doubt but to save my selfe could I have reasonable & faire dealings butt if I can not lett us end our accompts friendly for what is passed & lett me have what money is my due that soe I may imploy it heere or elce wheare for a livelihood, I am not soe redy to beleive striffe makers as you thinke I am all my exceptions are plaine & vissible in my owne busines without regardinge what you doe to others I can not thinke you less then £1,500 in my debt & doe accompt you my debtor for £1,500 till I have your accompt, I requested you to remitt me £500 in my letter of the 4th of November past to helpe me towards my greate some which I have to pay at Christmas but you are pleased to give me noe answer about it but runn me into streights to supply you with wares & then keepe my money in your hands whereby I am like to loose my credditt heere for want of your due supply if you deale with other men at this rate they must be men of better estates then I am or elce they may have just cause to repent it because you say you feare I shall come short of the accompt that I make of my estate in your hands it maketh me the more impatient for my accompt to see if I have not beene the servant in the trade if what you see me to say proove trew I shalbe far from maineteyninge myselfe like a marchant which I desire to doe as well as you intimate you desire to doe butt for effectinge your designe I must confess you have the better end of the staff for I am at the charge & hazard & you at the certaine advantage which is treble what I gett should I accompt hazard interest & loss by commodities, [*p. 130*] you wright that a broker which hardly putts pen to paper have 1 sterling per cento F[l]emish I presume you doe not alwaise make use of a broker altho you putt it to accompt which I could with the highest probability proove from your owne letter. Besides the provision of 3 per cento sellinge & 1½ per cento buyinge you charged in my last accompt pack howse hier for the goods retorned & sent to Hamborough brokeridge for wares sould & part of all letters & severall other things of that nature which was never don in a commission of any vallue but by your selfe or such as vallued not their commission. Mr Cockey upon the wholle I perceive you give me as rigorous an accompt (I meane in my former) as Holland ever produced by which I thinke I may safely conclude that you doe accompt me your friend to make the utmost advantage of you can lett me sinke or swim & therfore I am now in prudence obliged to looke to my selfe & if possible to bringe you to reason before I goe on further which if you denie me lett us come to a friendly conclution & remaine friends altho wee trade noe further, I am under some disturbed thoughts as well as distress for money & therfore I make it my request to you againe that I may speedily have my accompt currant & an accompt of what wares as to the sorts are on hand & what moneys are standinge out lett me alsoe have bills for the £500 which I formerly wrott for that soe I may be redeemed from those misseryes which I now am likley to be in throw want of them. Pray faile me not of them if you have any kindness left or would any wayse oblige

Your loving friend
Tho: Baret

[*p. 131*] Norwich the 9th of December 1674

Mr John Fittez

Sir, Yours of the 27th past have recevd & perused & am glad that the pack JF3 is safley arrived. I have now more serge de nîmes ready of collour to the patterns you sent me which I shall send forward, at the present I am not lickely to have any goods come over beeinge full of all sorts which sell to loss but if I had Mr Cockey can still give you directions as formerly altho the charges should be placed to my accompt, as to mill stones at the present I understand them not soe shall decline them as yet but as to the grave stones as sone as any are to be had that are good & reasonable pray send me <over> some over without any further advise about them, its possible some may come downe betwixt this & springe & therfore take the time for buying them when an oppertunity serveth lett me know how the price of madders rice with you but at present shall wright for noe comodityes till I see more hopefull markets which at present are soe much to loss as I choose to keepe my comodityes which putt me to soe great streights for mony that I must ernestly desire you per next poast to remitt me what ever mony you can possible gett upon my accompt which at this time will doe me a doble kindnes & therfore delay if not which will oblige

Your lovinge friend
Tho: Baret

Sir, I can buy as good payles as those you sent me for 2s I beleive I could have them for 22d heere in Norwich & therfore conclud he that sould you them did abuse you to take 24 sterling per piece.

[*p. 132*] Norwich the 23rd of December 1674

Mr John Fittz

I heerewith send you a small pack of stuffs marked No. WP1 conteyninge 22 pieces which please to enter as you use to doe formerly & putt the charges to my acompt, lett the pack remaine with you till you receive a letter from me to whome you shall send it for at the present I am not determined, my last to you was by poast of the 9th instant which I hope you received & will comply with it, this is the needfull at present from

Your lovinge friend
Tho: Baret

/No. WP1/
2 white serge russells No. 1 cost 43s per piece
6 mixt serge de nîmes 30 yards a piece No. 2 cost 108s per piece
14 mixt serge russells No. 3 cost 63s per piece
22 pieces

Norwich the 6th of January 1674[/5]

Mr William Peacocke

Sir, Your of the 14 of December last I received & have perused the contents of it by which I understand you are content to sell some goods for me in commission & therfore having the pack above ready by me I sent it to Mr John Fittz of Rotterdam marked as in margent[75] to lay it by him till I ordered to home he should send it & therfore if you please to send <to send> the inclosed to him with directions how he shall convey it to you he

75 There is nothing in the margin here.

will follow your order in it they went per Thomas Kipper whoe sayled last weeke & I hope is safe in Rotterdam before this time the wares are all fine & goods made better [*p. 133*] then ordinary & I hope will give content, if they should finde any fault with them lett me know what it is & it shall be amended in future. I use to sell the white serge russells at 27 or 28 guilders per piece & the serge de nîmes for 36 sterling & upwards per ell Felm[i]sh [*sic*] these are the lowest prices that I use to sell soe good wares for but I have sould them for 40 sterling per ell but I shall leave it to you to gett me the best price you can for my incoragement for I should be glad that you & my selfe might have soe good incouragement as that we might goe on briskly in trade together. This with tender of service is the nedfull at present from

Your friend & servant
Tho: Baret

Norwich the 6th of January 1674[/5]

Mr John Fittz

My last to you was of the 23d December last per shipps with a small pack No. WP1 which I hope is safley arrived per Thomas Kipper since which I have received none from you. This serveth to acquant you that I have consigned the pack above to Mr William Peacock of Amsterdam under whose couvert this cometh to you & therfore please to comply with his order about the same pack which will oblige

Your lovinge friend
Tho: Baret

[*p. 134*] Norwich the 6 of January 1674[/5]

Mr John Dey

Sir, My last to you was of the 13th of November per coverte of Mr Thomas Shephard since which I received yours of the 24 November past which is now before me but for your letters of the 13th I never received it & soe cannot tell the contents of it in ansure to this I perceive that you are disappointed of a shipp & soe could not send me any comodityes at this time which suiteth well with me for the season of the yeare was soe farr spent as I was unwillinge to have adventured, I perceive you have intentions to fraight a shipp in the springe but you beeinge incertaine in that alsoe maketh me at a stand what to resolve upon for that which hindered now will be the same then if the warre doe hold for our shippinge is much employed by Duch & French. The reasons you give for buyinge iron in the winter I hold to be very good but unles I were sure of conveyance it ware litle less then madnes for me to remitt my mony in to a strange contry & not know how to bringe back my comodityes hather for to bringe them by London is greater loss besides troble I am willinge to make a tryall but I would see my way cleare first I should be glad if I could finde out a way to vend my owne stufs which I make heare in your parts which I can not effect by Mr Shiphard for he will not medle with me because I am noe member of the company if I could finde vent for my owne st[u]ffes then I might attempt to bringe <them> my retorns by London but till then I must sett still or have my way cleared up to me before I doe ingage my selfe in remittinge mony either from London or from Amsterdam from which latter place I should chose to doe it because I have money there already & moneys dayley receivinge there and I presume its much to my advantage to remitt what is in Holland to Hamburge <in this thinge> then to bringe it first to England & then to remitt it to Hamburge in this thinge I would willingly be satisfied that is how much 1,000 guilders of Holland & £100 sterlinge will produce in Hamburge when I know this I shall be able to compute the difrence, as to sending calves skins they are here worth 12 per ell English which would turne to loss with you I know they are to be bought cheaper in other parts but I want a correspondent there, as to the buyinge of a shipp I should be willinge with it but I can not gett it made free but at a verry greate rate if at all & therfore if you had lett me know what a new shipp of 60 [?]last which computation I doe not understand for I would not buy one of more then 60 ton burthern according to our English accompt beeing fitt in all respects to goe to sea would [*p. 135*] cost I then would have made inquiry what it would cost to have it made free & soe consideringe whole whether it ware worth my purchase, you may doe the same abought the old vesalls you mentioned but with all you must lett me know their age & if they be stronge & good for if any wayse decayed I will not medle with them, I observe what you wright abought the prices of comodityes some of which might turne to accompt were the way cleared for them, pray informe of the corse of your exchange that is at what exchange when its mony for mony from England without loss or gaine on either side & how much one groat is off vallue in starlinge money by discovering this to me I shall understand your exchange in Holland 34s 4d is even money & evrey groat is 5s sterling please to afford an ansure to pray lett me alsoe understand the exchange betwixt Amsterdam & Hamburg

Your loving friend
Tho: Baret

[*p. 136*] Norwich the 27 of January 1674[/5]

Mr William Peacocke

Sir, Yours of the 25th instant I received my last to you was of the 6th instant with an invoyce of a pack of goods sent to Mr John Fittz of Rotterdam to follow your order in ditto pack marked No. WP1 alsoe inclosed in your letter was a letter to Mr John Fittes with order in it to him that he should upon receipt of it with your directions send the said pack to you as you should direct butt in regard your letter now received make noe mention of the receipt of mine beeinge of soe old date it doeth make me suspitious that it is miscared & therfore I request you to take some care by wrightinge to Mr Fittes at Rotterdam that soe the pack may not miscarry likewise & by next poast pray advise me how the case is with them, in yours I received sevrell patterns of wich I shall be mindfull & as soone as I can geet any ready shall send some to you but you desire to have some with an eye of <gold> yellowish which coller I understand not & therfore can act nothinge in it till you send me some patternes to be my guides for if you send me some any patternes in a very short time I can comply with them but without patterns for collours I can doe nothinge to content, as to madders I am alredy to deply to my loss ingaged in them indeed I am at present too full of all sorts of comodityes but hope by the springe I shall have occasion but the cefets[76] comodity that I doe *intend to* bringe my retornes in wilbe iron of which if you please lett me know how the prices doe rule & if very cheape may give order for some, I have beene inquiringe about glew which will not come under 48 per the 100lb but I doe not understand what you mene by its cleernes & well dryed & thin & large leafe ours heare is not that you can see throw itt but is of a darke <brow> brownesh collour & not very thinn but the leaves are prety brod four of them are neare as bigg as this letter but because it was a comodity that I understood not at the present I thought fitt to give you this advise about it, which is the nedfull at present but tender of serves from him that is

Your loving friend
Tho: Baret

76 i.e. safest.

[*p. 137*] Norwich the 27 of January 1674[/5]

Mr John Fittz

My last to you was of the 6 instant under covert of a lettere I sent to Mr William Peacock of Amsterdam that he might send it to you & alsoe give you his directions how you should send the pack No. WP1 to him which was in Kipper but I feare the letter is miscarred because I have received one from him dated the 25 instant which makes noe mention of its receipt & therfore deliver not the pack to any till you are sure you have his order for it. The last letter that I received from you bore date the 27th of November last since which I have wrott two to you besides that by Mr Peacock the principle of which bore date the 9th of December last in which was some what about gravestones but the most meteiriall was my request to you to send me an accompt what wares you have sould for my accompt & what moneys ware in cash & that you would remitt it to me & send me bills first poast but you have given me noe <accompt> ansure to itt which doeth not in the least give me content & therfore I doe now agayne desire you to send me my accompt & bills for the mony by the next poast for my occasions for mony are urgent, by complyinge heere with you will oblige

Your loving friend
Tho: Baret

[*p. 138*] Norwich the 26th of February 1674[/5]

Mr William Peacocke

Both your letters of the 6th & 22nd instant are before me as alsoe the price currant which is not of soe much use to me as the small one is which respects only iron brass & copper & therfore if you send any more lett it be only of that sort, I perceive that sueeds iron is reasonable with you beeinge 6 guilders per cento & I suppose it may come cheap if you can procure me 4 ton of narrow flat & 1 ton of inch squares reasonable pray send them per first good shipp & for the money if you shall have none of myne I will upon your advice send you a bill to receive it of Mr John Fitts of Rotterdam or Mr R[owland] Cockey which you best approve of. The iron must be good tuff metall or it will not serve my occasions you may alsoe please to send me with it 50lb weight of round brass bottums or black lattin[77] of 15 inch over

77 Latten: a mixed metal, usually yellow in colour, closely resembling or identical to brass.

none to exceede 16 but keepe as neere 15 as you can, in answer to your letters please to understand that for glew the person have sould his parcell before receipt of your letter which did not exceede a 300lb weight but next month he shall make more his price is 48s per cento English if you would have any bespoke upon advice it shalbe don, as to serge de nîmes they are now sould heere from £5 to £5 10s per piece as they are in goodnes but none are sould under that are any thinge good & for rusels they are if good sould now at 58s & 60s some meane wares are sould at 56s but those I sent you were made beter than ordinary & cost me as then advised but now I can suply my selfe at 58s not under if soe good I doe perceive that goods are sould most terribly under foote by some to beate others out of trade altho therby they discover much [*p. 139*] weakenes & I suppose when they retorne to their sences againe they will see they can not be afforded at the prices they have sould, I am now resolved to lett Mr Cockey have the trade to himselfe for a while & therfore if you can not sell my wares soe as to make me a saver by them at the prices before mentioned keepe my wares by you for I will not deale to loss & supply againe butt Mr C[ockey] is terribly clogged with bad goods yours are fresh good & new & I doubt not but will afford 36 or 38 guilders per piece which last price I know I could have for some particular collers that I have by me but they beeinge a litle more chargeable than others I will not send them over till they will fetch 40 guilders & till all are genrally soe sould there wilbe noe good to be don in trade, as to sendinge of damasks I can receive noe incouragement for its now driven to loss by M[ark] C[ockey] as I am truly informed by them that deale in them I meane by Rowland Cockey whoe tells me that all is now done to loss butt if were not I can hardly understand by your letter what colors you meane but especially what workes whether bigg or little, this with service is the needfull at present from

Your loveing friend
Tho: Baret

[*p. 140*] Norwich the 17th of March 1674[/5]

Mr Rowland Cockey

Sir, I hope this will finde you safley arrived in Holland & that you finde your wife & family in good health to whome pray present my servise. I should have beene glad to received a letter from you were in London but I suppose your busines would not permit, Mr Christian Langly acquainted me with your postscript in his letter which related to me I can not but wonder why you did not send me my bill of sales when you had it in

London it would have given me some <saftey> satifaction till my accompt currant had come & I am sure it would have come cheaper to me from London than from Amsterdam. Sir, you now will have the power in your owne hands to send me my accompt curant without layinge the blame of its <impatient> not cominge upon any other person I am very impatient for it & t[h]erfore lett it not be delayed for till that accompt is setled I am determined as I have before tould you not to send any more goods but as soone as that is fully & fairely concluded I have some parcells which may be sent to you, you intimated to Mr Langley that I am your debter but I will see my accompt before I can beleve it & I shall rest full content with what honest & just accompts make it, the shipps lay winde bound at Yarmouth in which you have your greate adventure of mixt russells serge de nîmes & white callimancoes I wish you good succuse[78] in your adventure I hope you will sell them better then you have sold mine for your brother the alderman tells me he sells none under 37 guilders & some better, truly Mr Cockey this action of yours in buyinge of these goods doe not shew well I know you will have some excuse because I would send none but when the reason was because you woud not deale fairely with me in my accompts & when you had don me reason theare that I would suply againe all your excuses will not wipe of the staine before any juditious auditors but I perceive its your desire to trample upon & throw off old friends & put your confidence in new ones whome I wish may not prove like brokinge reeds to you when you put your *gretest* confidence in them, <I have sould> [*p. 141*] I have sould some iron & therfore desire you to send me about 15 tonn well sorted I doe understand its to be bought 12 guilders per cento or there aboughts shipp it in two shipps & lett it be sent per first. This is the nedfull at present from him that desires to be accompted

Your friend
Tho: Baret

Norwich the 17th of March 1674[/5]

Mr John Fittz

Yours of the 8th of February last past I received and thorough some occations from home have defered the ansuringe of it till now which now I shall performe, as to your serge de nîmes sell at the best price you can gett

78 i.e. success.

to cleare your hands I would sell at 31 sterling rather then stant out but I cannot *yet* tell whether I shall supply againe to sell soe but if I finde the price you sell at to be any profit I will suply againe otherwayse it ware madnes in me to doe it, as to the russells which you have by you pack them up & send them to Mr William Peacocke as by my order with them you may send these two pieces of No. 3 & give him an invoyce of them & I shall discharge them in your accompt, I have not as yet drawne any mony upon you because I doe intend to draw 700 guilders upon you to be paid in cash mony which when done I shall advise you off I doe as yet defere it because I shall draw it at short sight, as to the grave stones follow my order as sone as you can but for madders there will be much loss in them, as soone as convenently you can give me my accompt of sales & accompt currant that soe I may by it understand what I have in hand & charge my bookes accordingly I doe belev I shall send you two small bundles of stufs per first shipps which keepe by you till further order. This with service is the nedfull at present from

Your loving friend
Tho: Baret

[*p. 142*] Norwich the 24 of March 1674[/5]

Mr William Peacocke

Yours letter of the 5th instant & that from Mr Hicks of the 8th are both before me with the patterns of serge de boyce[79] my last to you was of the 26 of February past, I have perused both your letters but really prices are soe extreme low that I have noe hart to send any wares over till the price doth advance which I hope now it doeth because Ald[erman] Cockey heere assures me that his son Mr Marke sells none under 37 guilders which I can hardley tell how to beleve because you sell under 34 guilders which is loss out of pocket I have servell[80] serge de boyce now by me & will next weeke send you a fresh pack in hopes you will rayce the price that I may be a saver elce it will discourage me for futer, as to patterns now sent I know the wares verry well for its of my owne makinge of them but I have given over making of them long since & shall not sett to them againe unles they will yeld abut 54 guilders per piece at this goodnes if they will yeld that price upon your advice I will sett to them againe, Mr R[owland] Cockey

79 Serge de boys, a worsted fabric made in England in the seventeenth century.

80 i.e. several.

have sevrell of these by him of mine which he sells at less than they cost me heere the truth is the uncle & co[u]s[in] of a name strive to undersell each other & I thinke to paine theire principles heare which makes me weary of dealinge with R[owland] Cockey but I request you not to speake one worde of it because it may make my consernes the greater with you if you can raice to such prices as I can but live of truly I doe beleve that he & I <doe beleive> shall part but I would have <you> all kept privet for reasons I could tell you were wee together. I have orderd Mr John Fitts of Rotterdam to send you 10 pieces of serge de boyce or russells & two pieces of new stufs the price of the first is 58s & the other is 88s soe they now will cost the lowest penney butt these cost me more when bought when I heare you have received them I shall charge them to your accompt. This is the nedfull at present from

Your loving friend
Tho: Baret

[*p. 143*] Norwich the 31 of March 1675

Mr William Peacocke

Sir, Yours of the 26 instant I have received & perused it my last to you was of the 24th instant which I hope is come safe to your hand. I am much trobled at the contentes of your letter you wright that M[ark] C[ockey] sells under 33½ guilders & his father doth protest to me he sells for 37 guilders & I will assure you that 37 guilders is loss if his wares cost as mine doth, I am in a greate straight what to wright whether to goe on & sell or elce to lett them lay by you till the price mend, I am loath to have M[ark] C[ockey] quite putt me out of trade & as loath to runn hazards to loss, for the present I shall leave it to you to make the most you can of those wares that you have by you & shall received from Mr Fitts but really unless you can amend the price I can <not> none more & doe wish the pack which I have now for Yarmouth were with me againe but when that cometh to hand lett it lay by till they will afforde a higher price, I am sure R[owland] C[ockey] could gett 37 guilders & better if he had the wares but I shall send none to him as yet till I can draw him to doe me reason, as to iron the price currant you sent me gave it at 6 guilders but you say its now 6½ which is deare but I shall leave it to you to send me 3 ton of narrow & 2 ton of square at the lowest price to be gotten at but you must send me none butt tuff Swedes iron for other will not serve my occasions, per next occasion for wrighting

I shall send the invoyce of the pack now sent forroward, this with serves is the nedfull at present from

Your freind & servant
Tho: Baret

If you have any friends in Hamburg I would desire you privately to request them to give you theire thoughts about one Mr John Dey a marchant in Hamburge whoe liveth neare the watterside & latliy marrid a widdow there desire to know who he is looked upon to be as to estate faire & honest dealinges & to his capacity in marchant affaires I desire you to give me as spedey an accompt as possibley you can because I have a neare realation that is somewhat consearned with him

[*p. 144*] Norwich the 6th of Aprill 1675

Mr John Fittz

My last to you was of the 17th of March past by post which I hope is come safe to your hand I have sent you in Smith one pack No. JD1 & one pack No. WP2 & here with I send you one pack No. WP3 all which send to Mr William Peacock of Mamsterdam [*sic*] per first convenience & I shall per post give him my orders about them, I hope you have sent the russells &c to Mr Peacock as advised I shall not draw any mony upon you as I last hinted but by next post shall order Mr John Langly from London to draw £60 or £70 at 2 usance which some he can best meete with all which please to accept & pay upon my accompt. This with serves is the needfull at present from

Your friend to serve you
Tho: Baret

Norwich the 7th of Aprill 1675

Mr John Richerds

Sir, Yours of the 9th of March past I received & have perused it in which you intimate that the wares which I have sent you are esteemed too deere which I am sorry for in regard I can not procure them cheaper if made up to soe greate a goodnes should you have occasion for any more they would cost the same price but if you would admitt to have them coarser

& thinner I could make them 10s per piece cheaper, I have sold of No. 1 & 2 for 50 guilders in Amsterdam & No. 3 for 45 guilders & these are the same sorts made intentionally for the same place but if I had a desire to trye an experiment with them in ther parts it is my delight to cause wares to be made to the heighth of goodnes which will make you seeme dear but they have a valuable consideration for it, I am glad No. 3 have mett with a markett I hope the rest will follow & soe give occasion for new supplyes & an advance of price for I beleive this price will hardly make me a saver unless I meete with some retornes [*p. 145*] which will turne to accompt heere which at present I am ignorant off butt if you please to lett me know what are the generall comodityes that you doe make retornes in I shalbe informinge my selfe which will turne best to accompt. Sir, I have ordered 20 pieces of mohares to be made me which shall come with in 2s per piece of what you hinte for at 35s per piece all charges on boarde at London if good wares its not to be doun, butt Sir I wish you had sent me what collour & sortment of collour you expected for this is such a coarce comodity that I never buy any in my way of dealinge unless a marchant in London should bespeake a parcell of my servant there & he send me downe his collour to provide them. These 20 pieces I shall sort as are usuall sorted & hope I shall hitt right with them I shall send 16 pieces of No. 3 & two pieces of a new stuff which will exceede the former in gloss & beauty of silke & I wish them good success. These wilbe ready in 21 days to goe from hence to London for the next shipps for your ports, as to iron its the cheifest comodity that I bringe home from the easterne parts whether I deale & I perceive is much cheaper in price than yours butt I have some chapmen that doe particularly use your Bilboa iron but it must be half square & half flatt of your smallest sort or some small part midlinge but there must be a care in the choyce of it that it be not thick in one place & thinn in another, of iron thus chosen I could dispose of 4 or 5 tonn if not more as soone as arrived in this place & therfore as soone as you have cash for my accompt send it home in iron till I shall have more in your hands & know better whatt to retorne it in. This with tenders of service is the needful at present from

Your servant to command
Tho: Baret

[*p. 146*] Norwich the 7th of Aprill 1675

Mr William Peacocke

Sir, Yours of the 9th instant I received my last to you was of the 31th of March past, I have perused your letter & doe observe you have mett with some sales which have brought your stock of wares low to supply which I have sent you two small packs the invoyce of which shall be underneath, the serge de nîmes are sould tollerable well but the mixt russells at 34 guilders are yet to low but I hope they will advance for they doe not turne to accompt yet I doe heare that M[ark] C[ockey] sells soe but they tell me its only to gett off his ould stock, R[owland] C[ockey] is out of this sort upon my accompt but like a worthy marchant he hath provided good store of his owne how honest these actions are he best knows I perceive you have sould the two white russells No. 1 for 27 guilders per piece by the name of callimancoes, R[owland] C[ockey] never sold me any under 28 guilders that ware soe good as these but now I have sent you some right callimancoes No. 4 wich I use to have sould for 50 & 48 guilders per piece, I doe not know that any ware sold under, I have sent you one pack No. JD1 which keepe by you till further order its designed for Mr John Dey of Hamburge but I would not send it till you can procure some accompt of him he beinge almost a perfect stranger to me but yet I hare he is honest which is what I much prise in a correspondent, if you should have a good accompt of him then send it away per first with a letter of advice & when I know what you have done I shall send him the invoyce per first poast, I have given Mr Fittz order to hast the three packs to you per first This with service is the needfull at present from

Your friend to command
Tho: Baret

/No. WP2/
14 pieces No. 3 finer the order cost 60s
9 pieces No. 2 cost 100s per piece
23 pieces

/No. WP3/
10 pieces No. 4 cost 76s per piece
15 pieces No. 1 cost 43s per piece
25 pieces

I think these packs are shipt in Smith I am sure all but No. 3 are he only waites a faire wind.

One pack No. JD1 to follow order therein

Mr Peacock as yet I never wrott to know what comission you intend to putt to accompt for buyinge & sellinge pray lett me know what it is for I finde some would impose upon me beyond the custome & I desire you would discover yourselfe to prevent future mistakes

[*p. 147*] Norwich the 7th of Aprill 1675

Mr Rowland Cockey

Sir, I received yours of the 5th instant I am truly glad that you are safely arrived at your owne habitation & finde your family in good health, my service to your good wife & to litle Lidia. In answer to yours Sir I have good reason to be discontented with your actions towards me & truly I shall not alter my thoughts till I have my accompt for I looke upon all as emty words till I finde reall affects & then the reason of them will in one moment alter me to any thinge in justice you can expect frome me, I spake Ald[erman] Cockey about sellinge for 30 guilders he told me he sell none soe but for 35 to 36 to 37 unles it be some old dogg house keepers which he may sell under, he told me he sold your wife for 33 guilders I told him what you writt & he told me you ware a lyer its his owne words, I have sett No. 32 & No. 23 on worke but I will be as true as stele to my word for when they are made I will not send one piece more till my accompt is recived & stated & therfore make as much hast of it as you <will> please for it can not come to quick for my solicitous expectations which thinke evrey post seven till I have it, I doe sppose that for mixt wooll russells worsteds & white callimancoes you will not sodainly be in want because the 40 pieces you bought of N. Morly & the greate parcell you bought of Nathaniel Denney beside[81]

[*p. 148*] /No. JF4/
2 pieces of white callimancoes No. 4 cost 76s per piece
10 pieces of mixt wooll russells No. 1 cost 58s per piece
8 pieces of mixt russells No. 34 cost 42s per piece
20 pieces

81 The rest of this page is blank, and the letter unsigned.

Norwich the 16 of Aprill 1675

Mr John Fittz

Yours of the 12th instant I received & perused it I have sent you the pack above with another marked No. WP3 which forward to Mr William Peacocke of Amsterdam, I hope you have received these per William Ambling & alsoe the other two per Edmond Smith in safty before this coms to hand, the prices you sould my last at doe not give content & therfore if you cannot get 47 to 48 guilders for the white callimancoes & 34 to 35 guilders for the mixt russells & 27 guilders for the white russells lett them lay by you & I will order you some other way for they will yeld the same elce wheare, I send you these because I would not have you out of sorts & if your customers will give such prices as I may live of it I am willinge to suply you in any thinge, my last to you was of the 6 instant I doe take notice of the grave stones & am desires to va[l]ue the accompt of there charges that soe I may be able to sett a prices upon them when arrived which I cannot doe till I know all charges, Mr Langly hath advised me he will drawe £70 upon you for my accompt I did thinke my accompt would have borne it but if it doeth not pray accept & pay his bill & I shall at an other time for beare you as much. This is the nedfull at present from

Your loving friend
Tho: Baret

[*p. 149*] Norwich the 30th of Aprill 1675

Mr John Dey

Yours of the 19th of February last I received & have perused the contents of it butt havinge had some extra ordinay buisnes which heare caused my absence from home I could not ansure it sooner nor can I now doe it soe fuly as I would bacause obliged to goe for London upon the 3 of next month & therfore take this breife accompt till further leisure. Mr Thomas Penton is deade soe nothinge to be done with him I have ordered Mr William Peacocke Jnr of Amsterdam to send you for tryall one pack as followeth

/No. JD1/
10 serge de nîmes No. 2 30 yards long cost 110s per piece
2 serge de russells No. 5 cost 65s per piece
2 serge de russells No. 3 cost 46s per piece
14 pieces

They are good wares & I hope wilbe to content as these turne to accompt I shall order you more. This is the nedfull at present from

Your loving friend
Tho: Baret

/£55 0s 0d
£6 10s 0d
£4 12s 0d
£66 2s 0d/

[*p. 150*] London the 12th of May 1675

Mr John Fittz

Your letters of the 24th 25th 29th & 30th last past I received both poast & shipping & also the gravestones and the iron with the bundle of brass bottoms marked TB, my last to you was of the 16th of Aprill in which I gave you the invoyce of the pack No. JF4 of which I gave you no accompt by shipping I shall in future give you account of the number of pieces which are in each pack but yet its very inconvenient to go by that rule because you see what great difference there is in pieces somtimes one piece mayeth equall to four or six but I shall answer your desire & then you may rule your selfe as reason shall direct, upon my coming hither Mr John Langley adviseth me that he hath drawne £70 upon you for my accompt & given you advice of it, which please to pay & place to my accompt. I have perused the invoyces of charges concerning the grave stones which run high but not to be helped I hope the last wares gave content I wish you so good marketts for them as to write for more. This is the needful at present from

Your loving friend
Tho: Baret

London the 12th May 1675

Mr William Peacock

The urgency of my occasions calling me up hither in such hast as I could not answer yours of the 23d & 30th of Aprill last post whereby I brought them hither & for answer, my last to you was of the 7th of Aprill past. In yours of the 23d of Aprill you advise for some goods which being to patterns I could not get ready before I left Norwich & now can order nothing till my returne which possibly may be two or three weeks I hope you have sent the pack of goods to Mr John Dey of Hamborough, because upon that good accompt you gave of him I have sent him the invoyce of them but you give no accompt whether he be a man *reputed* able in estate. If the pack be not gone pray send it per first. Please to send me 5 or 6 tons of iron 2/3 narrow flatt 1/3 square if you can buy it at 6½ guilders per cento but it must be right Sweeds tuff & good bending iron, if it be not I would by no means have it. This price of 6½ guilders is the highest price others give & therefore if you canot buy it so send none. You imagine I sett goods too high & so would be rich too soon. But in that you are under a mistake, but I will cast up my accompt my selfe & therefore if you [*p. 151*] canot sell goods at such prices as I do sett pray keep them by you for I had rather cease the trade then sell to loss & therefore sell not one piece for me under 35 guilders the worst you have at 34 I meane mixt russels, lett the lowest price for the white callamankoes be 46 guilders, & for the white russells 27 guilders & for the searge de nîmes 32 sterling per ell. This is the lowest price I will sell any at unless there should be some deffect to occasion it, if you shall think it a disparagement to hold up the prices of my goods because others do rashly sell to loss I must beg your pardon & sett still, but the truth is you will cause me to give over trade by demanding too high a comission from me, you demand 4 per cento selling & 2 per cento buying when as the custome of the countrey is but just halfe so much & therefore I now declare it to you that I will allow but 2 per cento for selling & 1 per cento buying. What you write about the Mr Langleys I could answer, for you do somewhat misrepresent them but yet I will allow you 3 per cento for selling provided you bring me no charges to account in Amsterdam unless it be freight of goods from Rotterdam which you pay there. But all other charges in Amsterdam you shall pay & beare them yourselfe whatever they be & for what goods you buy & send me I will allow you 1 per cento & no more, if you will not trade at these termes I will not trade at all, your gain is sure & I know you will be the greatest saver by the trade. I have written to Mr John Dye to advise you how you shall send the goods to him [?]suer from the company. This is the need full at present from

Your loving friend
Tho: Baret

[*p. 152*] London the 12th of May 1675

Mr John Dey

I have this night written to Mr William Peacock Jnr of Amsterdam to forward the pack of No. JD1 to you the invoyce of which I gave you in my last letter to you of the 30th of Aprill last past which I hope you have received, but because the company has been discourteous to me in my goods formerly sent therefore I am fearefull of these which make me intreat you to write to Mr Peacock about them & give him such directions about conveying them to you as that they may come to you in safety for I am loath to fall into theire hands againe, pray use your utmost for theire security & if these turn to accompt whereby I may setle trade I shall be ready to serve you, when you have any proceed to make returnes of lett it be in front or a tryall, the sortment generally is ¼ broad of about 3 inch English ¼ square about inch & 2/4 narrow or if there were a little more narrow it were no great matter, if you send for Yarmouth consigne it for Captain Huntington, if you send to London to Mr John Langley to follow my order, what I now doe is for tryall I wish it may succeed, I see there is no good to be done in shipping for they cannot be made free here. I should be glad to see Mr Sheppard here to whom I shall write this post for I hear not of his arrivall at present. This is the needful from

Your loving friend
Tho: Baret

London the 14th May 1675

Mr Thomas Shephard

Sir, My occasions being now in London where I did hope to have had the happiness to have wayted upon you, being informed that you would be in this place at this time, but upon inquiry finding you not as yet come over & supposing this may reach your hand before you leave Hamborough I was desirous to salute you by this & acquaint you that my last was to you of the 13th of November last since which I have received none from you, I hope that letter came safe to your hand although some former letter did miscarry, in it I did concur with your designe in sending them for Danzig or any other place which I hope you have done I shall be very glad to heare of theire disposall as also of your good health, please to accept the tender of service from

Your friend & servant
Tho: Baret

The Letter-book of Thomas Baret, pp. 152–3, May 1675
Reproduced with permission of the Norfolk Record Office

16: ps of Silke Stuffs No. 3. cost 60 ps ps ps
No. B. 2 2: ps of New Silke Stuffs No. 6. cost 80 ps ps ps
20: ps of Mowhares No. 7. cost 37 ps ps ps
38 ps

Norwich ye 10th of May 1675

Mr Geo. Richards

Sr my last to you was of ye 7th of Aprill Last past
since which I have receivd none from you
this serveth to Convey ye invoyce of one pack No. B. 2
ye pticulers are as above the Bill of Ladinge wilbe
inclosed to you by mr John Langley who will give
you a more pticuler accompt of ye shippinge of it
the No. 3. are better wares then you had before
therefore I hope will give better Content the 2 ps of
No. 6 are of a New invention & doe Cost as much
differinge from ye other as ye price doe mention I send
these only for tryall the Mohares No. 7 are as good
wares as are made of yt Comodity & ye prices are
reasonable the Charges to ye shipp beeinge added
to ye prime cost I hope I have sent you a good
sortment for sale beeinge such as Marchts usually
send to Spaine Butt if I should have mistaken
upon information in future I shall follow your
directions in my last I wrott to you what sort of
Iron is fitt off for my occasions heere to which
I shall only add yt if you Could send me for tryall
a Ton of Iron which is 3 inches Brode it would
suite my occasions well but I can not tell whether
you have any such scantlinge if you shall have
any future occasions for any of yt sorts wch I have
hitherto sent off I shall indeavour to have the
best for you this with service is ye needfull
at present from

Your ffrd & Servant
Tho: Barret

[*p. 153*] No. TB2
16 pieces of silke stuffs No. 3 cost 60s per piece
 2 pieces of new silke stuffs No. 6 cost 80s per piece
20 pieces of mowhares No. 7 cost 37s per piece
38 pieces

Norwich the 18th of May 1675

Mr George Richards

Sir, My last to you was of the 7th of Aprill last past since which I have received none from you. This serveth to convey the invoyce of one pack No. TB2 the particulers are as above the bill of ladinge wilbe inclosed to you by Mr John Langley whoe will give you a more particuler accompt of the shippinge of it, the No. 3 are better wares then you had before & therfore I hope will give better content. The two pieces of No. 6 are of a new invention & doe cost as much differinge from the other as the price doe mention I send these only for tryall. The mohares No. 7 are as good wares as are made of that comodity & the prices are reasonable. The charges to the shipp beeinge added to the prime cost I hope I have sent you a good sortment for collour beeinge such as marchants usually send to Spaine butt if I should have mistaken upon information in future I shall follow your directions, in my last I wrott to you what sort of iron is fittest for my occasions heere to which I shall only add that if you could send me for tryall a ton of iron which is 3 inches brode it would suite my occasions well but I can not tell whether you have any such scantlinge, if you shall have any future occasions for any of the sorts which I have hitherto sent off I shall indeavor to have the best for you. This with service is the needfull at present from

Your friend & servant
Tho: Baret

[*p. 154*] Norwich the 11th of June 1675

Mr Rowland Cockey

Sir, Yours of the 30th of Aprill last past I received & alsoe the iron per Mr Downinge with the inclosed accompts of sales & accompt of goods sent me & moneys paid for me which were drawne from London upon you, ever since the receipt of your letter I have beene absent from this place till a few dayes since & now fower dayes hence I am obliged to goe up to London soe that I can not peruse your accompt that part of it which I have till my retorne from London but I see you use me hardly in severall things which I shall mention to you when I come to give you my full observations upon your accompt, by your letter of the 30th you promised to send me the accompt of charges & accompt of debts standinge out & a particuler of the wares on hand all which are nessessary for the full statinge of an accompt & what can I doe with these which I have for the true statinge an accompt with out the other & therfore as you promised in your last that you would send them per first but have forgot it ever since pray now be mindefull of it & lett me have them. Mr Cockey I have now lay by me mixt russells <with silke mixt wooll russells &> *silke* mixt wooll bratts[82] or No. 32 & alsoe No. 23 butt as I have bound up my selfe by a resolution soe I will hould it not to send one piece more to you till I have my accompt stated & therfore heere they shall lay till I doe understand what you will doe which pray informe me quickly for elce I must looke out a market wheare & by whome I can, truly I did imagine I should have had a better correspondency then I finde, I shall not now troble you with any further complaints knowinge that I have to doe with one that is ingenious enough & may be soe to me if you please I am not sencible that I have given you any other [*p. 155*] cause, our madders proove a greate loss to us those at London are sould but noe money received as yet, when I come at London I shall looke after them & give you a further accompt of them from thence, those I have heere will not sell & therfore I have now sent them to London to gett the price for them there that I can for they are too good for this market I have sould one of them heere but shall not gett any money for it till August & then I am promised it but the dyers are such customers as I like not to deale with them, I have now occasion for a parcell of iron but I am fully suplyed with brode iron & Luke rods & therfore pray send me per first shipps 15 or 20 tonn of iron 2/3 of narrow flatt & 1/3 square I presume upon the new shipps cuminge inn that iron may be resonable you may alsoe send me two tonn of Suedes rods if resonable elce send none. Sir, I have noe resen to envy your new trade with Mr Greenwood Mr Morley Mr Denny & many more whoes imploy may be more than mine whoe am but one poore single man yet I doe not know but it may be equivalent to some if not most of them would you deale with me as in reason you ought I doe not envy your co[u]s[in] Marks trade but wish him prosperity & that he would soe farr consider himselfe as to manage his affaires with a litle more discretion then I thinke he doeth. Sir,

82 Bratos, a wool fabric made in Norwich in the seventeenth century.

I have reseived your kinde present of a Westphalia hamb & the roopad[83] beefe which I doe accept kindely & doe retorne your good wife harty thanks for them & please to accept & tender to your wife from me & mine most harty service whoe am

Your loving friend
Tho: Baret

[*p. 156*] Norwich the 11th of June 1675

Mr John Dye

I received your letter of the 14th of May past, by which I take notice that you received the pack which I sent you & are in some hopes of disposinge them to content which I shalbe glad of because it may introduce some trade. You are sorry that I send noe crowne rashes & truly I am sorry that I doe not know what you meane by them & therfore if you would have any you must send me a pattern of them or give me such description as I may understand for I am sure wee have noe such name for any comodity heere. I am sorry that warrs rise neare you which will make comodityes to raise prise & hinder trade but what can not be helped must be indured, I hope your place will stand free elce it weare an ill time to begin trade in, I have communicated the price of goods to your friends but they make light of it soe suppose its in vaine to troble them any more, when you have any money of mine to make retornes off doe it principally in iron, a sort of iron that is tuff & dus worke well both hott & cold is that which will give good content heere although it should not be of the finest mettall of all wee are much for to have our flatt iron both brode & narrow to be drawne even on the edges & thinn accordinge to the bredth of it if it be thick we call it coarce altho the mettall deserve another name what we call narrow is about 2 English & brode is about 3 but any scantling betwixt those two bredths is acceptable, squar[e] iron wee desire to have from 3/4 of an inch English to 1 inch & but litle above our most vendible the narrow doe exceede that proportion & the brode want it its best for me at this time because I want narrow & have a good quantity of brode by me however send me some brode [*p. 157*] because of tryall & because I am upon experiments pray send me a few Osenb[r]iggs for tryall & alsoe six or eight copper plates weighhinge about 40 or 45 English per plate but they must be taper that is broder at one end

83 Possibly roped.

then the other which is most acceptable with us, I wish you may meete with a quick sale for my goods that soe I may the sooner send you a supply & you may alsoe be the sooner able to make me these retornes which I have some present occasion for if you meete with a conveniency for Yarmouth consign them to Captain *Rich[ard]* Huntington for me if you send to London consigne them to Mr John Langly marchant in Great St Helens whoe is well knowne upon the Exchange. This with service is the needfull at present from

Your loving friend
Tho: Baret

Norwich the 10 of August 1675

Mr George Richards

Sir, I received both your letters of the primo June & 10th July past and am sorry that those silke stufs prove such a drugg I am sorry that I sent them over & doe wich that I had kept them back but now its two late and therfore pray putt them off as well as you can altho I gett nothing by them for its to no purpose to bringe them back againe that willent still add charge & since its like to prove loss the first loss is the best usuly if you can not sell them for mony rather then keepe them much longer truck them away for good Spanish woll if you can doe any good in the barter in future I shall send you only shuch comodityes as you doe advise for. I am glad that the mowhares give content & are like to turne to accompt I wish it may prove soe. Sir, when you have any effects fitt for it pray make me retornes in iron I heare ther is a shipp lading at Bilboa for Yarmouth if you could have freight in her for 4 or 6s per tonn more then <to send> to London [*p. 158*] I would wish you would send in her elce not for Yarmouth is the port whether I must bringe my comodityes butt be sure to agree the freight elce I shall be abused heere most grosley if you send any thing at any time on my accompt for Yarmouth consigne it to Mr Richard Huntington for me. This with tender of service is the nedfull at present from

Your reall friend & servant
Tho: Baret

Norwich the 11 of of August 1675

Mr Rowland Cockey

Sir, I received both your letters of the 2d & 5th of July past with a perticuler of what goods are on hand & alsoe an invoyce of a parcell of iron shippt in Edmond Smith whoe is now arryved. I have examened the invoyce and doe finde the iron is right cast up but you abate but 1 per cento fweight [*sic*] & payment which is a mistacke & indicatinge that you have made another mistacke of 2 guilders to my loss & in the provition of buyinge you charge 1½ which ½ is more then should be, exceptinge these errors the other is pretty right, I have & still doe wich[84] much patience waight for your accompt <current> of charges and debts standinge but I see you neglect it which is not the part of a friend nor can it be called civill dealinge as it doth not prove my descretion to permitt it soe it doth not turne to your reputation to have an accompt of towards five yeares now dependinge, although frenship to me will not move you yet lett the care of your owne reputation oblige you to give me an accompt currunt which hath beene soe long dependinge, if I knew what other arguments to give that would worke with you I should doe it but since I cannot I must only intreate you to send it me per first that soe I may fully know what loss insteade of gane I have gotten by tradinge to Holland which givth me to think of [*p. 159*] butt now I must <think of> make all best of a badd accompt. I have occation for a little iron in one & therfore by next shipps pray send me such another parcell of iron narrow & square as this last was. This is the nedfull at present butt tender of service to you & your lady from

Your loving friend
Tho: Baret

Norwich the 11 of August 1675

Mr William Peacock

Sir, I received yours of the 21st of June past which hath beene some time before me by reason that I was forced to take a 2nd journey to London in hast abought some troublesom busness which caused me to neglet all other busines but now I am retorned home againe having setled the affaire I went about to content. I have received none from you since that of the 21st of

84 i.e. with.

June last past by which I did suppose you would have sent me over sone iron before this time havinge sett you price 6½ guilders per cento for which price I have bought severall tonns which is come safly home since I received your letter & therfore either others can buy cheaper then you or elce you will not afforde it me soe cheape as others will possible yours may be better then thers altho I desire noe better & therfore I am desirous to trye it, pray send me by next shipp as bigg a parcell of iron as my conserns in your hands will admitt of lett it be 1/3 or 1/4 square & the rest narrow flatt which is the chepest sort lett it be tuff & well bending iron not spalt or brittle butt true & right Sweds iron and although the mettle be not of the finest it wille se[r]ve my occations, at my coming home I finde some comodityes abated in price & therfore you may sell mixt russells rather faile at 34 or 33 guilders none under & the white callomancoe at 42 guilders not less & the white russells 26 guilders or 25½ rather then losse sale & the serge de nîmes [*p. 160*] at 32 sterling per ell or at 31 if a customer takes a good parcell of wares these are the lowest prices that I can sett as wares rate now. I am setled againe at home & fitt to receive & ansure your advise & pray lett me here from you per first I shall alow noe more then what I did sett in my letter of the twlfth of May last for the provitation of buyinge & sellinge for in that I doe alow 1 per cento above the comman rate it doeth more then ansurer the small charges brokeridge inclosed, this with sevice is all at present from

Your loving friend
Tho: Baret

Norwich the 27th of August 1675

Mr Nathaniell Mathew

Sir, Both your letters of the 13th & 27th of July last past cam safe to my hands and are now before which I had sooner ansuered had not my occasions called me to London & some other places upon important busines which hindered me, upon my retorne I found the goods sent by Jacob Watson well arrived & safe in my warehowse which I have examined and observed but at the present not fully understandinge your invoyce & accompts beeinge different from other places I can not expose the goods to sale till by your next you doe answer me these followinge questions in refference to the invoyce you sent me in which I have taken the best care and advice & yet cannot soe understand it as to make the same rule agre in one parcell as in an other & therfore I shall run throw your wholle invoyce that soe you may direct me by your next.

The first is – two fatts q[uan]t[ity] 101 – at 12s – £60 12s 0d

I suppose this is 101 bundles at 12s per bundle Flemish money which I doe accompt to be 7s 2¼d per bundle starlinge money for the prime cost.

The 2nd is 829½ ells flaxen lininge at 10 guilders £34 11s 0d
844½ ells hempen lininge at 8 guilders £28 2s 0d
1674

[*p. 161*] This I can not tell what to make of it nor how to cast it up I did always accompt that 100 els Hamburg made 48 els English or thereabout I measurd over the wrapper findinge it marked 35¼ & it held 35½ ells English I measured noe more but desire to know if the contents upon them be English ells that I may warrant them soe without loss to buyer or seller, the flax is at 10 guilders the other 8 guilders I suppose this marke gl meaneth gilders but you doe not express whither it be at 10 guilders the 100 ells English or Hamburg or how much can be bought for 100 guilders, I have tryed it all wayes that I can invent but can not give my selfe satisfaction about it & therfore by next pray cleare it to me, pardon the troble I give you these are the first goods that I have received from your parts & must confes my selfe ignorant at present in your moneys & accompts but one invoyce beeinge explained to me I doubt not but to be able to understand the rest presently.

The last is the accompt for the iron which I can not make out either for weight or price, I did weigh the five brode barrs for plow iron which you did give at 295lb & made heere but 259lb, I weighed the 20 square barrs which you give at 570 & they made 609, the rest of the iron I could not soe sort as to weigh distinctly but all together I found 264lb not more by our pound then you make it but when I reduce it to our great lb by which wee heere sell iron I can make but litle above 40lb or two tunns English q[uan]t[ity] in 127 barrs or ends of all sorts, you should have lett me know how many barrs were of each sorte which would have much directed me in sorting them as well as to try how your weight held out by ours & alsoe by it I might have knowne whether the shipp master had dillivered me every parcell right but upon the wholle I compute your lb falls short of our about 7 per cento in this parcell but this rule doeth not hold true in the sqares or plow iron examined by themselves soe that I am yet at a loss how to fix a rule to myselfe to know exactly the difference betwixt your weight & ours & therfore in the next parcell pray be punctuall that soe I may be certaine in my examination otherwaise noe man can tell whether he tradeth to profitt or loss. The next thinge I can not understand is the price you make this iron to come to in toto £40 15s 0d and after say that is £2 10s 8d one with [*p. 162*] an other I suppose you meane that it cost soe much per shipp and together but I can not at the rate make it come to above £38 13s 0d Flemish money & truly it had not neede come to more for when all charges there & heere are added to the first cost it will come to as much as the goods will yeild for this iron when sould at six months will not yeild above 26 or £27 sterling money which if I doe calculate right can not be proffitt except the exchange in drawinge back your money can assist you with profitt, I doe not soe well understand the coarce of your exchange as I doe some others & therfore pray instruct me what coarce of exchange is even money with starlinge & how much every penny is in the rice or fall of the exchange, I perceive you have cast up the weight of the iron 4lb more than it is I have examined every particuler parcell of the iron & can not make it agree with your invoyce, I know its my ignorance but for my further instruction by next pray send me in a sheete of paper the severall somes cast up upon it that soe I may see your way & be thereby inabled to examin it after you that soe I may be certaine what price to aske for these comodityes which may turne to accompt, be not long in retorninge me your answer because till then I can not expose these goods to sale or be able to give you a judgment whether you are like to gett or lose by them, lett me know what you accompt a pound Flemish to be worth in sterlinge money whether 12s or more or less, as to the comodityes now sent my thoughts are these. The yarne will not proove verry vendible heere because its soe incertaine in the length as many persons refuse it for that some skeyns are considerably longer than others & the bundles are soe intermixt fine & coarce that it doeth disparage it the finest beeinge for one use & the coarce for an other whoe are different traders. The lininge I doubt not but will sell & the iron is verry vendible but whether to profitt or loss I can not resolve till I better understand your invoyce & then nothinge shalbe wantinge on my part to promote ther sale, I have perused your memoriall as to crowne rashes or perpetuanas[85] they are not made heere but fifty miles off where at present I have noe correspondency but could easily setle one there havinge good opportunity for it [*p. 163*] did I but understand it were like to turne to advantage but considring how my serge de neîmes sell with you & not yet understanding how retornes will turne to accompt heere it makes me at present wary of inlargin in trade to your parts but if I finde in future any incouragement of advantage I shalbe ready to inlarge in any thinge as occasion require you advise of but two pieces sould of what you have by you & those serge de nîems at 25 dollars per piece which I accompt to be rather

85 A durable woollen twill fabric made in England.

loss than profitt for I doe not accompt a dollar to be worth above 4s 4d at 5d sterlinge & the worst that are anythinge good will cost £5 sterlinge money first penny which price to give heere & sell them at Hamburg for 25 dollar I doe accompt it loss but because I am not soe well versed in your moneys as positively to determin it to be loss, I have adventured to send you an other pack for tryall the invoyce of which shalbe on the bottom heerof my way of tradinge is not in company but either upon my particuler accompt or elce in commission in which way I shalbe ready to serve you. The goods which I doe accompt most propper for this place & rediest for sale are Ossenbrigs or narrow hartfords[86] & iron which is tuff & will bend well & freely both when its hott & could & drawne thinn & even on the edges without cracks or flaws what iron have these propertyes will serve us although it be not of the finest mettall but beeinge cheape may turne to accompt the sortments wee best esteeme of is 1/2 narrow flat 1/4 brode & 1/4 square. The narrow flat to be about 2 inch English the brode about 3 & the square about 1 inch of the sorts of iron now sent I accompt the narrow Stockholme & the brode thin shafflon & the squares to be the only proper sorts for this place. The shafflon for cart wheeles & the long fine iron may doe well but the price is two deere. The ord[87] Gottenburge is two coarce but a litle mixt with the rest may goe off but it will disparage the rest because its not drawne thinn & even if it were I did not doubt but to sell a parcell of two or 3 tonns of it but for your plow these five barrs are more than I shall sodainly off it beeinge two thick for any use we have heere, please to give me your thoughts of such wares as you have already of mine & alsoe of those now sent whether they will sell or not [*p. 164*] alsoe lett me know whether they come to your hands cheper from London or from Amsterdam & what the difference that soe in future I may send that way which is with least charges if you send any goods hither its above halfe charges saved to send them directly for Yarmouth if an opportunity dus present & you could now have shippinge for Yarmouth for some of the goods before mentioned either upon your owne accompt or mine *vidz* Ossinbridges narrow hartfords or iron its best to accept it for that the winter will come on. I would adventure £200 my selfe in those comoditye for a tryall & doubt not but they may turne to accompt if well bought, you wright to have serge de nîmes well pressed but we press none at all but are at cost & charge to have them gentle should wee press them (as I

86 Possibly herford, a finer type of hammils cloth: *see* J. F., *The merchant's ware-house laid open, or the plain dealing linnen-draper* (1696), p. 23 (thanks to Lizzy Spencer for this reference).

87 Possibly 'ordinary'.

easily could for its but 1s charge) they would were badly as wee call it greasy these now sent are not pressed but if occasion did require I can doe it against next time if required. The wares now sent are good & cheape but I can not describe them to you & to send patterns of new stuffs doe but disparrage the wares when arrived therfore I must refer you to sight, I have beene too tedious noe more but that I am

Your friend to serve you
Tho: Baret

Remember me to Mr Dey if not saild & tell him I am satisfyed with his dillivery of my goods into your hands give me an accompt of the two white serge de russells & the two mixt ones which I sent with the serge de nîmes to him. The pack under mentioned I last night sent to Holland to Mr William Peacock Jnr of Amsterdam to send forward to you I suppose the shipp may sett saile from Yarmouth in two or three dayes if the wind present.

[*p. 165*] Invoyce of one bale of goods sent to Mr William Peacock Jnr of Amsterdam to forward to Mr Nathaniell Mathew of Hamburg marked as in margent *vidz*

/No. NM4[88]1/

8 serge de russells No. 1 cost 60s per peice	£24 0s 0d
4 mild mixt wooll silke tamels[89] No. 6 cost 64 per	£12 16s 0d
2 mascaradoes[90] No. 5 cost 58 per	£5 16s 0d
2 silvercloths No. 4 cost 58 per	£5 16s 0d
10 serge de neîmes No. 2 cost 100	£50 0s 0d
26 pieces	£98 8s 0d

Norwich the 8 of September 1675

Mr Nathaniell Mathew

Sir, Since my last to you of the 27th past I have received yours of the 17th & 20th August the first per post the latter from Yarmouth per covert both

88 Rendered as a merchant's mark, *see frontispiece.*

89 Tammel, a fine weave linen made in England in the seventeenth century.

90 Mascarado, a kind of 'say' cloth, made from worsted in Norwich in 1679 in imitation of silk 'mascades' from Canterbury. It was used for head-dresses. E. Kerridge, *Textile Manufactures in Early Modern England* (Manchester, 1985), pp. 56, 128 (thanks to Michael Pearce for this reference).

which letters are ansured in my long letter before mentioned and therfore at present I shalbe short. The reason of my not answer your letters soner was mentioned in my last which I presume is soe full as will give you satifaction in your desires, I shall alwayes retorne you ansure to your letters soe sone as I be able to give a good accompt of the afaires that it conserne. In your latter letter you doe intimate your want of serg de neîms & that if you had a 100 pieces you could sell them butt with all say they must not cost above £4 10s 0d but I can *get* none that are good under £5 per piece, I will rather not trade then deale in bad comodityes for my inclinations are to deale in such comodityes as shall bringe a reputation to the contry they come from as well as to my selfe & therfore I doe expect to have some considerable profit in what I doe which is now to be gotten if ever because it is a new experriment and you may soe order your affaires as to effect it if yow will because I bleve none others deale in the same comodity & therfore if you will follow my advise now the comodity is [*p. 166*] required rayse your prise & that will incorage me to be free in sendinge more over butt to sell at 25 dollars I doe accompt it loss out of purse & that considerably, two if you can sell them at 30 dollars I thinke it were but an in indefrent price & would incorage me to send more & at loss I shall hardly be incouraged for when I have to the first cost all charges in England & Holland & the charges to your self & some thinge for adventure 30 dollars will not yeld 14s per piece profit & I can gett as much *to sell them* heare & besides the intrest of my mony from the time I send my goods from hence till I received my mony agayne for them will be very considrable & besides a man must provide a bille in the sale of his goods to help to beare an accident if it shall happen otherwayse I may make a rufling in the wourld & beare the name of a marchant and at last leave off with loss, I doe intend to goe on slowly at present till I understand myself better in the proffitt & alsoe in the retornes how they will ansuer expectation, if they prove to content I shalbe ready to inlarge & I would advise you to follow the same rule and not to be too much graspinge at a trade or advisinge others to send over goods for the issue at last wilbe this if they be wise seeing noe considerable profit they will give all other & soe a trade will be lost & therfore I doe thinke it best that wee goe on by degreses & with all imagnable privacy raysinge comodityes to as high a price as can be & then to goe on soe as to feede not glut a marked I have alwayse found this to be saffest way, a small trade this managed hath made many a man ritch a large ruslinge trade hath made many a man a marchant but afterwards spoyled him for a man I have ben ingaged in many sorts of tradinge in the wourld & upon the hole doe find that a midlinge close trade well managed to advantagee which makes noe noyse in the wourld is the best way of tradinge & which I most effect & therfore sell none of the serge de nîmes now cominge under 30 dollars & the serge de russells No. 1 after the same propo[r]tion of advantage, if you can effect this I shall inlarge a trade & therfore with pations try it, except service from

Your loving friend
Tho: Baret

[*p. 167*] Norwich the 4 of September 1675

Mr Isaac Cropp

Sir, Yours of the 13 of August past I received and am glad to heare of your safe arrivall in Holland which I was ignorant of till I was advised of it by yourselfe. I perseive that Norwich stufs are at verry low rate soe that there is noe good to be don in sendinge any over which make me at present decline the trade till prices advance which I thinke are not likely to be upon the sodaine. Sir, had ther ben any <trade> incouragement of advantage I would have sent you some over per first butt since there is none shall defer it & retorne you thanks for the civility of your letter which with service is the nedfull at present from

Your friend & servant
Tho: Baret

Invoyce of two packs of stufs consined to Mr William Peacock Jnr for accompt of my self as followeth

/No. WP4/
12 pieces No. 3 cost 58s per piece
2 ditto No. 5 cost 70s per piece
1 ditto No 7 cost 78s per piece
3 ditto No. 6 cost 60s per piece
2 ditto No. 8 cost 26s per piece
3 ditto No. 2 cost 100s per piece
23 pieces

/No. WP5/
12 pieces No 3 cost 58s per piece
2 ditto No. 5 cost 70s
1 ditto No 7 cost 78s
5 ditto No. 6 cost 60s
2 ditto No. 8 cost 26s
2 ditto No. 2 cost 100s
24 pieces

/No. NM4/

Norwich the 8 of September 1675

Mr William Peacock

Sir, Your letters of the 20th & 30th past & 6th instant I found at at my house upon my retorne out of the contry all which I shall ansure at the end of my letter. The above I sent a way last weeke & suppose they are sayled as last satterday for Rotterdam. The No. 5 are 3/4 brode mixt russells the No. 6 are mild silk estamines[91] the No. 7 are russell with silk the 8 are paramides these are for tryall & the true cost of them is putt to them & therfore doe not sell them [*p. 168*] to loss, all I shall say of the goods is that they are good wares & as cheape as to be gotten, with these two packes is sent another pack marked as in the margent which per first send away to Mr Nathaniell Mathew marchant in Hamburgh these packes I ordere[d] Mr John Fitts to kepp by him till further order & therfore convey the inclosed to him which will cause them to be sent to you by first pray hast away that to Hamburg, in ansure to your letter I see you have sould some goods wherby to putt you out of some sorts which I suppose which I suppose [*sic*] these will supply I perseive that you doe not well undertand me conserninge iron which putt you to more truble in procuringe it than you ned for the sorts that I wright for are the comen sorts whether they be your inch brode or ours is not meteriall or if it be the 9/8 that you mention I can admit it if the iron be good only I would not have them above 9/8 they will be somthinge to bigg & for narrow flat I mean that which is about 2 inchs or 2¼ brode & almost ½ inch thick the thinner this ironn the better & cleaer or over drawne is a great convenancy for my particuler occation this sort of iron is expressed in your price currant by best Sweds iron flat I have had a great <iron> deale of AT & JDG but now I see that is tow high prised for me, I had a parcell that cam over about a month since exclent good marked FG & some <with> a brode starr with a fitt propo[r]tion of square & it cost but 6 & ½ all persons that have had of it doe comnendet for pure stuf & soft iron & therfore you shall not neede to be soe over curious in the scantling if the mettall be good I am advised from an other hand that this is to be bought for 6¼ which I may trie to compare with yours but I persume you can by as cheap as others & I hope you doe not buy at one price & send me at another, I perceve you have sent me a small parcell of iron which I shall seriously peruse when arrived, you wright that you have not enough in chash to pay for it which I wonder at beeinge soe small a parcell butt I hope that if it be not come inn yett its due & soe you

91 Estamene i.e. etamine: a worsted cloth manufactured in a wide range of qualities.

will be reimburse more before the time of payment for this iron cometh about for although you have no long time yet you have a litle butt houh ever you have effects enough of mine in your hands to secure you from loss for I would by noe mene have such a slur putt upon me as was upon [?]T [?] Dade because I have noe body to ingage for me upon the place, pray peruse your invoyce & you shall finde 2 per cento putt doune for provitotion which ought to be butt one per agrement and inded the costom of the contry is no more wher it is for retornes of comodityes in which you provition for sellnge & therfore praye mend your invoyce & send me a new one for if you doe not understand upon what accompt [*p. 169*] wee trade its best to leave off <trading> now whilst the accompt is small. I could dispose of 3 or 4 tonn of iron or more if you had chash of mine to purchase it with all butt since you now have it not pray give me notice when you have & then I shall order a parcell of iron to be sent me for it as bigg as my conserne will permitt till I doe order the contray, when you buy any iron for me lett it ¼ or 1/5 square & the rest narrow flat for I have enough of other sorts by me at present I want no battrey[92] unles it ware about 10 kittles from 24 inches to 22½ & of a suittable depth. This is all at present from

Your loving friend
Tho: Baret

Norwich the 8 of September 1675

Mr John Fittz

Upon my cominge home from London I found yours of the 9th July & primo August, in the first of which was your accompt which I have not as yet had time to looke into it this beinge our busey time to state our English accompts with those home wee deale w[i]thall butt I shall doe it care if be longe, this serveth to advise you that Captain Huntington hath putt on board marked Eldered & consined them to you three packs of stuffs at 73 pieces butt 20 of them are such small thinn ware as hardly deserves the name of of 10 pieces the packes are marked as in the margent which be pleased to send to Mr William Peacock Jnr by first oppertunitye, the iron per Smith is received & I doe understand that Mr Peacock have sent you a small parcell of iron & doe expect that R[owland] C[ockey] will send me another parcell all which send forroward as sone as can be for at present I

92 i.e. metal, or articles of metal, wrought by hammering.

want you havinge promised them. This with tender of servise is the nedfull at present from

Your loving friend
Tho: Baret

No. WP4 No. WP5 No. NM41

[*p. 170*] Norwich the 22nd of September 1675

Mr Rowland Cockey

Sir, My last to you was of the 11 of August last past since which I have received none from you, I hope the letter came safe to your hands & therfore I should not nede to give you the contents of it butt least it should have miscarryed I shall hint some part of it, the first part had relation to sone errors committed in the invoyce of the last iron sent me by Smith, the second part had relation to the accompt currant which I have soe long desired & you often promised but as yet you doe not performe it, the last part was an advice for a parcell of iron to be sent me by next shipps. Your ansure to this letter have beene expe[c]ted a good while for myne is now of six weekes dates. Sir, I request you would ansure my letters which is but the civility of marchants & alsoe performe my commison there in given because I have some occasion for a parcell of iron. My service to your Lady & except the same from

Your loving friend
Tho: Baret

[*p. 171*] Norwich the 22 of September 1675

Mr Robert Pease

Sir, Beeinge in discourse at London with my good friend Mr John Langly I did acquaint him that I was at present destitude of a good correspondent in Amsterdam there havinge latly fallen some crose thinges betwixt my last correspondent and my self which hath occasioned <my desires> our discontinance in trade, upon my makinge knowne my desires to him he did advise me to putt confedence in your self which Sir is the occasion of my troblinge you with this letter to know if you will please to undertake the sellinge of such goods as the manufacture of this place doeth produce as ffff[93] mixt

93 *See* note 35.

russells or serge de boyce & serge de neîmes & other new fashon stufs. Sir, if you please to undertake to dispose them for me & acquaint me of it per letter sent by the common post directed to me heere it will come safe & I will send you a pack for tryall per the very first shipps for Rotterdam which I hope may be with you in a very short time after I received your orders. Sir, please to accept the tenders of service from

Your friend & servant
Tho: Baret

[*p. 172*] Norwich the 22 of September 1675

Mr Thomas Shepard

Sir, I have latly received advise of the well arivell at London & good helth there which giveth me noe small content, I hope I shall have the happenes to see you in London at my cominge up which I suppose will be about the midle of November next & in the meanetime I should be glad if you would please to favor me with a letter relatinge to those goods which were sent to you from Holland uppon my accompt whether they be disposed off or still on hand in Hamborough of Danzigg or what is become of that unhappy parcell of which I would be glad to make somthinge or if they will not sell at all I must bringe them back againe, I have requested my friend Mr Langly the bearer here off to speake with you about them whoe may give me information if your occasion will not permitt, in the meanetime please to accept the tender of service from him that is

Your friend & servant
Tho: Baret

Sir, If I may be serviceable to you in this place please frely to command me

[*p. 173*] Norwich the 6th of October 1675

Mr Nathaniell Mathew

Sir, Yours of the 17th of September past I receive & have perused the contents of it, as to the yarnes pray send noe more upon any accompt whatsoever for heere is more than this place will carry off in 12 months I have indevord its sale as my owne but noe person will bid money for it, as to our stuff weavers they use none of it formerly they did use a litle but by experience finde our oune worsted yarne doeth better & soe they will buy none, I have indevord its sale to our lininge weavers but those that have allready seene it refuse it for the uncertainety of its length & goodness beeinge soe intermixt fine & coarce together that they doe prize our owne spininge farr before it, I have yet some other wayse to trye in which my indeavors shall not be wantinge & truly I can give you noe better accompt of your hamells[94] lininge since the receipt of your letter I have had two or three of the greatest dealers in that comodity in this place whoe would have taken the wholle parcell either of them had the goods beene to content but they all tould me they were the thinnest & narrowest they ever saw by thinness they meane the strikinge or woofe was not driven closse enough & for bredth these for the most part are not half ell brode which should be about 1/16 of an English yard above half ell, in short they found fault with every thinge but the color which they approved off & with all concluded that you had them upon barter or were not accustomed to buy this comodity but with all confessed they had seene none that were right good for these two yeares last past but better then these which they [*p. 174*] buy in London for 6½ & 5½ & would not offer me that price but your price beeing 7¾ & 6¾ I would not offer them lower & soe wee parted, they are gon for London & possibly when they retorne we may have some further discorce about them the peice this inclosed patterne cam off of they did seeme to approve of had the parcell beene as good & good bredths I beleeve I might have brought them neere your price. Sir, this place will only vend the best of all low prised cloths & unless the Ossenbrigs & hartfords which you intend to send be verry excellent good & good bredths send none for they will not sell, you wright that Ossenbrigs cost £3 3s 9d per cento ells English & our marchants tell me they pay but 8d to 9d per ell in London at 9d it cometh but to 75s & the charges added to you first cost will come about that price & they tell me they must be verry good that will give 9d per ell in London & therfore unless you can send verry good to be afforded at that price with profitt send none upon my accompt & the same I meane conserninge the hartfords, as for iron I may trye an other parcell of that if it be to be bought soe much chepaer than the last but the prices which you mention to sell for at London I doe wonder at because I can buy cheper at the iron mongers in London & have donn many a tonn but of this I shall wright more heerafter not elce at present but that I am

Yours to serve you
Tho: Baret

94 Hammils, a cloth used for shirts and sheets: *see* J. F., *The merchant's ware-house laid open, or the plain dealing linnen-draper* (1696), p. 23 (thanks to Lizzy Spencer for this reference).

Sir, If you send me noe linings upon my accompt then by first send me £150 sterling in iron sorted as formerly advised send to Yarmouth if you can if not send it to London consigned to Mr John Langly marchant in Great St Hellens [*p. 175*] & give timely advise if linings be sent me befor this arrive them send nothinge more till further order, whalebone[95] the best may sell heere but cutt whalebone is looked upon as a cheate heere & I beleive will prove a verry drugg & in barter they will never give you the best & this place is verry curious in theire comodityes, I have putt the yarne & hamells lininge to your accompt & the iron to my owne accordinge to your last invoyce. The iron now advised for is upon my oune accompt what elce you please to send of that or any other comodityes I shall place to your accompt. I am

Yours to serve you
Tho: Baret

Norwich the 13th of October 1675

Mr Nathaniell Mathew

Sir, Both your letters of the 24th & 28th September with the invoyce of the goods shipt in Teate I received by the same hand which presented me a bill of exchange payable to Mr William Hibbard at 2 usance for £200 starling to which I have given acceptance & shall provide for its payment, with the invoyce I did expect a bill of ladinge as is usuall in such cases & I doe much wonder you omitted it but I suppose next poast will bringe it for its not usuall to accept bills drawne for goods without a bill of ladinge as well as an invoyce to be first received but beeinge tender of your bill I did not now stand upon it I take notice of what you wright about the money drawne more then the goods now sent & the iron formerly received doth amount to which I shall give you creditt for beeinge allready in disburce for your accompt of hamells lining [*p. 176*] & yarne the latter of which I can finde noe body will medle with heere as yet & for the linings all complaine of the bredth & thinnes & profes they can buy as good at London for 6½ & 5½ but I shall not abate of your prices with out order, as for drawinge money in future pray doe not draw above £100 in one weeke & doe not over draw for as soone as I have any cash in hand on your accompt I shall advise you as alsoe of what sales I doe make & the same I desire from you,

95 Whalebone was used for stiffening stays and corsets.

your letters have soe well instructed me in your accompts that now they are as easy to me as our owne which inables me to acquaint you that the flaxen hamells are cast up 2d too much & the hempen 4d too litle & the iron is 4lb too much in weight & £2 0s 10d Flemish too much in price for if it were 4278 (which is but 4274) at £2 10s 8d per shiffpou[n]d[96] it cometh to but £38 14s 2d which error you must rectify as to the iron or elce I must give you credit in your accompt for the vallue, which way you like best of advise me per next & alsoe give me an accompt of particulers how the charges of the iron doe arise to £3 4s 0d in which I feare & am somewhat assured you doe over charge me, your invoyce of Ossenbrigs & hartfords is right cast up at price but the charges are extreame high & I perceive you putt me downe all towne dutyes which you as fre of the Company pay not, but Sir unles you bringe me off as cheape as if they were your owne you will give me small incouragement to continue for the charges will eate out the profitt & to this you putt provition for the disbursinges the charges for £252 to 2 per cento can not make £5 5s 0d. This is bitinge & not customary in other parts & therfore I doe expect it to be altered otherwaise I shalbe correspondent to your profitt & laffed at for my [*p. 177*] ignorance, you may sell my serge de neîmes at 27½ to 28 dollars per piece the other sutable new fashon stuffs leave a fagg end for loss & therfore unless it be provided for in the sale of the first wee doe but cheate ourselves, I suppose none have of these but your selfe & therfore you may rule price at your pleasure but if others have any I am sure they can not sell soe good soe cheape for those I send you I could have sold in London for 6s per piece & have sold worse for more, I am not convinced that 8s per piece will cleare all charges I am sure it will not throw Holland what it may by London I can not tell but may trye when occasion serve for those serge de neîmes you had first which collour did not please you may sell at 25 dollars or 24 dollars but these that come new which are good collour hold them up & make them pay for the others or put them off with them, your frind that advised you iron flatt will sell for £14 per tonn at five months payment doe not advise you amiss for I can sell soe heere & somethinge better but its all sorts brode narrow & square in proportion, but for square at £15 5s 0d I dare say he is mistaken for I can sell cheper by 20s per tonn but take notice that £14 per tonn shall not cleare you £13 6s 0d if the freight from Hamburge be noe more than its from Holland but I suppose its more, I have advised Captain Huntington of the contents

96 Shippound, schippound; a unit of weight used in the Baltic trade, varying from 300–400lb.

of what is in Teate whoe is not yet arrived as per advice of the 9th instant. This with service is the needfull at present from

Your friend & servant
Tho: Baret

[*p. 178*] Norwich the 13th of October 1675

Mr William Peacock

Sir, Yours of the primo October I received & perused it which gives me good satisfaction that I shall receive just dealings from you which I noe way question. I have now perused that iron you sent me which is not soe thinn & smooth drawne as Mr R[owland] C[ockey] use to send me this full of flaws or cracks which make it not soe commendable for sale as the other is, I hope the mettall is good which I shall have occasion to trye when I can meete with a custom[e]r for it butt the black bottums you sent me were the worst that I ever saw for not one of them but hath either hole or crack throw the midle of it that nobody will buy them he that sold you them dealt verry ill by you one might say knaveishly, as soone as you have where with to send me a parcell of iron pray send it for I could make use of it, as to R[owland] C[ockey] I wish he did deale otherwaise with his friends than he doth for at the last the discredit will light upon himselfe altho at present the loss light upon others I am sure, I may say soe for my owne part I have ordered some light grey serge de boyce & serge de neîmes to be made when they come of shall send them but I doe not like soe light collour for they will fade with verry layinge yet I shall trye half a dozen or six pieces. This with <tender> service is all at present from

Your friend to command
Tho: Baret

Give me accompt of Mr Mathew as soone as you can.

[*p. 179*] Norwich the 13th October 1675

Mr Robert Pease

This was a letter of noe other busines then to inform him how I began trade with R[owland] C[ockey] & to invite him to undertake my commission & give order for to send him some goods on tryall.

Norwich the 27th of October 1675[97]

Mr Rowland Cockey

Sir, My last to you was of the 22d of September past which was mostly a coppy of a letter of the 11th of August past. The last letter that I received from you was of the 5th of July past. Sir, I have deserved noe such slights as these from you I can tell how to shew respects as to know how to expect kindness at least civility from a friend as hitherto I have accompted you but I see I did mistake myselfe & therfore hence forward shall demeane my selfe sutable to such mistakes, I am now takinge horse for London as soone as I come there I shall draw upon you £200 sterling at single usance & £200 starlinge at dobl usance by myselfe or Mr John Langly when its don I shall give you due letters of advice, I doubt not but you will honor my bills with acceptance because you have a greter conserne of myne in your hands both in money and in goods. Sir, your unhansome[98]

[*p. 180*] London the 9th of November 1675

Mr Nathaniell Mathew

Sir, Your letters of the 5th, 16, & 22d of October past I received with the invoyce of the goods shippt in Teate upon your private accompt. Teate is at last arrived safe at Yarmouth, where my order lay for the dispatch of the said goods to Norwich, where all due care will be taken of them in my absence, which will not be above 14 days & then upon perusall of them I shall be more large in my writing & advice concerning them, but at present cannot being absent from my books, your bill of exchange shall be duely & punctually paid. Till further order send no more goods: for I find here as well as at Norwich bad marketts & very low prices. Ossenbriggs I heare sell at 9d hartfords 7d & less hamells 5¼ & 6, which are no incouraging prices, I feare Norwich is no markett for your steele, for wee use only fagotts & them the very best, this with service is the needfull at present from

Your loving friend
Tho: Baret

97 Letter crossed through.
98 Letter stops abruptly here.

London the 9th November 1675 £200 sterling at 36s 4d Flem[ish]

Sir, At doble usance pay my first per exchange unto Mr Robert Pease or order two hundred pounds starling at thirty six shillings four pence per pound the value of Mr John South & place it to my accompt as per advice

Tho: Baret

To Mr Rowland Cockey
Merchant
In Amsterdam

[*p. 181*] London the 9th of November 1675

Mr Robert Pease

Sir, Yours of the 8th currant I received here, have perused the contents of it & shall answer it at my returne to Norwich, which will be about 14 days hence. Sir, I am much troubled with & about Mr Rowland Cockey for I can neither gett him to give mee an accompt nor to answer my letters & therefore as my last refuge at present I must try if he will accept or refuse bills accordingly I have as above sent you a bill upon him for £200 sterling at doble usance which pray favor mee to gett accepted, & if he should refuse pray lett it be protested & returned with all the formalities of a protest for I am now resolved to try what honesty is left in the man. But I beg of you to carry it so privately, that he may not in the least suspect but that it is a true bill given to Mr John South for money paid heere pray carry it as such & give mee your answer before I leave this place, direct your letters as formerly the poastmaster here takes care of them, this with service is the needfull at present from

Your friend & servant
Tho: Baret

London the 9th of November 1675

Mr Rowland Cockey

Sir, My last to you was the 22nd of September past since which none from you, this for advice that I have this day by poast drawne upon you a bill of exchange for £200 sterling at 36s 4d per cento Flem[ish] payable at doble usance to Mr Robert Pease or order for the value of Mr John South, which please to honor with acceptance & due payment. Sir, my urgent occasions did oblige me to draw this bill knowing you have cash for my accompt. My reputation is much engaged in your acceptance of this bill & therefore I doe againe most seriously recomend it to your care which will much oblige

Your loving friend
Tho: Baret

[*p. 182*] London the 19th of November 1675

Mr Nathaniell Mathew

Sir, Yours of the 28th of October past came yesterday to my hand in this place where I am obliged to remaine about 14 days to attend some law matters of importance to me & question not but to make my returne in three weeks at longest, my last to you was of the 9th instant to advise you that Teate was arrived, but had a very dangerous voyage, yesterday I received advice that the goods were safe come into my warehouse, & upon my returne shall do my best to putt your goods to sale & to gett the best price for them the markett will afford, as to your yarnes I cannot as yett find any that will meddle with it, but I shall not slack my endeavours, I wish you had sett a moderate price at first upon your linnings & then they might have been sold before this time but now most of our dealers in those commodities have supplied themselves here & truly yours are not so good of the sorts as I wish they were, whereby I doe feare I shall not find a market for them till spring, your steele I am informed is no proper commodity for that place & for your whale bone I can give no accompt as yett but shall make all the hast I can to returne & then shall lett you know what I can effect in it. Truly I am troubled that you have been so adventurous to send so many improper goods, which I feare must be sold at considerable time when ever I can come to a market for them for ours is but a dull place to raise ready money in, because the linnen drapers heer court them with good time & pennyworths. As soon as any are sold I shall acquaint you with it the price, person, & time, but I must desire you to draw no money upon me for goods unsold. As soon as there is any cause for drawing I will acquaint you, butt till then I can accept no bills if you should draw. My advice from Norwich is that the Ossenbriggs are pretty good wares, but the hartfords are meane, which I am troubled at, because all goods with us which are not the best of theire sorts, are very druggs & more loss by them than in London where is a generall markett for all sorts [*p. 183*] but for good wares Norwich will afford a markett. As soon as I do returne I designe to advise for some more cloth, but as yet shall not determine any thing. I wonder that you have not advised mee of the arrivall of those goods from Mr Peacock of Amsterdam which I am somewhat solicitous about, & therefore per next pray give me an accompt of them, & let me know whether you have sold any goods for mee or not, for as yett you have advized me only of the sale of two pieces which giveth mee so small encouragement that I almost resolve to send no more into your parts, but to correspond with you to buy goods for me & draw the money for them. I have at present occasion in Amsterdam for some of those goods which lay dead by you & therefore by the very first ship send to Mr Robert Pease marchant in Amsterdam for my accompt the 10 pieces of searge de russells No. 1 & also the two pieces of white serge de russells No. 3 & 4 or six pieces of the last parcell of serge de nîmes No. 2 & for the rest of the wares put them of as soone & as well as you can & I shall order you what to returne them in as soon as the money is in cash I have per this poast advized Mr Pease of this order, which pray comply with all per very first opportunity least the first should fall in so as to hinder all passage. Your bill is now neer due which shall be punctually paid. This with service is the needfull from

Your assured friend
Tho: Baret

[*p. 184*] London the 19th of November 1675

Mr William Peacock

Sir, I have now before me here both your letters of the 8th of October past & the 8th instant, which I could not well answer till now. The contents of both are much the same, complaining that others buy, at least, sell cheaper than than those wares you have of mine can be afforded which you do impute to my over rating them & seem to be discontented that others undersell you, whereby you are only warehouse keeper to my wares. Sir, I have no reason but to think that you do report the actions of those persons aright, but I will assure you its to my admiration they should do so for I dare be any mans bondman that can buy wares so good as those I send you to make his money of them againe at the prices you mention, but if men will be mad I can not help them but I am loth to be mad with them, I am willing to sell if I could but save my selfe but to sell to loss will oblige me to lay all downe & give it over, I had rather buy for you than have <you> sell for mee whilst those prices rule & truly you have given me such discouragement by your last letters that I will not make one piece more to sell at these rates you mention when they will yield more I may then make againe, the truth is I have some wares upon my hands & therefore I shall be content to putt them off upon which accompt you may sell serge de nîmes at 30 sterling per ell & the russell at 31 or 32 guilders if you can gett it. Sir, I do only recommend my business thus to you, if you can so sell as I may live I will continue trade, but if I can not I will quite leave off the Holland trade: for what I have now by mee pray sell them as high as you can, & if I can possible take incouragement I will continew, bee not over covetous to follow other mens steps in underselling your new goods to theire old ones to get the [?]repute of a great trade. Consider is it not better to sell a few well than at a soddaine to sell many to the loss of your [*p. 185*] correspondent & trade also. I know I can sell as low as any considerate person can, but if any man be so mad as to sell to loss although I may do so for the present to cleer my hands of goods I shall not continue it. I know that R[owland] C[ockey] has no silk russells that are good & I profess mine cost me about £4 per piece first [*illegible*] but I assure you I will never make another piece againe. Sir in the whole I referre my selfe to you, as I like the prices you sell at, so I shall ac[comp]t you know wares use to rise when Exchange rise. This with tender of service is the needfull at present from

Your loving friend
Tho: Baret

<Norwich> London the 3rd of December 1675

Mr Rowland Cockey

By my letter of the 9th of November past I did recommend to you the honouring of a bill of exchange, which I then drew upon you, with acceptance & not hearing from you did conclude you had done it accordingly yet wondred you had given me no advice of it, but about 10 dayes since my mistake was made manifest to mee: for being upon the Exchange I had deliver[e]d to peruse the bill of exchange returned with protest for non acceptance for reasons you would advize the drawer & for that time till now I have waited for your letter of reasons, but none is come nor have I received one line from you since yours dated the 5th of July past, with the protest showne mee was a demand made of the money charge & loss which I could no waise avoid or refuse & therefore to patch up my broken creditt I paid them, & here inclosed I send you the receit for my loss. The staine of my creditt (I returne you thanks for it) was your intent. But

Mr Cockey know it, although I returne you no hectoring letter for it, yet I resent it deeply & bless God its not in your power to break it, although you have done more toward it than all men ever before. My ready complyance with its satisfaction have gained mee so much creditt from the same person as that he hath trusted me againe & delivered mee £200 for which I have given him a bill of exchange upon you. The copy of which I have sent you on the back hereof [*p. 186*] & do seriously recommend its acceptance to you, as you honor that little creditt I have left upon the Exchange at London. With this marchants bill I have also drawne a bill of exchange for same some payable at same time to same person with reason why I draw it, either of these being possitively accepted the other to be void, but if not accepted I have orderd the last to be protested, the contents of which is true. Sir, although you respect not my creditt yett I doe yours no person being knowing in what I now doe but my selfe & the persons through whose hands it cometh to be presented to you which is the least I could doe in returne of your unhansome act to me if you make it more publick its your owne fault, for I desire to honor you & show my selfe

Your reall friend
Tho: Baret

London the 3rd December 1675 £200 sterling at 36s 11d Fle[mish]

Sir, At doble ussance pay my first per exchange unto Mr Robert Pease or order two hundred pounds starling at thirty six shillings eleven pence per pound the value of Mr John South & place it to my accompt as per advice

Tho: Baret

To Mr Rowland Cockey
Merchant
In Amsterdam

Received this 22nd of November 1675 of Mr Thomas Baret for a bill of exchange & all charges upon it which cam back by protest from Mr Rowland Cockey of Amsterdam
£200 14s 6d

per John South

[*p. 187*] London the 3d of December 1675 £200 at 36s 11d Flem[i]sh

[Rowland Cockey]

Sir, By the poast of the 9th of November past I drew a bill of exchange upon you for £200 sterling at doble usance to Mr Robert Pease for value of Mr John South, which bill for non acceptance you suffered to come back with protest for reasons you would advize the drawer, which reasons I have now expected about 10 days since the protest was presented me but have none or any letter from you since yours of the 5th July last past, notwithstanding I have written severall to you contening orders for goods, before my last to advize of the bill then drawne. It is now ever since primo June Anno 1672 since I received an accompt from you, to which accompt I then or presently after acquainted you of the errors passed in it. By my letter of the 9th July <u>1673</u> I did solicite you to send mee my accompt currant & by many letters since to you I have repeated the same which you have answered with a promise it should come by next poast & with excuse you were ashamed it was delayed so long. But as yett I am without it notwithstanding its an accompt of about 30,000 guilders if not more with the ballance of the accompt before mentioned. By severall letters all along in our correspondency I have requested you to remitt my money to mee as it came to your hand for you sold my goods (two kinds at least) at 2 per cento rebate & yet would remitt me very little although it were in cash, but forced mee to draw upon you to my great loss. In November <u>1674</u> & severall monthes foregoing I wrote to you angerly & pressing for my accompt & declared I would send no more goods to you till I received my accompt, but had severall prepared for you when that came, about May or June last you wrote mee word that you had about 90 & odd pieces of goods upon hand & that there might be about 6,000 guilders betwixt us towards a parcell of iron about 12 tun then sent & the charges upon the accompt, but wold send me no accompt currant & since the 5th of July you have been totally silent [*p. 188*] I use the words about such a time, because I am absent from home & have not your letters before mee, elce should give you day & date. & therefore upon these reasons: Sir at doble usance pay to Mr Robert Pease or order two hundred pounds sterling at thirty six shillings, eleven pence per pound the value of Mr John South & place it to my accompt as per advice

Tho: Baret

To Mr Rowland Cockey
Merchant
In Amsterdam

This bill was sent to Mr Robert Pease, but Mr Cockey had no copy sent to him of it

London the 3rd day of December 1675

Mr Robert Pease

Sir, Yours of the 26 of November past I received, but that letter only of all my letters missed mee here & went downe to Norwich which maketh my answer to it beare the longer date as soon as I received it I did acquaint Mr Langley what you writt about woolls from whom you will here further. I received R[owland] C[ockey's] protested bill, which truly is like him: for I have feared his honesty a long while, although in the protest he sayth its for reasons to be given the drawer, yet notwithstanding he hath not writt one word to me about it, nor hath any friend spoken to mee in his behalfe, I am angry at it but must show no more than will doe me good. I am truly thankfull to you for your kindness, & I will assure you no person but Mr Langley (who is as much against him as my self although not so concerned) knowes any thing of this transaction. I love to act my business privately & I know its your desire to doe the same, & for his credit [*p. 189*] which I respect more then he doth I am glad all things are acted with privateness. But Sir I must begg another favor of you in Mr Souths name to present him with the inclosed bills of exchange for acceptance I have given him a coppy of one with an accompt what order is given upon them please to present to him the common bill which I presume he will not refuse againe but if he doeth then please to present him with the other with reasons why I drew the £200 if he doeth alsoe refuse that then please to lett the last bill with reasons be protested if he will have noe respect to his creddit I can not helpe it Sir I have some serge de neîmes & serge de boyce laying at Hamburge in the hands of Mr Nathaniell Mathews which by reason of the company I thinke lay not verry safe and therfore I have ordered the said Mr Mathew to send a pack of them to you for my accompt which please to looke after & when received advise me of it Monday next I am for Norwich & shall then send forward some goods to you. This is the needfull at present from

Your friend & servant
Tho: Baret

[*p. 190*] Norwich the 22nd of December 1675

Mr Rowland Cockey

By last poast I received the protest of my last bill for non acceptance which putts me to a verry greate troble & confusion not beeinge able to understand these actions or what you designe or intend to doe with me, you have now twice protested my bills spoyled my creddditt will give me noe accompt of my estate in your hands nor wright a letter to me to intimate your reasons why you doe thuss or what you doe intend to doe with me. I leave it to the whholle world to judge if these be faire actions I must confess my selfe much perplexed at these things but I see to wright to you availeth me litle & therfore I might be silent but that the concerne is soe greate & neere to me that I must be wrightinge to you for my accompt & for the reason of your actinge thus with me which I desire you would intimate to me by an answer to this letter by first poast. I know my goods in your hand are but a troble to you & therfore I have requested Mr William Peacock Jnr to call to you for them accordinge to the accompt of wares restinge which you sent me the 2nd of July last past & were in all 81 pieces all which or what of them are now unsold pray dilliver to Mr William Peacock Jnr upon his demand of them & his receipt for them shalbe your sufficient discharge, I have given him a note of them & their nomber & therfore pray faile not to dilliver them to him upon demand which will oblige

Your loving friend
Tho: Baret

[*p. 191*] Norwich the 22d of December 1675

Mr William Peacocke

Sir, I have both your letters of the 26th past & 10th instant before me which I have perused & shall now answer them although Mr John & Peter Wiggett be noe nessessitous men yet it doth not follow but their factor may sell their goods at such low prices as they may loose by their wares as I am confident they doe at the prices you mention if the wares be as good as mine butt to pass by that discorce in your letter you assure me that my giveinge you generall libberty to sell shall not be to my loss & therfore I shall leave you at libberty to gett the best price for my goods which the market will afford if it be a liveinge price I will continue it if not I must give it over as I heare one or both of the Cockeys have or doe intend. Sir, I now have a litle other imployment for you to doe for me, inclosed I send you the last letter I have had from Mr Rowland Cockey for now he will neither send me my accompt nor accept any bills I draw upon him nor wright any letters to me soe that I am putt to greate streights to know what to doe with him to bringe him to accompt with me & therfore I desire you by next poast to send me word what coarce I must take with him in Holland to force him to give me my accompt, at the bottum of the inclosed letter of his (which pray keepe safely by you & retorne it to me againe) is what wares are restinge of mine in his hands, pray doe you goe to him as soone as you have this letter & dilliver my inclosd letter to him which reade & seale up before dillivery & then demand my goods of him & take them home to your howse presently pray doe not delay it in the least but lett me know by next poast that its effected [*p. 192*] if he should refuse to dilliver them then pray forthwith take such speedy coarce with him for the recovery of the goods as your law will permitt I have some reasons which afterwarde I shall discover to you for my beeinge soe ernest with you not to delay the effectinge this thinge. Because this letter doeth not mention the nomber of all the goods therfore I have on the margent heereof sett downe the nomber of all I am but now come home from London soe could doe nothinge about beans & pease nor am I versed in that way, I am

Your friend & servant
Tho: Baret

I doe suppose now you have money come in enough to send me a parcell of iron & therfore desire you would doe it per first & lett it be all narrow flatt because that is cheapest my wares in Mr Cockeys hands are not sealed as yours are & therfore its the nomber that must gide you to know they are mine

/12 No. 15 & 35
10 No. 4
4 No. 29
5 No. 30
11 No. 13
1 brode No. 13
6 No. 16
3 No. 34
1 No. 22
2 No. 21
6 No. 24
6 No. 28
2 No. 32
2 No. 25
11 No. 14
3 No. 10
1 No. 36
1 No. 28
87 pieces/

[*p. 193*] Norwich the 31st of December 1675

Mr Nathaniell Mathew

I have now before me yours of the 16, 23rd, 29th of November & 14th currant which I found heere at my cuminge home, all but the last I did defer there answeringe supposinge by this time you might have beene in London sutable to former advice but not knowinge but that you might have altered your thoughts I shall ansuer them all together & begin with the last of them which concernes the bill of exchange, your friend that wrott you word it was not paid at day wrights you falce for I had the bill dillivered up to me upon the 27th of November beeinge Satterday & it was not due till the day followinge beeinge Sunday the bill beeinge presented to me heere I had accepted it to be paid heere & at my goeinge to London had provided the money for it & left it ready with orders to pay the bill, the goldsmith in whose hands it was seeinge me in London spake to my servant to know where I would pay the bill, I sent him word that I had made provition for it at Norwich where the money lay ready butt to ease him of troble if he would alow me the customary time of exchange from Norwich to London which is never less than 14 days I would pay it him at London which he did willingly accept, upon which accompt I gave him two bills at 14 days each £100 upon Mr Hinde & Kerwood & because the goldsmith whoe had the bill then wanted money upon the Monday followinge beeinge the second of the bill beeinge due I payd him £100 & toke out one of the bills I gave on Hinde, this is the verry truth of the thinge & I wish you friend whoe ever he bee doeth satisfy his credit noe worse than I did your bill & had he given the carrage of the business aright I doubt not but it would have prevented your reflections on me in the fore part of your letter [*p. 194*] which I could not soe easily have passed over but that I conclude you under a misinformation, as to the rest of your letters I shall answer them in generall for the linings advised of sent to London I shall not medle with you or any other thinge unless they come to Yarmouth for the charges come too high to profitt by them & next I will trye how these succeede that I have allready the Ossenburg you sent are some of them especially six Ravenburgs[99] verry good wares but some of them verry meane & there is soe many underbands amongst them as spoyles the parcell in the next I will have noe underbands, the hartfords seeme better conditioned but I see its noe proper comodity for this place & will lay long by me for they are two thin a cloath for our sale, as to your yarne & hamells lininge I am discouraged

99 Ravensburg: from a linen-producing town in Germany (thanks to Sally Tuckett for this definition).

at them as to the first I have gotten one man to trye a bundle of it & he tells me he feare its not stronge enough beeinge made into sum implements for weavinge he saith it workes with him pretty well & if his masters finde noe fault he will buy more if this dus take I shall not feare its sale but in a long time by small quantitys if this faile I know not what to doe with it I sould this bundle at 10s as to the linings I have offered them at 6½ & 5½ & can not sell them they say they are bad bredths & thinn not driven up closse but I hope when springe comes on they may off its good wares or none must off heere to save ones selfe by & for barter heers noe good to be don unless you would take old fashon stuffs such as are out of date in England & then I could putt them & the threed off butt in all barters I conclude one must be cheated, for the steele I can as yet get noebody to fasten of it they never saw such before & are afraide of it but I this day gott a smith to trye some of it which putts me in hopes I may gett it off [*p. 195*] for he doeth give it commendations but this is a large parcell for this place & will take time but I am informed its sould at London for 28s to 32s per cento at 120s to the cento & you sett it to me at 40s, as to the whalebone I have had noe great experiment of it yet verrily thinke its noe such drugg as I feared but am informed that 16d per lb is the highest price any will yeild diverse have tould me they will come & see it but have not as yet, the truth is trade is verry deade with us heere this winter & money extreame scarce pray by next lett me know the verry lowest price I shall sell your comodities at I am noe underseller & I doe assure you whatever I can gett shalbe every penny to your accompt & he is a verry knave should doe otherwaise, as to serges & perpetuanas I must confess I have noe good correspondcy which makes me unwillinge to adventure in them havinge as yet had noe verry good success either for you or my selfe. Since the wrightinge above I have beene abrode & discoursed sev[er]all about your whalebone whoe have promised to come see it but they protest to me they can buy it of marchants heere in towne whoe bringe finns from Holland & cutt it heere at 10s or 11s the dozen which is 12s English this price doeth amaze me whilst you sett it at 18d per lb for me to sell at & therfore sett me your lowest price to sell or keepe at that soe I may not aske such prices as may fright persons from dealinge with me in other comodityes, as to my goods with you I perceive you have sould 16 sixteene serge de nîmes the price of which together is good but its in vaine for me to send more because you can supply the market bought at £4 10s 0d per piece & I can not supply under [*p. 196*] £5 per piece & therfore I may justly expect to have mine lay by when you can soe much undersell me & true I am loth to give six months time for I must bringe it back against per exchange or comodities in the latter of which is noe profit more than the other you say he that will rate his goods at pleasure at home & sett a market abrode must sell his goods himselfe, the first I have not done the latter I ever will doe which not giveing you content will make me drive but a small trade for if I can not doe better by runinge hazards then at home I will take the quietest coarce & keepe my estate in Engeland but I am too tedious, accept the tender of service from

Your lovinge friend
Tho: Baret

[*p. 197*] Invoyce of one pack of goods sent to Mr Robert Pease of Amsterdam for accompt of Thomas Baret consigned to Mr Fr Greenwood of Rotterdam for conveyance as follows.

20 serge de boyce No. 1 cost 55s	£55 0s 0d
2 silke ditto No. 2 cost 74s	£7 8s 0d
6 silke tamilens[100] No. 3 cost 60s	£18 0s 0d
2 serge de neîmes No. 4 cost 98	£9 16s 0d
6 with serge de boyce No. 5 cost 42	£12 12s 0d
2 paramides No. 6 cost 27s	£2 14s 0d
38 pieces	£105 10s 0d

/No. RP1/

Norwich the 31st December 1675

Mr Robert Pease

Sir, Yours of the 17th currant received & perused, its needles to retorne Mr Rowland Cockes bill or protest I see his humor & condition & must deale with him some other way which he will not well approve of, I retorne you thanks for your paines & must begg your assistance in future when occasion serve pray acquaint me what you thinke of him for I feare his condition is bad or elce he would not have acted severall things which he lately have don. The above is an invoyce of a pack of goods sent for tryall they are all good of their sorts I wish they may finde markets to continue as well as begin a trade for I have more redy upon your order, whoe am

Yours to serve you
Tho: Baret

100 Possible variation of 'tamel'; possibly a variant of 'tamin' or 'taminy', a lightweight glazed woollen fabric (thanks to Sally Tuckett for these suggestions).

[*p. 198*] Norwich the 12th of January 1675[/6]

Mr Robert Pease

Sir, My last to you was of the 31st past since which none from you, this serveth only to acquaint you that the pack mentioned in my last is putt on board of Marke Eldridge whom I wish safe with you, Mr Rowland Cockeys dealinge with me doe verry much disturbe me & the more becase I am ignorant how to fre my selfe from them beeinge never before ingaged in an affaire of this nature & therfore I doe crave your advice & directions how I should gett my wares out of his hands which remaine unsould & alsoe an accompt what he hath done with my other goods to whome sould & for what, I am informed you have a ready way in Holland to force a person to give an accompt by callinge him before the Lords &c butt I am ignorant of the way & therfore request that by next you would please to direct me in it for I must take some such coarce in it since noe faire meanes will draw him to doe me reason & truly by my accompts which I make heere I can not conceive him to have less then £1,000 sterling or verry neare of myne in his hands in goods debts & moneys but what ever it bee I am willinge to stande to a faire accompt could I gett it as I begg it soe I hope you will assist me in my streights & I doe assure you in what ever I am able I shalbe ready to serve you, I must alsoe request you by the first shipps to send me 150 pound weight of clover grasseede & 28lb weight of nonesuch seede & as much of saint foyne seede its for to sow my grounds[101] with all & therfore I desire it may be the verry best of the sorts & new seed of the last yeares grouth, this with tender of service is all at present from your friend & servant

Tho: Baret

[*p. 199*] Norwich the 7th of February 1675[/6]

Mr Nathaniell Mathew

My last to you was of the 31st of December past to Hambrough which I perceive by yours of the 29th past from London cam not to your hand but suppose it may to which I refer yow, in ansuer to yours from London I am glad of your safe arrivall in England & should be glad to see you heere for my occasions will not permitt me to come to London till Aprill at which

101 Baret had recently purchased the Heggatt estate at Horstead. *See Introduction.*

time I may spend a month there, as to your goods heere I am sorry you have sent them to such an unfortunate place as will not afford a market for them, the highest price that I am offered for your hamells lininge is 6¼ for the wholle parcell together which I refused last weeke your lowest price beeinge 7d & 6d which is 6½ together, if you will take that price I presume I may have it upon the retorne of your letter at three months time, as to the yarne this place will never vend it I have only sould one bundle at 10s, as to your whalebone I have don my best & they tell me they neither want any nor will buy any till Aprill, I have sold one barrell of steele & as yet the party have not given me his experriment upon it whoe tould me if it proved well he would buy the parcell & this is all the accompt that I can give you of your comoditys & am truly sorry that I can give you noe better which is a dayly troble to me & I am in the same condition about my hartfords linings for I cannot sell one piece of them heere, pray lett me know what price they beare at London for I feare I must remoove them thither this is an ugly tetchy place for a market & doeth much dishearten me in trading when my retornes neither turne to accompt nor sell redily, I have sould the Osenbrigs but soe verry low as discourage me but I hope trade will mend. I have perused the patterns you sent two of [*p. 200*] which are not the make of this place the other are serge de neîmes & most of them good wares & all good colors & if you can buy such wares at £4 & £4 10s 0d you can doe more than I can for the most of these are prime wares & 10s per peice is hardly disserned in this comodity, you have a fancy that I doe over rate my goods but you are much mistaken altho you will not beleive it if my price be deerer than others its because they are made much better then others for our stuffs are not like brass farthins all of one stampe & vallue thers noe sort but I can vary 10s some more in true & reall goodnes but since your market will not admitt it I am sorry I sent such but since they are there pray sell my goods at Hambrough at the best price you can gett whether profitt or loss & I shall send noe more such againe, if you please to come to Norwich & will take a bed at my howse you shalbe hartily welcombe. Sir, I presume by this time you are satisfyed that I did duly comply with your bill of exchange & that the discorce you sent me about it was a mistake. This with service is the needfull at present from

Your loving friend
Tho: Baret

[*p. 201*] Norwich the 7th of February 1675[/6]

Mr William Peacock

Sir, Yours of the 21st January past I received & perused my last to you was the 22nd of December past in which upon reasons then given I left you at liberty to sell my goods at the best price the market would afford. I have observed what you wright about R[owland] C[ockey] whoe still addeth one unworthynes to another for he hath not writt one word to me notwithstandinge what he tould you he had done & therfore I doe expect nothinge wilbe don but what force oblige him to & therfore I will noe longer delay & as for his creddit he is to take care of that for he hath alredy lost that with me & soe all I have or shall take care for is to get cleare with him & get my estate out of his hands by faire meanes if he please if not by the utmost extremity he will force me to use for I will leave noe stone unturned but because you thinke thretnings may serve turne therfore I shall trye that at present, in the inclosed which seale & dilliver I have pretended to have sent you a letter of attorney to sue him if this will not doe by retorne of next poast I will really send you one but doe you now carry it as if you had it by you & give me the isue of it by first opportunity. I observe what you wright about iron but I desire a parcell may be sent me presently for I want about 3 or 4 tonn of narrow flatt iron to sort out what I have alredy by me & therfore send me some although it be the less for it will helpe off what I have by me. This with service is the needfull from

Your loving friend
Tho: Baret

[*p. 202*] Norwich the 7th of February 1675[/6]

Mr Rowland Cockey

Sir, For the procuringe of my accompt currant from you & the receivinge of my goods out of your hands I have used all the faire meanes that I could possibly invent which I perceive will not worke any thinge with you but you answer all my kindnesses with the utmost slight & discredit you can putt upon me & therfore now I am resolved to use the utmost extremity of law which I can & therfore I have by this poast sent to Mr William Peacock Jnr a letter of attorney to sue you & call you before the Lords or in my name to use any extremity the law of the place will admitt against you for I will noe longer be delayed then the coarce of law will oblige, if this proove to your domage or discredit thanke your selfe for had you civillity or common sence you would prevent it by delinge honestly with him that hath by all wayes courted you to it whoe still desires to be

Your loving friend
Tho: Baret

Delay not but dilliver what goods you have of mine to Mr Peacock Jnr upon first demand although my accompt currant for a short time be defferred.

[*p. 203*] Norwich the 7th of Feburary 1675[/6]

Mr Robert Pease

Sir, Yours of the 24th past is now before me & I hope the pack of wares sent you are safely arrived ere this time, I have perused the envoyce sent with them which was as they then cost since which time this beeinge the deadest time of trade some of them are abated in price which will up againe as soone as springe comes on the comodityes fallen are as follows

No. 1 – 1s per piece, No. 4 – 3s per piece, No. 5 – 1s, No. 6 – 1s

These are as low as now soe good wares are to be bought but I am loth to abate it because they must up to it againe but I leave it to you to doe as you see cause possibly it may introduce a trade butt I am not content to purchase a trade without profit for I must loose by my retornes which is to be considered, as to R[owland] C[ockey] he deales verry ill with me (not to give him a worse caracter altho he deserves it) I can not tell how to press you to act for me publiquely against him because our correspondency is but small & may not deserve soe greate a kindness but I doe see that I must per force gett my goods & accompt from him, I have tryed all faire meanes with him & can effect nothing nay I can not procure soe much as a letter from him since July last notwithstandinge what he hath putt upon me by protestinge bills & findinge you unwillinge to act against him, I did by an other hand demand my goods of him which he refused to dilliver but at first tould him he would dilliver them & then that he had written to me & would send my accompt but did neither, I am willinge to act by all faire meanes & if you would please to speke with him upon my accompt as persuaded by your friend [*p. 204*] Mr South I should be thankfull to you that soe I might hear what his ansuer would be to you but I am sure nothing but rigor will bringe him to reason & therfore if I can not persuade you to act in it I must request you to advise me to some honest man that will doe it for me to whome I shalbe willinge to alow any resonable satisfaction for his paines & must request you to be privately assistinge him with your advice, its the highest charity to assist me to gett out of AK— hands I know you have advocates for such matters with you as well as wee have heere & I am resolved if I can to bringe him to reason one way or other & therfore if you will not in the first pray be assistinge in the later which wilbe a greate kindness to

Your assurd friend
Tho: Baret

Norwich the 23d of February 1675[/6]

Mr John Fittz

Sir, I hope this will finde you in good health not havinge heard from you or written to you of a good while since by your last accompt you had severall goods restinge on hand I desire that by next poast you would send me an accompt currant that soe I may see how things stand betuixt us, pray fail me not then because I would take order with one that is now with me about some of the goods which rest on your hands not fitt for your market but are fitt for his & he is to leave England in three weeks at furthest & I would order the busines whilst he is with me, not more at present I am

Yours &c
Tho: Baret

[*p. 205*] Norwich the 23d February 1675[/6]

Mr William Peacock

Yours of the 10th currant is before me, my last to you was of the 7th instant, your ansuer to it & the effects it had on R.C. I am verry desirous to know which I hope may be good for I heare he is retornd againe to exchange which I am hartily glad off but I doe not understand your letter conserninge him where you wright you send me his letter but for the list youle keepe it but heere was nothinge inclosed & I hope you have not cutt the list from the letter that were ill done for its best to have them together & soe I would have them retorned me when I wright for them, you say noe body hath over fallen him but Mr Thomas Kirby seased his goods & amongst them some of mine which I hope he will consider off & dilliver to you, if you had pleased you might have acted upon my letter as sufficient authority it conteyninge the equivalent to a letter of attorney but I perceive you were too deeply ingaged your selfe & friends to act for me as you might but I hope he hath dilliverd them now what remaine & that your brother in law will dilliver you the rest for I ought him noe money altho Mr Cockey did pray give me an accompt what he will doe in it & demand them frindly of him, I have seene Mr Mathew and shall order some goods to him from you but at present I know not what you have not haveing had any accompt from you since our first beginninge & therefore by next poast pray send me an accompt currant sale of goods goods restinge & debts standinge out by which I shall know what to order him, I am providinge a parcell of serge de boyce but till I know what they will yeild wherby to consider whether profitt or loss I will send none over for I had better buy none then sell to loss, be quick in sending me your accompt that soe I may know what to doe with Mr Mathew before he leave England

Your
Tho: Baret

[*p. 206*] Norwich the 23rd of February 1675[/6]

Mr Robert Pease

Sir, Yours of the 11 & 14 instant are now before me my last to you was of the 7th which I hope is come safe to your hand before this time your ansuer to which wilbe welcome to me, I am sorry for R[owland] C[ockey']s mishapp &c

I perceive you have sent the clover seede which I am glad of but as yet heare not of Kippers arrivall for the other seeds lett them alone for they can not come time enough for my occasions, I see you have received my goods but to a bad market for the prices you doe mention are loss, in my last I gave you the louest prices now to be bought at what will sell to profitt altho small profitt dispose of the rest keepe by you for I hope when springe cometh on markets will advance if not I will then take market price as countinge first loss the best but I feare your marchant under bid you for the last invoyce I had which is not long since serge de boyce were sould at 31 guilders &

better, I am sorry we have soe bad a begining but hope for a better endinge, with service presented I rest

Your friend & servant
Tho: Baret

Send me the cost & charges of the clover seed for I must helpe a friend to some of it & know not what price to take

[*p. 207*] Norwich the 23rd of February 1675[/6]

Mr George Richards

Sir, My last to you was of the 10th of August last past since which I have not heard from you by letters or otherwaise I hope this will finde you in health the intimation of which by a letter would be acceptable to me. I am sorry my commission prove soe troblesome to you, I wish I knew wherein to be more serviceable to you & I should be ready to comply with your orders. Sir, I request you to send me an accompt what of my goods are sould & what remaines on hand & what probability there is of disposinge them by sale or barter for I leave you to doe with them for me as you judge best for my advantage, its greate loss to bringe them back hither againe but if ther be noe other way retorne them when you thinke fitt altho I judge it best to trye what this somner trade may doe to their disposall before you retorne them but because I would not be too troblesome to you I shall leave it to you to doe as you shall see cause, please to accept the tender of service from

Your reall friend & servant
Tho: Baret

[*p. 208*] Norwich the 25th of February 1675[/6]

Mr John Fittz

This only serves in hast to acquaint you that now in the port of Yarmouth by new advice & directions from above they seaze upon all iron whatsoever that comes from Holland except what is really & prooveable to be Lukes iron in prosecution of which directions they have seized all the last parcell of iron which cam from Rowland Cockey for John Andrews, I have seriously perused the law in the case & doe finde the seisure to be good & I doe verrily beleive the wholle is lost to J[ohn] A[ndrews] unless he workes to his advantage privately, the shipp is in the same condition forfited & the master lyable the truth is there is noe avoidinge of this busines because the marchant must proove it to be Luckes iron to clere him selfe & that is hard for him to doe, I had not been soe mindfull & inquiring into this busines but that I feare it wilbe my oune case to manage in behalfe of Mr Peacock for yesterday by poast Mr William Peacock Jnr sent me word that he had bought some iron & would send it downe for the first shipp ready which makes me feare it should be sailed before this comes to hand but I hope it will not & therfore I desire you that if any iron from Mr Peacock comes to you to be sent to me keepe it by you & send none till further order & if it should soe happen that the iron be shipt before this comes to hand take it out againe & if the master should refuse for the troble or the like tell him his & the danger in the thinge & they are goods can not be runn & therfore tell him plainely you will have them out if he dus yet refuse goe to him with wittnes such as may sware it & demand the iron out & tell him in these verry words that its Suedish [*p. 209*] iron & noe iron of the growth production or manufacture of Holland but it & the shipp for bring of it are both forfited & if he should yet be soe mad as to refuse it & at resnable termes too tell him from me that if there be loss upon the iron I will assure him he shalbe prosecuted for his shipp with the utmost rigor & for want of an informer to serve him tell him I will turne informer my selfe if he doeth not as he should doe. In hast I rest

Your loving friend
Tho: Baret

Pray by first send all the goods that you have of mine to Mr William Peacock Jnr for he hath present occasion for them all & give me advice what you send that soe I may charge them to his accompt & discharge yours pray delay not for he is in present want of them.

Norwich the 25th February 1675[/6]

Mr William Peacock

I have yours of the 26 & 28th before me my last to you was of the 23 to which I refer you. I have observed your letters you say my goods are sould which I am glad off but doe not say at what price soe that I can not tell what incouragement there is for sendinge more yet I shall send downe a pack this night which was designed for an other place & soe the nomber may disagre with what you have had but the wares are fitt for your occasion. I doe not know what you meane by ([*illegible*] says). As to R[owland] C[ockey] I am assured he wilbe in England sodainely soe shall defer a litle while, I have ordered Mr Fittz to send you what wares he hath by him of mine which will give a pretty supply till the other arrive, the invoyce shall come by next for I am in greate hast sendinge this by an extraordinary way to prevent the cuminge over of any iron to me for now in Yarmouth they seize all but Luke iron & putt the marchant to proove it to be soe which is hard to doe, I have perused the law in the case & doe finde that all iron but what is truly Luke [*p. 210*] iron is forfited & lost & soe is the shipp that bringe it & what is come by the last shipps is all seized & wilbe lost & therfore what ever iron that is not really Luke iron which you have ordered hither whether it be on your owne or my accompt with all imaginable speede cause it to be stopt in Holland till further advice, if it be on shipboarde cause it to be taken out if the master should refuse tell him his danger if that will not make him unlade it take two witnesses that will sware it if occasion require & tell the master in these wares that it is Sueeds iron (if it be not really Luke) or what contry iron it is & that it is not of the growth production or manufacture of Holland & that its forfited when it comes hither & that his shipp is forfited for bringin of it over & that if not withstandinge all this he will bringe it over the loss wilbe to himselfe & that for his wilfulnes I will cause the shipp to be proceeded against with the utmost rigour, I perceive you have bought about 12,000lb of Luch sqaure iron to send hither but its upon your owne accompt for I will not medle with it nor have I any occasion for it, my advice was only for narrow flatt as you will see by my orders & therfore place this to your owne accompt & in future observe my orders better or elce I shall never know what I wright for I hope this timely notice will prevent all danger, accept service from

Your loving friend
Tho: Baret

Pray buy or send noe more iron upon my accompt till further order

[*p. 211*] Norwich the 9th of March 1675[/6]

Mr Rowland Cockey

Sir, Yours of the 21st past I received & since that a recommendations by Mr Thomas Andrews for both which I give you most harty thanks they beeinge favors which you have denyed me for a verry long time, I am verry sorry for the mishap which hath befallen you notwithstanding the unkindness that you have soe often acted towards me & indeed to be plaine with you I have admired at your blindnes in not foreseeinge this & timely preventing of it notwithstandinge you have had soe many hints even from my selfe, I doe not love to add affliction to affliction & I doe hope a friendly debate of affaires will not be accompted soe for I can not doe less whilst things doe stand as now they doe, I gave you my resolve for not sendinge any more wares till accompts were setled neare two yeares since which I will still hould to since that by severall letters especially my last I have plainely tould you what coarce I would steere with you which I shall not in the least vary from unless you state my accompts & deliver up my goods accordinge to my orders which I have sent you for till this accompt be fairely & justly stated & determined I will leave noe stone unturned to force you to it, I love not this way of dealinge but you constrayne me to it & you have soe long putt me off with faire words that now nothinge but actions can worke upon me to conceive you reall & when I finde them to my content I may enter upon other discorce but not till then my service to Mrs Cockey I am desirous to be

Your loving friend
Tho: Baret

Upon my last letter Mr Peacock did demand my goods of you & you refused to deliver them sayinge there was an other accompt in my hands to you & now <to take away that objection I acquaint you that of the [*illegible*] sent in company there is three resting unsould the particular of which is is ready to send you when you send me mine by which you will see the misrable accompt of loss they will come to> [*p. 212*] that shalbe ready as soone as you send mine for I can not full state it till you send my accompt, Mr Cockey if you have any respect for your selfe or me dilliver my goods to Mr William Peacock Jnr upon his next demand which wilbe the last frindly one after refusall expect the worst

Tho: Baret

Norwich the 8th of March 1675[/6]

Mr William Peacock

Sir, Since my last to you of the 25th past none from you, I was then discouraged in sending for iron because of its beeinge seised at Yarmouth but now I am informed that those which were seized are sett fre againe & therfore pray by first shipps send me a parcell of narrow flatt iron but send me noe other sort upon my accompt for I have alredy a full supply. I hope

Mr Fittz have sent you the stuffs in his hands accordinge to my advice given him I have now shipped in Carver the pack followinge

/No. WP6/ 23 pieces No. 3 cost 55
1 piece No. 7 cost 74
2 pieces No. 2 cost 94
4 pieces No. 1 cost 40
30

which are good both wares & collour & price resonable according to ther goodnes as to the serge de neîmes which you have & those that Mr Fittz send you gett them all packed up & marked as in margent[102] & send them per first for Hamborough to Mr Nathaniell Mathew, you may stay till the pack above arive & send them with the other & soe cleare your hands of that comodity for with your parts there [*p. 213*] is noe good to be done in it, pray demand my goods once more of Mr Rowland Cockey & if he dus refuse it shalbe the last friendly demand that shalbe made of them & therfore I have inclosed sent you a letter of attorney which please to putt in full execution as soone as is possible & pray make noe delay which he hath too much vexed me with allredy since the begininge heerof, I have received yours of the 10th instant & as to the inch square iron I have above & by my last informed you that its not for my occasion or sutable to my order & therfore if it should come hither please to give your orders what shalbe don with it & it shalbe followed butt of narrow flatt send me a parcell per first but gett it resonable for the market is verry low heere. The remainder of your letter is answered above, pray delay not to effect my busines with Mr Cockey to gett my goods from him but have a care that you discharge for nothinge but just what you have I shall take care for my accompts & what money is in his hands afterwards. This with service is all at present from

Your loving friend
Tho: Baret

If you can not come by the goods or that he will not dilliver you others in leiu of them to the vallue of £500 sterlinge or that he will not give you security for soe much in part of what he owes me pray delay not but arrest his body & lay it in prisson for I can beare noe longer delayes

Yours
Tho: Baret

102 Merchant's mark in margin.

[*p. 214*] Norwich the 17th of March 1675[/6]

Mr Nathaniell Mathew

Sir, Yours from London I received. Mr Baret & my selfe doe desire you to send us by the first good opportunity for Yarmouth the goods below mentioned, that which wee now wright for is only for a tryall till wee meete with that opportunity we soon hope for. Sir, wee desire your care not only to send choyce goods but also to beate downe the price as low as you can, the old sayinge is good goods well bought are halfe sould, if you can meete with 30 or 40 pieces Oznibridge whites good ware you may add them to the parcell, the slezy lawns[103] I neede not tell you for you well know there is a vast difference in that comodity the more to be heeded in buyinge in them & a few diapers if you follow the method as for London you can not err, you may please to pack the slezy lawns in three bundles or four which you thinke best the other goods you neede noe direction iff this parcell of goods amount to £400 that insurance be resonable you may insure £100. I am informed two or three vessells bound for Hamborough are now in Yarmouth Rode, wee desire you to advise soe soone as you have shipt the goods the drawinge the money that wee leave to your prudence I presume you neede not draw all upon a post if you can conveniently draw the halfe one poast three or four weeks after the remainder but not understandinge the custome of buying in goods there shall aproove of what you doe mee not doubtinge but you will doe for us as for your selfe, what money you shall have occasion to draw upon our accompt draw upon Mr John Langly if you please at any time to give us the prices of any goods that are vendible in this parts shall thankefully receive itt. I have noe more to add onely that I am yours to command

Christian Langley[104]

[*p. 215*] 100 pieces gray Oznabrugs *viz* 30 pieces Tekling[105]
30 pieces Rawenburg[106]
40 pieces Ozinbridge

103 Lawn: a fine, plain cotton weave. 'Sleazy' is derived from 'silesia' because of the coarse, cheap nature of the fabric, *see* note 108.

104 This is a copy of a third-party letter, presumably forwarded to Baret from either the author or the recipient.

105 Probably 'ticklenburg', a course fabric of hemp, linen, or linen mixed with cotton, named after the German town of Tecklenburg, where it was first made. It was similar to, but coarser than, Osnaburg (thanks to Sally Tuckett for this suggestion).

106 Ravensburg: *see* note 99.

18 sheets copper 6 square } from £28 to £32 per sheet
6 taper }
6 copper bottums from 18 to 24 inch over
150 pieces sleezy lawnes from the lowest to the highest
A small parcell diaper value of 30 or 40 £

Norwich the 18th of April 1676

Mr Robert Pease

Sir, My last to you was of the 23d of February since which none from you. This serveth only to advise you that now I thinke it will grow fit time to dispose of my goods & therfore I leave it to you to putt them off at the best price the market will afford, when I know what that price is if it gives incouragement I will send you more. This with service is all from

Your friend & servant
Tho: Baret

Pray by next lett me know the wholle charge & cost of the clover seed.

London the 5th of May 1676

Mr Nathaniell Mathew

Sir, I have received your letters & perused the contents of them as also the patterns inclosed & am sorry that I can do nothing in them for I am heere lyed to attend some law suits which my customers force mee to enter into with them to get my just dues, now that I am a leaving of all trading in this city & since they are so unworthy with mee I think it best for my advantage to sett close to itt & attend it this sommer although I doe neglect trading a while, which I am the rather inclined [*p. 216*] to, because the warre is like to be somewhat severe in your parts this sommer, which will make trading not only low & dead, but hazardous & when I have cleared my selfe of London I shall be more free & at liberty to enlarge with you, Mr Peacock had advized mee that he hath sent you 14 pieces of searge de neîmes, which with all other comodities that you have of mine pray sell by first, at the best market price you can gett & draw in what money is standing out on my accompt for the wares formerly sold & employ it in buying that parcell of wares that Mr Langley & my selfe wrote to you for whereby you need draw the less money upon us, halfe the cost & charge of the parcell advised for, you must draw upon Mr Christian Langleys sole accompt, the other halfe upon my owne, but out of my part deduct what moneys you have of mine standing with you. The money for your hamells begin to growe due, which I shall gett in with all speed possible & when received advize you of it. In your bone[107] I follow your order & lett it lay by till you direct I have had one or two to see it, but they will not offer above 10d per £ as yet I have not as yet sold all the steele or the hamells but upon my returne which will be very soddainly hope a markett, you have some stuffes of mine which I desired you formerly to send to Amsterdam, by your next advise mee what of them are unsold & I will order them back to Amsterdam for its to no purpose to have them lay there if not fitt for the markett. I am

Your friend & servant
Tho: Baret

[*p. 217*] London the 5th of May 1676

Mr John Fittz

Sir, I received yours of the primo May instant in this place & have perused the contents of it. Marke Eldred is safely arrived. Mr Peacock I suppose will bee in Norwich by that time I returne from hence and shall further enquire into the occasion of his complaint & the miscarryage of information upon the iron which I perceive is very considerable to my loss if it be not allowed to mee, although there is no reason that I should pay for others miscarryages, which I think ought to be putt to his accompt that occasionned I am here without my letters & accompts, butt truly I doe not remember that you have sent me an accompt currant lately, if you have & that I have received it tis at Norwich. But to prevent any further delayes pray by next send me an accompt currant to date & I will by the next returne order you what shall be due upon it. Your next I hope will find mee at Norwich I am

Your friend to command
Tho: Baret

107 i.e. whalebone.

London the 5th of May 1676

Mr Rowland Cockey

Sir, Yours of the 14th past I received, which I did intend to have answered sooner, but was prevented by my journey hither & some extraordinary business which has taken up my time since I came hither. In your letter was a bill of exchange for £100 which I presented & after many delayes & sometime allmost absolute refusalls with good words & arguments I gott Mr Langley to accept it, but I doe assure you they shew a greate deale of averseness & unwillingness to it, before hee did it I doe observe the particulars of the wares deliverd Mr Peacock & the provition &c you put downe for doing of it which is unreasonable & I shall not allow it & I presume you rather putt that downe to fill up the paper than expecting it would be admitted. [*p. 218*] But I shall referre the further discource of that to our meeting to settle the accompt which I hope will be soddainly & the sooner the better, both for yourselfe & mee that so when the accompt is stated & setled wee may consider of future affaires for I doe holding resolution of doing no more with you till this accompt be first setled & the longer you are a doing it the worse will bee for yourselfe, for the sooner this is ended the sooner another will begin. I am glad to see such beginnings of your cleering up your creditt & showing yourselfe in actions what hitherto you have only professed in words. Remember me kindly to your wife & accept tender of service from

Your loving friend
Tho: Baret

By your poastcript you advise that the accompt of sales should come by next poast but as yett I have received none, pray speed them & passing the accompt for your delayes doe but hinder you selfe in further business.

Norwich the 24th of May 1676

Mr Thomas Shephard

Sir, I have not beene unmindfull of our discorce together about white or pickold herrings & a trade of iron, as to the first it seemes to me upon further inquiry to be attaineable if we had the command of a shipp for that purpose & then it might be carried on with privacy & I verryly beleive to content but without a shipp of our owne to command at pleasure noe good can be don, its possible some thinge of good may be don in hiringe of a shipp for the first time but after that it would discover the trade to the owners & others which would spoyle the trade [*p. 219*] for ever after, he that hath a master at his owne command may expect privacy but he that hires others servants must expect his designes shalbe divulged & then they are never to be acted over againe which make me advise that it may be the undertakinge of an other yeare & not of this, as to iron it may doe well to be undertaken presently for I have discorsed my friends & customers heere about it & would I now promise them to deliver them 60 or 80 tonn heere in three or four months time to their sorts & scantlings which are common sorts they would not buy elce wheare but reserve themselves for my parcell & I beleive 200 tonn in a yeare would not be two much for this place but I would begin with a smaller parcell least theire should proove some miscarrage in sortment or the goodnes of the mettall. Sir, if you please to communicate to me the price beyond sea with the charges upon it & what place you will bringe it from & how a shipp may be procured at best rate to import it into Yarmouth & how our moneys may be best ordered for its procurement at the easiest rate I am ready & willinge to goe halves with you in this experrimentall undertakinge & the sooner it be undertaken the better, if you doe concurr with me please to give me your resolve per first that soe I may make ready my advice & instructions for you. I can at all times sell heere as deere as Mr Western sells in London with the charges hither added & some times for more, its to be considered whether the warrs beyond sea will not make the adventure hazardus if it would I should decline it for present. Sir, I leave the wholl to your consideration & am

Your friend & servant
Tho: Baret

[*p. 220*] Norwich the 26th of May 1676

Mr Nathaniell Mathew

Sir, Yours of the 9th instant per poast I received, my last to you was from London of the 5th instant by which you will understand how I am involved in scurvy suites & trobles in getting cleare of my London trade which will for this somer keepe me soe much at London & soe litle heere that I determine to ceace all trade for this somer for I can not be heere to tend it as it should be & its better to drive noe trade at all then not minde it as it should be & its the same for law suites which I will set close to that I may the sooner finish them & then next yeare god willinge I wilbe for tradinge againe beyond sea for I will deale noe more in London where in my way that hither to I have there used I meete at closinge with brokers fooles & knaves which I will clere my hands of, really I am sorry for your sake as well as my owne that I am forced to alter my intentions of supplying you with goods as I intended & doe resolve to performe god willinge next yeare but if it were your owne case upon the reasons given I know you would act as I doe & therfore wright to your agent at London for what you thinke fitt & in any thinge I can be a furtherance to him or you pray frely command me & I will act or advise, as for myselfe I doe expect to be in London 14 days hence I have conferred with Mr Langley & toald him that because there is noe sodaine or constant conveyance from you to Norwich that I would not be conserned with him in any goods that shall now come either hither or to London for heere they will come too late & to London the charge of commission upon commission will eate out the profitt & therfore although formerly I wrott for some goods [*p. 221*] with him now I forbid sending any upon my accompt but what or how I shall order in future or in the close of this letter. Sir, I am sorry that you should have soe just cause to complaine of the 14 pieces sent you from Holland, my frind there hath not don well or followed my order for I did advise to send good wares & collours & some variety for experriment but to have them abused as you doe intimate doe much troble me, if any accident had befallen them he should for his owne credit have freshed them up before he had sent them away, this miscarrage I shall intimate to him that I doe not take it well but since they are now with you pray lett them be made up handsomely & cleared from the dirt & soyle which you say they have contracted & fitt them for sale, I doe thinke you doe undervalue them shrewdly but I know in the dispose of them you will doe your best for my advantage I had rather sell them for money altho at the lower price but if you can not gett that to content then barter them away for some vendible comodity heere or at London & give me advice what it is you gett in barter & then I shall order whether I will have them come hither or to London, as for the rest of my goods pray sell them for the best price you can gett or barter them away if that will turne to best accompt but pray barter only for good goods & such as are vendible heere or London for bad wares or drugg wares wilbe to incredible loss heere or London for its a verry deade time for trade in both places & all comodities are too plentifull & exceeding low, I wish you could barter them for any of those comodities that Mr Langly wright for for those will sell heere for least loss, I see you have sould me seven pieces which I am glad off I wish the rest were [*p. 222*] gon with them I am promised the money for your hamels next month but they doe complaine much of them & shew me some they bought since at same price two fingers bredth broder verry neare & thicker wares, since my coming home I have had two persons promised to come see the remainder & I have stayed at home at their time but as yet they have failed me, I doe expect your directions about the whalebone, I have now received my accompt of charges about your goods from Yarmouth & doe finde that I am out of pocket upon your accompt about £19 sterling beside the £2 that you had of me heere at Norwich I doe not question but that the money which you sould for last somer on my accompt is now come in & therfore be pleasd to remitt it me by bill of exchange by first opportunity or if you can not remitt it I will order a frind to draw it upon you from London but I know the best way is for you to remitt it to me & therfore I desire it may be. This with tender of service is all at present from

Your reall friend
Tho: Baret

[*p. 223*] Norwich the 7th of August 1676

Mr Nathaniell Mathew

I have received your severall letters of the 13 16 & 20th of June past & alsoe yours of the the 11th of July past all which I shall now answer. I gave you an accompt formerly of my beeing involved in soe many troblesome businesses that I could not minde trade for this sommer but should be at better leisure next if god spares life & then I doe intend to renue trade which coarse nessessity in part but prudence wholly obligeth me to the answering of your letters which conserne Mr Langly with me I have referred to him & hope he hath don it to your content elce he is to blame knowinge my other conserns to hinder me in answer to your severall letter received. The goods which you sent to Mr Langly & me are safely arivd a good while since but they are somewhat domaged as Mr Langly tell me for I have not had time to give them a generall veiw leaving the orderinge to him but I doe observe these follouinge errors to have beene committed by you, the white Ozenbriggs are not right Osenbriggs by the marks but are verry slim wares such as I would not by any meanes have had & we tould you wee would have only good of the kinde these wilbe a drugg & to our domage they are alsoe cast up falce in the invoyce 2,745 ells at £5 per cento comes but to £137 5s 0d & you make it £143 8s soe you are debter £6 3s 0d, the slezias[108] I hope may doe but you have erred in not sending

108 Slesia; silesia: an inexpensive lightweight linen fabric, made near Hamburg, Germany, in the historic province of Silesia, *see* note 103.

some lower sorts for we wrott to have from the lowest to the highest & you have only sent the highest which is an injury in soe greate a parcell & you have cast up the rebate 12s short soe that you are debt[or] for it, the rest of the goods are pretty good in generall but some of them are very bad the insurance 2½ per cento £4 I understand not soe that for the errors in the accompt we shall reckon with you afterwards & for the present for honor of your bills we have acepted them to the vallue of £507 8s 0d my proportion of which is remitted to London for punctuall payment at day & I know Mr Langly hath ordered his part which I question not wilbe performed, for any further trade at present Mr Langly & selfe have had noe conference but as these goe of to incouragement [*p. 224*] may give you farther troble in a short time for next month is a generall mart which I hope will incourage, as to my private conserns in your hands I am much trobled about them meeting with soe ill success & therfore by the first opportunity for Yaremouth send me back what goods you have by you of myne unsould & I will make the best market I can of them heere & for Octtos debt which trobles me I leave it to you to make the best end of it you can but I am for the quickest payment although with loss if he will give halfe doune take it but you can get more at some litle time & security take that for ther goods in my hands I have requested Mr Langly to use hid [*sic*] indev[or]s for disposing them to ther advantage, Nuremburge toyes doe sell heere verry cheape but if Octto would give some for his debt at tollerable rates I would take them but I must intreate you to act for me as you would for yourselfe if goods with you fall now surely they wilbe cheaper two months hence & then it wilbe good buyinge, accept service in hast I rest

Your friend & servant
Tho: Baret

[*p. 225*] <Horste[a]d> Norwich the 20th of September 1676

Mr William Peacock

I was verry glad to heare of your & ladyes safe arivall in Holland wheare I question not but you were welcombe & by this time I suppose the treates & entertainements are soe over as it wilbe noe unpleasant thinge to divert you with a litle busines for now I am in want of some iron but when it comes heere it wilbe a verry drugg or I must loose by it if I sell it quickly but now I have none by me but rods & I doe not love to be out of sorts in that comodity & therfore send me 10 tonn or 15 tonn of iron by the first good opportunity for I understand its now pretty reasonable, lett the sortments be as followeth, 3/5 of narrow flatt from 2 inch to 1½ / 1/5 of brode flat from 3 to 2½ / 1/5 of square of 1 inch & for your directions the line which is drawne on the top of the letter[109] is the exact length of an English inch if the square less it were better for me if they would come at the same price but they will not yeild any thinge more heere for the quallity of the iron it must be tuff whilst its hott & cold which you may know by its easines to bend whilst its cold lett all the brode & narrow iron be the thinnest you can gett & observe that it be drawne even on the edges not broder in one place than an other & observe that it be not full of small cracks on the edges for that is an infallible signe of britle or spalt iron when hot altho it bends never soe well when its cold, pray observ[e] these directions as much as possible you can for I know its impossible to buy a parcell of iron but some barrs wilbe defective pray gett it a good penniworth for you have money in cash to performe it with & make as much hast *to send me this parcell* as <possible> you can send me over a list of the goods you have by you that soe I may retorne it to you with prises to them that soe you may expose them to sale by the first opportunity, I give you this troble because by your discorce or Mr Cockes accompts I know not how to putt price to them that you will understand, I have some wares by me which I will send over to you by the first opportunity *pray present* my service to Mr Robert Pease & tell him I should be glad to heare of his welfare by a letter [*p. 226*] & present him with half a crown as a token which you brought over from me to him & place the money to my accompt. My service &c

Tho: Baret

Norwich the 13th of October 1676

Mr George Richards

My last to you was the 23rd of February last since which time I have not written to you but dayly hoped to have received some retorne of the goods which you have sould for me & an accompt of the rest but beeing disappointed in both it occasions this to desire you to send me an accompt by the first opportunity what of my goods are sould & for those which are restinge on hand pray retorne them by first for England to Mr John

109 This line has not been included in the copy.

Langley & for what is sould make me retornes in good Bilboa iron sutable to the sorts I formerly advised you of, the accompt now is of a long date & therfore I desire it may be closed with expedition I am sorry it gave me incouragement to inlarge but must be content, accept service from

Your friend & servant
Tho: Baret

[*p. 227*] Norwich the 13th of October 1676

Mr William Peacock

Yours of the 13th instant I received but noe other since you went to Holland then what my last answered. Mr John Fittz beeinge in towne I have stated my accompt with him & for ballance have given him a bill of exchange upon you for 195 guilders of cash money not to be paid in banke which bill is dated the 30th September last & payable at sight which please to pay & place to my accompt. I have beene soe busy in followinge my workemen that I might turne them off that truly I forgot to advise you of it till now, as to R[owland] Cockey he have now given me an accompt wherein he makes himselfe creditor not withstandinge when he was arrested he did confess himself debtor for £250 sterlinge the accompt is long & intricate & I have had noe leisure to peruse it but ere long I shall fall close to examin it & then I may say more to it, present my service to Mr Pease & tell him I shalbe glad to receive a letter from him I wright not to him to save charges, Sir I doe thanke you for the token which your Brother C[hristian] L[angley] brought from Yaremouth for him & my selfe & others, as to the newse of warr twixt England & France I heare not of it & therfore send forward the iron by way of Rotterdam which is but a short cutt & safe yet for security lett it come in two severall vessells. This with service to your selfe & Lady is all at present from

Your loving friend
Tho: Baret

[*p. 228*] Norwich the 13th October 1676

Mr Nathaniell Mathew

Your severall letters of the 18th of August & 7th & 11th September with the four fatts of toyes are all come safe to hand but the invoyce of the toyes I can not understand nor can I get any body to interpret it to me soe that I am forced to send it to London & if I faile there I know not what to doe, I presume you have had accompt your bills are payd to content I perceive you wonder I doe not pay into your friends hands the money that I have received for linings & steele but you neede not for the some is soe verry small that its not worth puttinge to any accompt but by your selfe to mine for I am out of about £20 sterling for charges & you had £2 of me & the ballance of your accompt to me was £29 odd Flemish & there are some errors to rectify all which comes neere the some I have received for you & therfore the ballance I shall place to your accompt heere, the goods that I have of yours I have spoken to Mr Langly whoe promiseth to use his utmost indeavors about them I perceive you now have disposed all my goods but at soe long time as discourage me for sendinge any more but at present you have not given me an accompt of theire sorts & prices which I doe expect, I am sorry that I forgott to retorne you thanks for the kinde present you set me &c – – – you send me patterns for serge de neîmes some are silke & some are other stuffs & sarges & would have me match those patterns for you which is an imposible thinge to doe, if you had given me comission to gett them as neere as I could in which I would have don as for my selfe [*p. 229*] I would have adventured to procure your parcell but your commission beeinge soe streight I will only attempt for ten peices & will goe as neere to your patterns as I can & shall draw the money accordinge to your order, pray be mindfull of Ottos debt, accordinge to your order I shall shipp away the whalebone for London to Mr Sanders, accept service from

Your loving friend
Tho: Baret

London the 26th of October [16]76

Mr Nathaniell Mathew

[*no letter*]

[*p. 230*] London the 30th of October 1676

Mr William Peacocke

Sir, My last to you was of the 13th instant since which I have received none from you. Last weeke I sent downe to Yaremouth to be shipped off for you by Captain Huntington one pack q[uan]t[ity] as follows *viz*

/No. WP7/	1¾	mixt russell No. 5
	22	mixt russells No. 3
	2	white callimancoes No. 4
	25	pieces

They are wares that I had made a pretty while agoe & therfore I putt noe price to them but leave you to sell them for my utmost profitt, they are better wares by 3 or 4s per piece then what are ordinaryly sould, pray send forward the iron that I wrott for lett it be sent in English vessells from Roterdam & I doe not feare any domage from the French, accept service from

Your loving friend
Tho: Baret

London the 14th November 1676

Mr Robert Pease

Sir, My last to you was of the 18th of Aprill with a full order for the disposinge of my goods which I sent you since which I have received noe letter from you, this serveth to inquire of your welfare & to request you to send me an accompt not doubtinge but the goods are long since disposed, Sir I request you would please to give me answer by your first conveniency. I did present my service to you by Mr William Peacock when he left English & requested him to spend a halfe crown token with you. This with service is the needfull at present from

Your friend & servant
Tho: Baret

[*p. 231*] Invoyce of one pack of goods upon accompt proper of Mr Nathaniell Mathews of Hamburge & by his order dillivered in London to Mr Edward Sanders for his accompt as foll[ows] & marked as in margent

/No. NM1/	2 serge de neîmes cost 100s per piece	£10 0s 0d
	5 ditto cost 98s per piece	£24 10s 0d
	2 ditto cost 96s per piece	£9 12s 0d
	1 ditto cost 95s per piece	£4 15s 0d
		£48 17s 0d
	To packinge ropes & canvace &	£0 8s 0d
	To carrage of the goods to London	£0 11s 0d
	To provition	£0 19s 0d
	In toto summa £	£50 15s 0d

London the 14th of November 1676

Mr Nathaniell Mathew

Sir, I am just now leavinge London & have dillivered to Mr Sanders the pack mentioned above & inclosed send you the invoyce of it which I doubt not but is to your content & will further incourage you in the trade, I have drawne my bill upon Mr Sanders for the money accordinge to your order payable to Mr John Langley upon the 16th of December next & doubt not but your orders will take care for its due payment I should chide you for your omissions in this affaire butt I am in hast to goe home, accept service from

Your loving friend
Tho: Baret

[*p. 232*] London the 14th of November 1676

Mr Edward Sanders
£50 15s 0d

Sir, Accordinge to Mr Nathaniell Mathews order for drawinge upon you please to pay to Mr John Langley or order upon the 16th of December next the some of fifty pounds & fifteene shillings & place it to the accompt proper of Mr Nathaniell Mathew as per advice of

Your servant
Tho: Baret

To Mr Edward Sanders
Merchant
In London

London the 14th of November 1676

Mr Edward Sanders

Accordinge to the order of Mr Nathaniell Mathew I have drawne a bill of exchange upon you payable the 16th of December next to Mr John Langley or order for £50 15s 0d sterling which please to accept & pay & place it to the accompt of Mr Nathaniell Mathew as per advice of

Your loving friend
Tho: Baret

[*p. 233*] London the 17th of November 1676

Mr William Peacock

Sir, Yours of the 20th instant I received & doe assure you my buildinge is now over, soe that I have time to think & consider of tradinge & my money is soe spent as that I want & haveing time for it must take care to get it in that soe I may have tooles to worke with, I might send over comodityes &c but now I will looke to have somethinge considerable come back againe & therfore to be serious I have perused the contents of your letter (which had noe price current in it) & I doe assure you I had noe more letter than what I have intimatd to you, I am well pleased you have paid the bill to Mr Fitts as to R[owland] C[ockey] he & I shall doe well enough, I question not when we come to accompt together which wilbe next weeke or weeke after for its the first worke I will sett to when I retorne as you thinke my heade have beene two full of buildinge (which I confess) soe I thinke yours have beene of something elce otherwaise you would have given me a particular of the goods restinge before this time when soe often desired that soe I might fix a price for their sale & not lett them lay by as stones, I am now for mindinge quick trade or none either send me a particular by next or retorne me the goods by next shippinge & really I am at a stand to thinke your meaninge in not sendinge me the iron that I wrott for, you have effects enough in hand to send it upon if my credit were not worth 2d I know these late parcells are not the cheapest for the plenty comes in the months past & if you have a parcell comeing must I stay to make you a market, either deale squarely with me or letts close our accompts [*p. 234*] and have done for now, I will sett close to effect busines or knock off all, as to the iron you have made me as a foole to bespeake customers & none comes, either send it me by next or give me better reson why you doe not for you give me reson to thinke you triffle with me, as to the goods now sent I know the most if not all are verry vendible colors & for callimancoes I know by what you have written to others a man can not make his money againe, if you wright to me for any thinge send me word what it will yeild & at what payment & if I finde it will turne to accompt I will send elce not, Mr Peacocke I am now for trade againe accordinge as I finde incouragement by the profit of goods & the quick retornes of money if they will not answer I have totally done for trade. My service to you & to your lady whoe am

Your reall friend to serve you
Tho: Baret

Mr Nathaniell Mathew debtor to charges
Ultimo November 1676 as follows
To a bill sent the 18th of December 1676 with the following letter £22 4s 7½d

Norwich the 18th of December 1676

Mr Nathaniell Mathew

Yours dated in October last (for the seale tore out the date) I received & now beeing retorned from London have taken the first conveniency I could to send your bill of charges as above, accordinge to your desire in ditto letter I have gotten the invoyce of the toyes don into English & was forced to unpack the fatt No. 11 not beeinge able to understand it without [*p. 235*] & upon its unpackinge doe finde it to be the greatest cheate that ever was putt upon a man for all the toyes of greatest vallue are taken out & things of noe use or vallue putt in the roome of them which are not mentioned at all in the invoyce & the No. of verry few agree wherby it is plaine that it hath beene rifled & new packt to putt a cheate upon me & therfore take noe more of Ottos toyes upon my accompt but torment him for my money & alsoe that he makes restitution for this abuse, if you take any more they are upon your owne accompt not mine for this is a cheate most notorious the things wantinge are as follows *viz.*

<table>
<tr><td>144 slatt bookes with leaves
288 ditto
36 polished slatt bookes
23 large slatt bookcs
24 pa[r]tridges made of wood
264 small roses read</td><td>there is not one of all of these</td></tr>
</table>

40 nest boxes fine painted there is but 6
50 painted boxes q[uan]t[ity] otters or adders thers not above 20
66 read boxes with tradsmen thers not half of them
140 howsehold goods browne No. 28 thers not one of this sort
242 bullitts within ninepins thers not above 1/3 of them

I have not as yet but as soone as I can get leisure I will take a particular accompt of them that soe I may expose them to sale by a true invoyce, had I sould them by this I should have beene accompted a knave & have exposed my selfe to have made good the invoyce the fatt now is litle above halfe soe good as it would have beene had it beene right to the invoyce butt in short the wholle parcell will never yeild me half the money they cost me & I beleive at last I must send them for London, but enough of these which which vex me when I see them, as for sending for more goods at present I am totally discouraged for what ever I receive turns to loss when that money comes in which is now standing out I shall order goods for that [*p. 236*] your goods are now soe cheape in Holland that the exchange from that place which is verry high beeing considered they are brought cheper from thence then from your parts, as to your goods that I have by me I have don the utmost that I can to sell them & can not gett a chapman for them, as to your steele its soe feirce as our workmen can not use it & I know not what to doe with it yet my indeavors shall not be wanting for its sale & the hamells linings are soe narrow as I can not persuade any body to buy them altho I would sell them under the price of the last you know that I have only what cam from Mr Wallers which are worse than the last were whether he sufferd them to be culled & soe sent me the refuse I can not tell, your whalebone I have sent to Yarmouth & soe for London to Mr Sanders accordinge to your order but upon my cuming home I finde they are not yet gon away from Yarmouth the officers obstructinge them as not beleiving them to be the same which were formerly entred I have ordered them a certificate & if that will not doe when the weather breakes up which is now extreame I will goe downe to cleare them. Sir, I doe assure you I have don my best to dispose your goods but if you will not beleive it I can not helpe it, as to Mr Sanders I wrott him worde that you had ordered me to buy some goods for you & to draw £100 upon him but I feared I should not get your quantity to content & soe thought I should not draw above £50 or £60 & desired to know if he had any orders to accept my bill but he gave me noe answer to my letter till I was in London & then refused it, if he writt more then this he mistooke my letter or wrott his owne conceptions upon it, as to my moneys standing out you [*p. 237*] offer to secure them at 2 per cento & to remit me the money if I will alow the rebate if I alow the rebate I shall not neede to alow the 2 per cento ensurance I know not what you doe demand for the rebate were it reasonable I might agre with you & therfore when you send me my accompt lett me know what it is & I shall give you my farther answer, I hope the invoyce of the searge de Neîmes is to the content I am sure the wares are good, pray be mindfull of honoring my bill with good payment & if you have occasion for any more goods which this place dus afford if you give me your orders I will doe my best for the advantage, accept service from

Your loving friend
Tho: Baret

My last to you was from London with the invoyce of the serge de neîmes dat the 14th November 1676

Norwich the 22d December 1676

Mr William Peacock Jnr

Sir, Yours of the 8th instant I received & have perused the contents of it & that pretty excuse you send for not sendinge the iron which is highly prejudiciall to me but to make me amends you must alow me the interest of the money layinge in your hands which by this time I presume is neere 3,000 guilders & when the frost breakes up I will have it come all in iron sorted to my last order & I would have it come by first shipps & therfore neglect noe good opportunity for my advantage in buyinge it in, its most likely that now in this deade time of trade a good pennyworth may be gotten but the time I must leave to you beeing upon the place but neglect noe opportunity that soe I may have a good parcell come by first shipp for I have present occasion for it, as to the particulars of the goods restinge I can not well understand [*p. 238*] it as you sett it doune & therfore I have drawne out the particlars as I thinke you meane which are under written, if they be right send me word by next letter if not give a true one & lett me know in what condishon those remaininge of what you had of Mr Cockey are the particulers follow *viz*

wares remaining unsould
of the pack last sent per T Baret
11 pieces of serge de boyce
2 white callimancoes
13

wares remaining unsold
of what I did formerly
receive from Thomas Baret
5 pieces No. 6 silke sayes
2 pieces <ditto> No 3
7 pieces
13 pieces brough from above
40½ pieces brought from other side
60½ pieces in all

wares resting of what was received
from Mr Rowland Cockey for the
use of Thomas Baret
1 white bratt No. 17
1 ditto a doble piece No. 16
1 piece ditto No. 16
1 white russell
9 drogetts[110] No. 13
1 gold collour bratt No. 18 a doble piece
3 silke sayes[111] No. 28
9 ditto black & white No. 14
2 ditto goldish collour No. 32
2 pieces No. 25
5 spotd serge de boyce to send back
1 ditto with silke to send back
1 ditto noe good color
2 pieces ½ silke say No. 10
1 black bratt
40½

Mr Rowland Cockey & I are now cuminge to even our accompts if wee can & he doeth charge you with 62 pieces of wholl goods ditt[o] to you & you doe charge the same No. but neither he nor you give me the particulers that soe I can not tell how to charge you or discharge him in the particulers which breeds a great confusion in both your accompts & besides you told me that many of them were broken up & some cutt off & some were but half pieces & remnants, I sent him none but wholle pieces & therfore what is wantinge he must make good to me & therfore by next poast that soe I may not stay for it for his accompt send me an [*p. 239*] exact particuler of the goods you received from him & the condishon they were in whether wholl pieces or remnants if remnants what they held that soe he may answer for what fall short, I see you now charge half a piece restinge of the goods received from him I sent none such & therfore unles you have sold the other half he must answer for it, pray faile me not of an answer of this letter by verry first, I am

Your loving friend
Tho: Baret

110 Drugget, a plain woollen cloth (thanks to Sally Tuckett for this definition).
111 Fine quality fabric, originally made from wool, made from silk from the fifteenth century.

Norwich the 19th of January 1676/7

Mr John Fittz

A friend of mine Mrs Eliz[abeth] Rayley[112] have persuaded me to undertake the management of a small concerne of hers in stuffs to Holland which by misdirection she have sent consigned to you, the goods were sent to Captain Huntington last weeke to send forward, I have undertaken her concerns & therfore pray doe for her as you would for me & wright all letters to me & I shall communicate them to her, pray be carefull in this small afaire & it may be an inducement to farther, the invoyce is underneath, I am

Your loving friend
Tho: Baret

Invoyce of one small pack of stuffs for the accompt of Mrs Eliz[abeth] Rayley consigned to Mr John Fittz

/No. ER1/ 10 pieces white russells cost 38 £19 0s 0s

[*p. 240*] Norwich the 21st February 1676/7

Mr Nathaniell Mathew

Both your letters of the 22nd of January past & 5th instant I received in answer to which as to sending any more goods on my owne accompts I am resolved against it for the presente because I can as yet bring nothing back againe which dus turne to any accompt soe much as to save my selfe & therfore I will first trye how I can bring home that saveingly which I have allready at Hamburg, if I can doe that then I wilbe for trade againe but to bringe good back againe I will trade noe more if I gett 10 per cento out I loose that & a greate deale more in the retornes & therfore now I will trye what I can doe by retorninge my money & therfore retorne me by bill of exchange what moneys you have of mine, I presume those debts long since credited are now come in, when I have experimented that I can doe any good this way then I will trade againe but not till then for I have lost soe much allready by trading to your parts that I am quite disheartned,

112 Possibly Elizabeth Rayley, Baret's sister, who married William Rayley, a Norwich merchant. Their descendants inherited Baret's estate in Horstead. In the early-modern period, 'the term 'friend' had a plurality of meanings', and it was common to use 'friend' to designate kin: N. Tadmor, *Family and Friends in Eighteenth-Century England* (Cambridge, 2001), p. 167.

as to the goods in Mr Sanders hands I bought them for your accompt & therfore I doe expect that by next poast you will send me a bill to receive my money in London in March next accordinge to your promise by letter its hard that I should loose the interest of my money its more than I gett by the comission for them but with you I shall not stand upon it thers not a week pas over my heade but I doe indeavor to sell those goods that I have of yours but can get noe body to buy them as yet, noe indeavors of mine shalbe [*p. 241*] wantinge had they beene right good they had sould long since you have a verry falce notion of seirge de Neîmes none can be made at £4 but must be verry thin such wares as I would not buy or make upon my owne accompt I should be ashamed of them & such is the nature of this stuff that if it be thin altho made of fine materialls yet the wale wilbe brode for its the thick makinge of this stuff which makes it fine waled. The parcell of seirge de Neîmes at London are the best wares that everyon had from me & will gaine you reputation, as to the toyes I shall make a protest of them for they are not as the invoyce but I will medle with noe more of them for I doe understand that Otto payes other men better & soe I hope he will me with a litle patience. I shall send to Mr Sanders the white stuff you wright for its a light grey camblet[113] made in imitation of haire but verry fine it will not weare well in breeches because its subject to fret at the knees where it weares with corners in the foults but in any loose garments as coate or cloake it weares incomparably well, its the goodnes of these stuffs as of haire cambletts that makes them frett in close garments. This with service is all at present from

Your reall friend
Tho: Baret

I wrott to Mr Peacock about the half piece of serge de neîmes which you say he sent you & he sends me word that he sent you none but wholl pieces, & therfore by next cleare it that soe I may know how to charge it whether to you or him for its not resonable that I should loose it betwixt you.

113 Camlet: originally a costly eastern fabric, this probably refers to a substitute, a mixed fabric of wool and cotton.

[*p. 242*] To Mr Peacocke Jnr

1 piece of white bratt No. 17 27 yards long will now cost	68s
3 pieces No. 16 53 yds each	96s
1 piece white Russell 26½ yards long	35s
9 pieces drogetts No. 13–29 & 30 yards	46s
2 pieces No. 18 29 or 30	68s
3 pieces No. 28	
9 pieces No. 14	
2 pieces No. 32	
2 pieces No. 25	
5 spotted serge de boyce	
1 ditto with silke	
1 ditto noe good collor	
1 piece & 25 Duch ells No. 10	
1 black brat 53 yards long the single piece cost	
4 pieces barakenes[114] No. 30 30 yards long	
2 pieces No. 22. 52 yards cost 2s per yard	
2 pieces serge de neîmes No. 15 cost if good per piece	
49 & 25 Duch ells of No. 10	
19 Duch ells of searge de Neîmes	

Mr Peacock

These are the prices the wares above would now cost if they were to be bought but because they are old I leave you to make the best market you can of them to my advantage for I doe assure you I doe rate them soe low as I verryly thinke I could not gett soe good soe cheape but indeede worse would serve the market & therfore pray make the best you can of them but keepe them not long, what is not vendible send back when you please, I have now perused the list of the goods you received from Mr Cockey in which I perceive there is a considerable domage putt upon me for I never [*p. 243*] sent him any piece for two in one although 54 yards long but only sent them for one piece in number although I might wright them one doble piece & he hath counted them to you for two each & besides I never sent him any remnants & therfore I accompt that I am wronged by him & desire you to demand of him or her or those that dillivered the goods to you as follows

114 Barragan, barragon, barracan: a coarse cloth.

2 pieces No. 16 those are doble pieces of 54 yards long elce there wants *4 pieces*
1 piece No. 18 single
1 piece silke callimancoes No. 22 single
1 piece black bratt No. 16 single
1 piece serge de neime No. 15 single
15 ells of No. 10
25 ells of serge de neime
6 single pieces & 40 ells of No. 10 & No. 15
2 single pieces of No. 16 or elce in all 4 single pieces & 2 doble No. 16

If I should have soe mistaken your noate as not to enter all downe that he hath delivered one doble piece for two single which were sent but as one pray doe you add them to the nomber & make demand of restitution for them & if they refuse to doe it pray make protest of it send it over to me, Mr Cockey have now left England & me much disappointed he did faithfully promise to come to me that soe we might rectify his mistakes & soe setle a true accompt that verry day which he left Norwich & went for Holland, truly I pitty the mann for I verry beleive he is not in his right sences at all times of all the accompts that ever I see I never saw soe confused an one nor soe unjust an accompt but now I must doe with him as well as I can, as to Nathaniell Mathew I know not what to say I feare I am in same condition with you & in some respect [*p. 244*] worse for I have accepted four fatts of toyes & opened the best which is notoriously falce to the envoyce but he pretends ignorance & the party shall make it good I have sould them for £30 which cost me with charges £50 but I heare you scaped such another bargain, for generall answer to your letter I have sett 40 pieces of serge de russells to worke *vidz* half black with an eye of white & half white with an eye of black of which I shall make all possible hast they are such collours as not to be had unless bespoken soe will take some time, you now have directions about all wares that you have of mine & therfore pray speed their sale & send me the iron as soone as you can but lett noebody know when or what you send me for the Cockeys are verry angry that you & I deale together but I beleive neither of us care for it, for the more privacy what you send me lett Mr Steinlock of Rotterdam shipp it off for I understand he doeth Mr Langleys & your business there, I have sent over to Hamburgh about the piece of searge de neime for he doeth owne but 13½ soe I expect his answer since my begining this letter, I received yours of the 2nd March instant & am much trobled at your delaying to buy me the iron before its raise in which I thinke you are to blame but if it were not to be had it could not be helped & truly now the price is soe high at 7¼ that there wilbe more loss then by the exchange all things considered & therfore send me over only what iron you have allready bought for me which I perceive is but a single quantity lett that come by [*p. 245*] first & remitt me £200 by bill of exchange, you see I have allready lost considerably & therfore use your best indeavors to gett me an exchange to my advantage doe not delay it especially the one half because I am in want of money to carry on my affaires, I would have the wholl some remitted to me if the exchange be any thinge favorable for I want it you should send me word what wares will yeild for if there be profitt I would now trade againe. My service to you & your Lady lett me have an accompt of sales from last I am

Yours to serve you
Tho: Baret

Norwich the 6th of March 1676/7

[*p. 246 is blank*]

Thomas Baret's letters to Sir Josiah Child, 1695

[*p. 247*] Horstead neare Norwich in Norfolk the 5th of April 1695

Most Honoured Sir

Were I in the presence of Sir Josiah Child[115] I should *not* have the confidence to speake to him because I doe not know that ever I saw him <in my life> but under the umbrage of my penn I begg leave to acquaint you that a curiosity to see the funeral of our late most gracious Queen made me take my horses for London the end of February & whilst *I was* there I stept into a booke sellers shopp & tooke up a booke intituled A New Discourse of Trade by Sir Josiah Child, I cursorily ran over the heads & finding it entertaining a notion I have had for many yeares for emprovement of trade (in which I was once not soe profitable a member as I might have beene altho I was not wholly negligent but as you truly observe had not land beene soe <low> *cheape* I might have traded still & I really owne I wish I had continued it still) this *old* good will to trade & new to emprovement of my lands made me purchase your booke which since my coming home I have read over & over with greate satisfaction, but I begg your pardon if I should say I can not agree with you in sevrall consequences which you draw referring to our inland trade but especially in refferrence to land, I must acknowledge you are the most understanding person in trade especially the outland trade that ever I met withall <I see> you are familiar with all the fowre quarters of the world but I see it fareth with you as it doth with one that standeth on the topp of a high hill (I humbly beg your pardon for the similie) wheare all that layeth upon the declivity of the hill he stands on beeing beneath the right line of his eye passeth with a less curious observation then what is at a further distance, soe the true occasion of [*p. 248*] the sinking of the rents of land layeth but in part within your vein the other & misterious part with your leave I will discover to you in some short hints which may be afterwards inlarged upon if you command them you most truly assert that <lowning> bring in interest to 3 per cento will double the price of land that is £100 land

115 Sir Josiah Child (bap. 1631, d. 1699), English economic writer and merchant.

per annum[116] will then sell for as much more than it will doe now but this will not hinder but that your £100 per annum now may & will sinke to £80 per annum & lower if care be not timely & speedily taken to prevent those evills I am about to complaine of which are the true *moles &* wormes that spoyle land & beggers all that depend upon it & hinders improvements &c, your *accompt of* seven <reasons of the> pressures upon land may doe somewhat in their severall places but they are two remote to have soe sencible an effect upon land as you seeme to intimate. The true reason of all is our tennants & all persons that have dependance purely on the product of land are beggerd & have not wherewith either to pay landlord improve by by marling &c or pay workemens wagis by the contrivance of three sorts of undermining tradesmen *viz* brewing maulters, grazing butchers &d perticuler sort of peeple called jobbers but this last can hardly be called a tradsman, the countryman hath but three wayes to use his land by *viz* sowing corne fatting cattle or breeding & keeping of leane cattell for the plow & other uses & for the paile or to rent in <leane> markets *for leane cattle* & all these are intercepted by one or other of the forementioned persons in former times bruing & maulting were two distinct employments & soe were grazing & butchering & maulting & grazing were verry <verry> genteele imployments for gentlemens younger sonns & therby have beene raised verry considerable estates both which wayes are now quite lost as to the profit of them *viz* the brewers have joynd maulting to their other trade & now will buy noe mault but use what he makes & soe the maultster for want of customers was forced to give over unless it be a very few litle ones in the country to serve private familyes soe that the brewing maultster is now become the only buyer of the corne of the country *unles some time when the merchant byeth* & combine together & give but what price they please & when they have a little before hand will bringe corne from [*p. 249*] 10s to 6s per coomb & under in less then two months time by pretending they want none when if their chambers were examind they are not halfe stockt for the yeare <have not nine months stock by them when as they ought to have 15 months that is> for when they leave maulting they ought to have stock by them till four months after they begin to mault againe for new mault will not have lost the fire tast sooner. Thuss the old maulters use to doe thuss one way of using land *in Norff especially* is spoyle for noe man can grow a coomb of barley at 6s charge & then the tennant throws up his farme unless he be abated *& whoe can blame him* nay I know the brewing maultsters have given but 4s when there was noe reason for it but that if they had given more they should have gained

116 Thanks to Gavin Robinson for transcribing this abbreviation.

soe much less but to state this would fill a sheete & soe I leave it at present. The second way is spoyle by the butcher turning grazier for by that meanes he knows what catle cost leane what they cost fatting & soe he will not alow a livelyhood to the countryman for his paines when he can buy cheape he will kill none of his owne if the countryman be stout then the butcher kills his owne till he hath humbled him & forced him to sell & then he spares his owne, to sett out this fully would fill a sheet of paper & soe I shall leave this for the present. The third way is spoyled by the jobber whoe buyes up all sorts of catle *fatt & leane* in faires & elcewheare & then drives them to other faires wheare he either raiseth the faire by offring more then he intends to give or glutts a faire & then at last sweeps when he hath brought downe price to his minde & thuss they abuse all faires they come into by this time. Sir, I presume you may see that land is in the management of thre trusty guardians but I feare to offend your patience & therfore shall abruptly breake off beggin your pardon & leave to subscribe my self

Your humble servant to command
Tho: Baret

To Sir Josiah Child at his seate by the Greene Mann neare London

Horstead the 8th of May 1695

Sir, I can not but retorne you my humble thanks for the honor of yours of the 19th past & seeing Stretham at the bottum of it pardon my boldnes if I wish all happines may attend you & yours in your new relations by your virtuous grand daughter.[117] Sir, I doe not rejoyce that you have the misfortune to have lands <upon> *in* your owne hands but yet it pleaseth me that you have soe sensible arguments which are on my [*p. 250*] side to persuade you the three things I mentioned are greivances upon land in your reply to interest of money mistaken <in page 49 about> *a litle below* the midle of <that> page 49 you have these words. (Soe that I doe conclude the present fall of rents is not naturall but accidentall & to be ascribed principally to the late improvement of Ireland) by which passsage I thought you had not beene soe deepely insighted into the greivances I mentioned as I now perceive you are but it greives me to thinke you apprehend them not to be remedied & secondly that you thinke them not soe mischeivous, this latter doth not surprise me because the laying of all

117 Child's granddaughter, Elizabeth Howland, married the future 2nd duke of Bedford on 23 May 1695.

trade open to all persons (except what is upon a joynt stock) seems to be your opinion your wholl booke through*out* as to ou*t*<ght> land trade & some few inland *trades* that have sole dependance upon it I subscribe to your judgment but to inland trade in generall & land in particuler I begg your pardon if I discent from you, I owne that outland trade inland trade & land are like thre sisthers which have a neare relation to each other but like sisthers they take their propper nourishments sevrally & must be managed in thre different manners for the same rules may be advantagious to one which may be prejuditiall to the others, & might I be permitted without offence in future I might offer some reasons for my opinion, as to the laws you please to mention I have examined them as to brewin & maultinge grazing & butcheringe & they doe not reach either of them as to what they spend themselves *by brewing or butchering*, as to laws against jobbing I have not consulted them but if ever I see the other remedied I will spend <my> *some* tyme upon that. Sir, I have now stated the bruing-maultsters case & I thinke putt my last hand to it yet if any more objections then what are there should be sent me I would doe my endevor to give an answer to them the discource runs large to two sheets of paper closs <& thick> written on all sides [*p. 251*] if when I have gotten it faire written over I did know wheare to leave it *in London* for your perusall that it might come safe to your hand I *should effect it &* hope it might give you satisfaction at least I should esteeme it better or worse accordinge to your opinion of it, this with many others of differinge subjects are the entertainments of my winter evenings in my solitary & widdowers living *MM*[118] if I err in these things its by well meaninge which almost meritt a pardon from ingenuous persons & that I may obteyne yours is the request of

Your humble servant to command
Tho: Baret

To Sir Josia Child at Wanstead in Essex neare London

MM[119]

I can not pass the honor of your invitation to Wanstead in my passage to London without retorning my due & thankfull acknowledgement for soe undeserved a favor which I shall presume to make use of if ever my occasions should draw me neare that way but my acquaintance in London

118 Denoting insertion, written below.
119 This section intended for insertion above.

how greate soe ever it was formerly is become soe small in <one &> twenty yeares absence that I did *not* now know twelve faces in London that were not either my country-men or relations which are become soe small a number that affords me <small> *litle* encouragement for soe long a journey, my last was a mixt occasion, curiosity & to see a mistris which turned to noe accompt soe I presume I am now fixed from travailing yet I could not but take a serious vein of the place neare Kings Oake in the forrest wheare upon Whitson Eve 1674 I was robbed bound hand & foote & left to heare the nightingalls singe &c

[*p. 252*] Horstead the 6th of December 1695

Sir, As modesty obleigeth me not to trouble Sir Josia Child with much wrighting soe a gratefull acknowledgement of the respect you shewed me at Wanstead commands me to lay before you my thoughts upon a needfull subject at this time *viz* the rectifying of the coyne of England the reading of a passage in the Kings speech & the commands of a friend a member in Parliament made me permitt my phantasy to inlarge it selfe into the two discourses above written, the latter of which was the first in this order of my wrightinge them but having given away that without taking a coppy of it I am forced to present it you imperfect by an abstract. Sir, I submitt them both to your sensure because they seeme alitle opposite to your sentiments in a booke which I highly prize.

Sir, I was under some hopes that from your selfe or that gentleman into whose hand you putt the discourse contra brewing and maulting by the same person I should have had your thoughts upon that subject but your greate & weighty busines hath entertained you otherwayse. The evill grates soe <closs &> hard with us heere that it <mindes> obleigeth me to indevour to gett it redressed this session of Parliament in order to which some members of <this> Parliament have promised me to doe their utmost to effect it & to manage it themselves for its a publique greivance & I can not make it my private charge or loss of time to attend it altho it *should* miscarry if you would favor me with your instructions how to manage it at a distance & afforde it your kinde incouragement amongst your friends & acquaintance you would for ever obleige

Your humble servant
Tho: Baret

To Sir Josiah Child at his seate in Wansted in Essex neare London

Bibliography

MANUSCRIPT SOURCES

The National Archives, Kew

PROB 4, Prerogative Court of Canterbury, Engrossed Inventories

PROB 11, Prerogative Court of Canterbury, Registered Wills

Norfolk Record Office

MS 6360, 6B8, Letter-book of Thomas Baret, 1672–1698

MS 21490, Register of the Dutch Church in Norwich

TRAF 619, Will of Thomas Baret, 1709

NCC will register, Famm 353 (1710), Will of Thomas Baret, microfilm 95

PRINTED PRIMARY SOURCES

J. F., *The merchant's ware-house laid open, or the plain dealing linnen-draper* (1696)

T. Fuller, *The History of the Worthies of England*, volume II (London, 1662; 1840 edition)

PRINTED SECONDARY SOURCES

J. Ball, *Merchants and Merchandise* (London, 1977)

J. Bischoff, *A comprehensive history of the woollen and worsted manufactures* (London, 1968)

R. Brenner, *Merchants and Revolution: Commercial Change, Political Conflict, and London's Overseas Traders, 1550–1653* (London, 2003)

A. Cappelli, *Lexicon Abbreviaturarum* (Leipzig, 1928)

R. Chenciner, *Madder Red: A history of luxury and trade* (Abingdon, 2000)

P. Clark and P. Slack, *English towns in transition, 1500–1700* (Oxford, 1976)

J. Cooper, 'Economic Regulation and the cloth industry in seventeenth-century England', *Transactions of the Royal Historical Society*, 20 (1970), pp. 73–99

P. Corfield, 'A Provincial Capital in the late seventeenth century: the Case of Norwich' in P. Clark, ed., *The Early Modern Town* (New York 1976), pp. 233–72

— 'Norwich on the Cusp – from second city to regional capital', in C. Rawcliffe and R. Wilson, eds, *Norwich since 1550* (London, 2004), pp. 139–66

— 'East Anglia', in P. Clark, ed., *Urban History of Britain II: 1540–1840* (Cambridge, 2000), p. 38

B. Cozens-Hardy and E.A. Kent, *The Mayors of Norwich, 1403–1835: Being Biographical Notes on the Mayors of the Old Corporation* (Norwich, 1938)

P. Croft, 'Trading with the Enemy, 1585–1604', *Historical Journal*, 32.2 (1989), pp. 281–302

C. Daniell, *Atlas of Early Modern Britain, 1485–1715* (Oxford, 2014)

S. Decker, 'The silence of the archives: business history, post-colonialism and archival ethnography', *Management and Organisational History*, 8.2 (2013), pp. 155–73

S. Groenveld, 'The seventeenth-century Anglo-Dutch wars: economic or political issues?', *Low Countries: A yearbook* 4, (1995–6), pp. 172–89

S. Haggerty, *'Merely for Money'? Business Culture in the British Atlantic, 1750–1815* (Liverpool: Liverpool University Press, 2013)

E. Hobsbawn, 'The Crisis of the Seventeenth Century', *Past and Present*, 6 (1954), pp. 33–53

A. Hopper, J. Agnew and E. Alley, eds, *The Great Blow: Examinations and Informations relating to the Great Blow in Norwich, 1648* (Norfolk Record Society, lxxxii, 2018)

J. Israel, *Dutch Primacy in World Trade, 1585–1740* (Oxford 1989)

J. Jones, *The Anglo-Dutch Wars of the Seventeenth Century* (Essex, 1996)

E. Kerridge, *Textile Manufactures in Early Modern England* (Manchester, 1985)

H. de Bruyn Kops, *A Spirited Exchange: the wine and brandy trade between France and the Dutch Republic in its Atlantic framework, 1600–1650* (Leiden: Brill, 2007)

X. Lamikiz, *Trade and Trust in the eighteenth-century Atlantic World: Spanish merchants and their overseas networks* (Suffolk: Boydell & Brewer, 2010)

E. Lipson, *The History of the Woollen and Worsted Industries* (London, 1965)

J. Levy and K. Barbieri, 'Trading with the enemy during wartime', *Security Studies*, 13.3 (2004), pp. 1–41

P. Millican, *A History of Horstead and Stanninghall, Norfolk* (Norwich, 1937)

J. Murray, 'The cultural impact of the Flemish Low Countries on sixteenth and seventeenth-century England', *The American Historical Review*, 62.4 (1957), pp. 837–54

D. Ormrod, *The Rise of Commercial Empires: England and the Netherlands in the Age of Mercantilism, 1650–1770* (Cambridge, 2003)

G. Parker and L. Smith, eds, *The General Crisis of the Seventeenth Century* (London: Routledge, 1978)

J. Pound, *Tudor and Stuart Norwich* (Sussex, 1988)

U. Priestly, 'Marketing of Norwich Stuffs, c. 1660–1730', *Textile History*, 22.2 (1991), pp. 193–209

— 'The Fabric of Stuffs: the Norwich textile industry, c. 1650–1750', *Textile History*, 16.2 (1985), pp. 183–210

G. Rommelse, *The Second Anglo-Dutch War* (Hilversum, 2006)

— 'The role of mercantilism in Anglo-Dutch political relations, 1650–74', *Economic History Review*, 63.3 (2010), pp. 591–611

— 'Mountains of iron and gold: mercantilist ideology in Anglo-Dutch relations (1650–1674)' in D. Onnekirk and G. Rommelse, eds, *Ideology and Foreign Policy in Early Modern Europe (1650–1750)* (Farnham, 2011), pp. 243–66

G. Rommelse and R. Downing, 'Anglo-Dutch Mercantile Rivalry, 1585–1688', in M. Isenmann, ed., *Merkantilismus, Wiederaufnahme einer Debatte* (Stuttgart, 2014), pp. 169–95

P. Seaward, 'The House of Commons Committee of Trade and the Origins of the Second Anglo-Dutch War, 1664', *The Historical Journal*, 30.2 (1987), pp. 437–52

P. Slack, 'Great and good towns, 1540–1700', in P. Clark, ed., *Urban History of Britain II: 1540–1840* (Cambridge, 2000), pp. 347–76

N. Tadmor, *Family and Friends in Eighteenth-Century England* (Cambridge, 2001)

S. Talbott, *Conflict, Commerce and Franco-Scottish Relations, 1560–1713* (London, 2014)

— ed., 'The letter-book of John Clerk of Penicuik, 1644–1645', *Miscellany of the Scottish History Society*, XV (2014), pp. 1–54

— 'Trade and Commerce', in J. Hogg, ed., *Using Primary Sources* (Liverpool University Press, 2016–)

— '"What cannot be helped must be indured": Coping with Obstacles to Business during the Anglo-Dutch Wars, 1652–1674', *Enterprise & Society*, 22 (forthcoming 2021)

P. Tortora and I. Johnson, eds, *The Fairchild Books Dictionary of Textiles* (8th edition; New York, 2013)

H. Trevor-Roper, 'The General Crisis of the Seventeenth Century', *Past and Present*, 16 (1959) pp. 31–64

F. Williamson, *Social Relations and Urban Space: Norwich, 1600–1700* (Suffolk, 2014)

P. Wilson, 'Was the Thirty Years' War a "Total War"?', in E. Charters, E. Rosenhaft and H. Smith, eds, *Civilians and War in Europe, 1618–1815* (Liverpool: Liverpool University Press, 2012), pp. 21–35

Index